EUROPE
A Manual for
Hitch - hikers

GW00371662

Editor
Simon Calder

Published by VACATION-WORK, 9 Park End Street, Oxford

First edition by Simon Calder, Colin Brown
and Roger Brown
published in 1980

Second edition 1985

EUROPE—A MANUAL FOR HITCH-HIKERS
Copyright © Vacation Work 1985

ISBN 0 907638 29 5 (hardback)
ISBN 0 907638 28 7 (softback)

Acknowledgements

We are indebted to the following hitch-hikers for their help with this
second edition:

Gill Badoit, Michael Baker, Tim Berkeley, Iain Giles, Max Glaski, David
Gray, Douglas Hutchinson, Robert Mallakee, Karen Mitchell, Alan Ng,
Evelyn Pfeiffer, Uwe Ratz, Kathy Ricketts, Simon Ryde, Chris Savill, Ulrich
Schwab, Anne Shutt, John Speyer, Brian Spurrell, Anders Sterner, Gary
Willis, Rob Woon.

Illustrations and country maps by William Swan
Motorway maps by Roger Brown and Simon Calder

Printed by Gibbons Barford Print, Centenary House,
Wednesfield Road, Wolverhampton

Contents

Preface... 7

Introduction

Rules of Thumb
How to Hitch 9
When to Hitch 9
Where to Hitch 10
Competition....................... 10
Gimmicks and Tricks 11
Signs.................................. 11
Other Things to Take 12
Choosing Your Lift 13
Short Lifts........................... 14
Number Plates..................... 15
The Language Barrier 18
Planned and Paid Lifts 19

Route Planning
Crossing the Channel 19
Routes and Maps 21
Crossing Frontiers 24
Trains and Boats and Planes 25

The Usual Warnings
Psychopaths 25
Demon Drivers 26
Central Locking 26
Health 27
Insurance 27
The Long Wait 27

Best and Worst in Europe.. 29
Hitching out of Towns 30
Motorway Hitching 33

Western Europe
Austria 35
Belgium, Netherlands and Luxembourg 40
France 58
   Andorra 74
   Monaco 74
West Germany 75
Great Britain 100
   Eire 113
Greece 115
Italy 120
   San Marino 139
   Malta 139
Spain and Portugal 140
   Gibraltar 151
Switzerland 152
   Liechtenstein 156

Scandinavia 157
   Denmark 159   Norway 162
   Finland 161   Sweden 164

Eastern Europe 167
   Bulgaria 173   Poland 178
   Czechoslovakia 174   Romania 182
   East Germany.............. 176   Yugoslavia 183
   Hungary 177

Country Maps

Austria 39
Belgium and Luxembourg 45
Netherlands.. 52
France 67
Germany (West and East) 85
Great Britain 109
Eire and Northern Ireland 114
Greece 116
Italy 128
Spain and Portugal 147
Switzerland 155
Scandinavia 158
Eastern Europe 168

Motorway Maps

Belgium
A10/E5 46   A1, A7/E10 47   R1, A14/E3 48
A3/E5 46   A16 47   A15/E41 48

Netherlands
A1/E35, E8 53   A4, A13/E10...... 55   A28/E35 56
A2/E9 53   A16/E10 55   A12/E8, E36 57

France
A1 68   A10 69   A6 71   A9 72
A13 ....68 A4 70   A7 72   A8 73

West Germany
A1 86   A45 92   A7 95
A2 88   A4, A48(E) 92   A8 97
A3 89   A5 93   A9 99
A4(W) 91   A6 94

Great Britain
M1 .... 110 M4 .... 111 M5 .... 111 M6 112

Italy
A5 129   A10 132   A2 135
A4 129   A12, A11 132   A3 135
A9 131   A22 133   A14 137
A7 131   A1 133   A16 138

Spain
A7 148   A2.............149 A68 .... 150 A8 150

Preface

Mass tourism and packaged holidays are now the norm in Europe, so why would anyone choose to endure the uncertainty, discomfort and perils of hitch-hiking? And with the present range of tempting offers from coach and rail operators, why are the motorways of Europe still teeming with hitch-hikers?

The unique features of hitch-hiking provide the answers. Firstly, hitching is extremely cheap: with a little initiative and goodwill from your drivers, it is possible to travel from Glasgow to Athens for free. Secondly, when it seems every other tourist on the Continent is being herded from charter flight to standardised hotel room, the hitch-hiker casts his fortune to the road with no idea of where he will spend the night. Thirdly, there is simply no better way to meet the natives than to have them pick you up from the roadside. And finally, there are worse ways to travel than by chauffeur-driven car.

Since the first edition of *Europe—A Manual for Hitch-Hikers* was published, the road network has become even more complex and daunting. Suppose you're in a car going through the Ruhr: at which of the many spiralling junctions should you choose to get out in order to hitch on to Munich? Which number plates should you watch out for? If you're tired of "real" hitching, what's the telephone number of the local car-sharing agency? And when you finally get to Munich, which underground line will put you on the right road to hitch out again?

The information in this book provides the answer to these questions and thousands like them. It deals with all varieties and speeds of hitching: from London in the rush hour to Warsaw at the height of the official hitching season. It tells you how to hitch north from Helsinki, west from Cork, south from Naples, east from Heraklion, and between all the major cities in Europe. Most of the book is concerned with rapid transit hitching, covering long distances with minimum fuss and maximum speed. But you can successfully apply the principles described to any kind of hitching adventure.

Europe—a Manual for Hitch-Hikers deals only with hitch-hiking and the associated ideas of car-sharing and hitching trains, boats and planes. It is not watered down with material on places to eat, sleep or visit. The tourist offices of each country provide sheaves of free hand-outs on specific places, and there are plenty of guide books where you can get information of this kind; but no other which deals exclusively with hitching in Europe.

The extensive revision and expansion of this edition would not have been possible without the generous help of the many hitch-hikers who sent in suggestions and amendments as a result of the first edition. Any further ideas, information or corrections are most welcome. Please write to me at Vacation Work, 9 Park End Street, Oxford OX1 1HJ. If your material is used, you'll receive a free copy of the next edition.

Simon Calder

Introduction

Hitch-hiking has probably existed longer than the wheel. But only since Daimler and Benz invented the petrol-driven vehicle one hundred years ago—giving man the opportunity to travel great distances with the minimum of effort—has hitching been raised from a casually optimistic pursuit to a very practical form of travel. Hitch-hiking has achieved a degree of respectability in two stages: first during the depression of the 1930s when honest but suddenly destitute men took to the roads in search of work, and secondly during the second world war when petrol was rationed and there were constant migrations of soldiers up and down the country.

The concept of hitch-hiking was originally almost synonymous with hiking. You started walking, and if a vehicle came past, you put your hand out. Long distances were not a practical proposition, so you often reached your destination without actually hitching a lift. With today's volume of traffic, the emphasis now is much more on hitching than hiking. On a busy road, you just choose your location (which is what this book is mostly about) and dig your heels in until someone picks you up. But the old hiking method is still good on quiet country roads, where the incidence of traffic may be two vehicles an hour or less; nothing can be more satisfying than a leisurely hitch-hiking holiday on such roads in the remoter parts of Greece, Spain, Portugal or Yugoslavia.

Rules of Thumb

How to hitch. Choose a suitable stretch of road (see *Where to Hitch*), display a sign if you have one, adopt a permanent smile, and stick out your thumb. However, in a few areas of Europe (notably Corsica and remoter parts of Greece) a raised thumb is interpreted as "up yours". In such places a raised palm is preferable both for getting lifts and for personal safety.

When to hitch. Timing is obviously important to your chances of getting a lift but the optimum time for hitching depends upon where you are. Hitching a minor road in the middle of the night might not produce a lift for the simple reason that there is no traffic. On the other hand, night hitching at service areas on major motorways will often bring a lift more quickly than during the day; there is little competition, and drivers are more keen on company. Hitching on public holidays tends to be slower than on working days, and Sundays in countries like Austria can be nearly as bad as thumbing around rural Lincolnshire in mid-winter. At peak weekends in summer, some of the main European arteries are choked with vehicles with no room for temporary passengers. The start and end of the annual French *vacances* is a completely hopeless proposition for hitch-

9

hikers. Hitching out of large cities at any time of year is particularly bad during the afternoon rush hour, when the traffic volume is too high to enable cars to stop safely, and most of those that do stop will be going only a few kilometers into suburbia.

Competing with dozens of other hitch-hikers is another problem associated with large cities. There are constant queues of hitch-hikers at the main exits from cities like London, Rome or Paris; these queues diminish slightly late at night. In summer, the channel ports—Calais, Boulogne and Ostend in particular—tend to get choked, as do the major through routes across France, Belgium and Germany.

There are also isolated crises when roads suddenly become blocked with hitch-hikers. The end of term at Madrid University is like a swarm of locusts disbanding in all directions. Market day in Belgrade is the same, when hundreds of peasants (and their associated goats and chickens) try to cram themselves into the empty lorries as they leave the market in the afternoon. In cases like this it's often best to just sit back for a day and wait until the crisis has passed.

In general, the best time of day is early in the morning, when you will find a lot of drivers setting off on long journeys. If you're on the road before 7 am, you will also meet a minimum of competition from other hitchers. In southern countries, beware of the *siesta* (which can run from 1-5 pm). Its effect is to wipe out all but long-distance traffic, and it may be as well to take a rest yourself.

Where to hitch. Choosing a good location is the key to successful hitching. First you want to stand somewhere where there's going to be some traffic; your chances are better on a trunk road than on a farm track. Once you've selected your road, the next criteria are that the drivers can see you and that they can pull in without causing a major accident. Motorway service areas are good bets, as are many motorway slip roads (although hitching from some is illegal, and others carry very little traffic). On other roads, try standing at roundabouts, or, failing that, at a T-junction or traffic lights—in fact anywhere where the traffic has to slow down or stop. If you're dropped off on the open road, it might be worth walking until you find a suitable location, such as a lay-by, where cars can pull off the road. Avoid standing on bends as this is hazardous to everyone concerned. At the same time, avoid long straight stretches of road where traffic moves so fast that it doesn't have chance to see you, let alone stop.

Competition. If you're stuck in a line of a dozen international hitchers, you'll simply have to wait your turn or try some of the gimmicks and tricks below. But in eastern—and to some extent southern—Europe you'll find a great deal of local competition. Soldiers, schoolkids and little old ladies use hitching as a routine way of getting to and from the nearest large town. It is infuriating to find yourself swamped by people travelling five miles when you're trying to hitch five hundred. You have two options. One is to stand out from the crowd by displaying your flag and sign for a faraway destination. The other (and probably more successful) is to ingratiate yourself with the locals. If you can turn yourself into a local celebrity, they'll go to great lengths to find you a ride, even for example by standing in the middle of the road and forcing the traffic to stop.

Gimmicks and Tricks. Although your choice of location is the most important single factor in avoiding long waits, there are other ways of reducing your waiting time. Hitch-hikers are fairly evenly divided over the use of gimmicks, but some tricks (like a man hiding behind the hedge while his female companion pretends to be hitching alone) are universally condemned as unethical. Instead try to brighten the motorists' day by, for example, displaying a "Just Married" sign, preferably translated into the vernacular. Simon Ryde reports that the French in particular find the idea of an impecunious British couple having to hitch as the only way of honeymooning abroad absolutely hilarious and stop in droves. This is not a custom that comes naturally to them. Similarly, a sign saying "Good with children and animals" may attract the family motorist, and will at least set you apart from the crowd.

There is also considerable diversity of opinion on the question of whether you should scout around asking drivers for lifts, for instance at motorway service areas. This is an effective way of getting lifts, but it can be most uncomfortable if the driver doesn't really want to take you but feels too guilty to refuse. The situation can be worsened even further if there's a language barrier. Still, even the hardiest opponents of this method of hitching may sometimes find themselves in desperate situations where the only chance of getting a lift is to ask someone. To minimise embarrassment, ask if the driver can offer you a lift to your specific destination. A negative reply can then mean "No, I'm not going that way", "No, my vehicle is full" or even "No, I don't like your knee length kaftan or your 15 mates", without the driver needing to be more specific. Whatever techniques you employ to get a lift, your chances are best if you look casual, but clean. It helps to have what the French call *une bonne tête*, implying a pleasant, unthreatening demeanour.

Signs. Another major division of opinion concerns the use of signs. Many hitch-hikers use them all the time; others prefer to travel without a sign unless absolutely necessary. In case you reach the threshold of necessity, try to ensure you have the raw materials at hand. This need only be a chalk or a broad felt-tip pen, and you can use your imagination to find a suitable surface: any old bit of cardboard will do, or even a pair of sandals. You probably won't have to go as far as David Woodworth of Vacation-Work who set off from Land's End with a T-shirt emblazoned with the words: *John o' Groats. Please.* To start you off, there's a sign at the end of this book; however your choice of destination is rather limited.

Many combinations of materials have been tested in the search for the ideal sign. For best results, use a dry marker such as *Velleda* pens on white plastic. You can change your destinations instantly by rubbing off the original. It turns to powder and brushes off easily, so you don't need to wander around Europe with ink-stained hands. Use a black or blue pen, and make your sign number-plate size: drivers will be able to read it and it will fit neatly into your pack. Fluorescent or illuminated signs are worth considering if you plan a lot of night hitching.

Bear in mind that many other European hitchers now use signs: it is essential that yours is the clearest and the most polite. The above techniques will enable you to stand out from the crowd, and thus give you a head start.

On really long journeys, you may be at a loss as to what to write on your sign. The answer is not to set your sights too far away, yet to name a destination sufficiently far away to sift out the long distance traffic. A "Madrid" sign on the way out of London is (usually) futile because it will only tell drivers that you're aiming for one of the channel ports. A Madrid sign would be more in its element when you're hitching out of Bilbao or Barcelona. When composing your sign, it's best not to think more than about 500 km ahead. This upper limit should be reduced when travelling through the more densely populated countries, like the Netherlands or Germany, where a large city some 200 km away would probably be far enough. Since drivers draw their own conclusions from your signs, you must guard against the possibility of reducing your options too far. A "Geneva" sign, when leaving Basel, might indicate that you will accept no lift except one going all the way to Geneva, whereas in reality you might gladly accept a ride as far as Bern or Lausanne. One way round this, and a particularly useful device when you're approaching a major motorway junction, is to inscribe your sign with the additional word for "Towards" (or whatever the local equivalent is) to indicate the direction, not necessarily the destination, that you want. The other essential word to add at the end of your sign is the native word for "Please" (see *The Language Barrier,* below).

Once you've written your sign, don't hide it under a bushel (or anything else). Display it proudly, even if you feel daft walking through suburban Paris with a sign for Lyon. It is not unknown for drivers leaving their homes for a long journey to spot a hitcher complete with sign strolling past the front door and on impulse decide to take him a few hundred kilometers.

Other Things to Take. Along with sign equipment and the hitch-hiker's usual paraphernalia of rucksack, clothes and sandwiches, the following items are essential for a successful trip.

Passport. If you don't intend to venture into Eastern Europe, a Visitor's Passport (£7.50 from Post Offices, valid one year) will suffice. If your travels take you into an Eastern bloc country, not only will you need a full passport (£15, valid ten years) but also the appropriate visas. Costs and regulations vary; details are given under *Getting In* for each Eastern bloc country. A supply of passport photographs will be required to obtain visas, whether in advance or at the frontier.

Travellers Cheques. Avoid the normal 1% charge by obtaining commission-free cheques from the Leicester or Leeds building societies. Even if you don't have an account, there is nothing to stop you opening one, then immediately withdrawing all your funds in travellers' cheques.

Foreign currency. Even if you plan to travel straight through a country, a small amount of the appropriate currency will enable you to take buses out of cities, buy coffee for your driver and so on. It is very expensive to exchange a few pounds' worth of currency in Britain, so it's better to change money on the ferry or at border kiosks. Better still, try to find travellers who are just leaving the country you're arriving in. You can agree a mutually beneficial exchange without losing a cut to the sharks who run *bureaux de change*. Camp sites and youth hostels close to frontiers are often good unofficial foreign exchange markets.

Cheque book. Useful as a standby, assuming you have funds in your account at home. But even a rock-solid account with the Bank of England will be useless unless you obtain a Eurocheque Encashment Card in advance from your bank. The one exception is the National Girobank, whose Postcheque card is valid at Post Offices throughout western Europe.

Credit Cards. Handy for "proving" your financial stability to suspicious border officials, and for buying a ticket home should you lose this book.

Insurance. See *The Usual Warnings* for a few good reasons why you should take out an insurance policy or, at the very least, form E111.

Student card. For discounts at museums, theatres and many other places, obtain an International Student Identity Card. This is considerably easier if you happen to be a full-time student. Otherwise, the FIYTO card for non-students under 26 may yield discounts in lieu of an ISIC card. Both can be obtained from student travel offices.

Address Book. After a trip or two across the Continent, you should have a fine collection of addresses culled from friendly drivers and fellow hitchers. Preserve them carefully for the occasions when you're dropped off at nightfall close to one of these people, and can impose upon their hospitality. It's clearly only good manners to reciprocate by giving out your own address freely, and acting as host to those visiting your country.

Driving licence. Your ordinary British, Irish, Canadian or American licence is valid almost everywhere in Europe. You'll need it if you agree to share the driving—but also ensure that the driver's insurance covers you to drive.

Pen and paper. To regale the readers of future editions of this book with your tales of rides across Europe in Ferraris or three-day waits outside Stockholm.

Books. Tolstoy's *War and Peace* is recommended to fill in time on the Autoroute du Soleil in August.

Swiss Army knife. Helps you to cope with impromptu roadside picnics, open all manner of bottles, and carve up cardboard to make a sign of reasonable dimensions. Choose only the genuine article, made by Victorinox. You'll never know how you managed without one.

National flag. Your own, if you think it will go down well with the natives. Otherwise, someone else's national flag and a good story.

Choosing Your Lift. If you're on an all-motorway long-distance trip, you have to be a bit fussy about the lifts you accept and the lifts you turn down.

Accepting the first lift just because it's taking you an extra ten—or even fifty—kilometers in your direction, might eventually prove to be a time-wasting policy. It's far better to check your map and decide where the next good hitching spot is (usually the next major services, although you may prefer to try your luck at a busy slip road). This then defines the minimum lift you will accept. Make a mental note of any towns *before* your next hitching spot, as well as any towns that are off on a tangent, for instance if you're coming up to a motorway junction: these are the lifts you must turn down.

Having mapped out your route and decided on your minimum lift, you are ready for the first car to stop. When a car pulls up, it is best for you to ask the driver the direct question: "Where are you going?" This should elicit the name of a town as a response, so you can decide whether to accept the lift (have your map handy for reference).

Other questions may elicit misleading replies. For instance, if you're holding up a sign for Stuttgart, and you ask the driver: "Are you going to Stuttgart?", the answer "Yes" may just mean that, in his opinion he can offer you a useful lift in the general direction of Stuttgart. Having received the false information that the driver is going to Stuttgart, you might jump in, and then only gradually realise that he intends to drop you at an illegal motorway junction just south of Mannheim. If there's a language problem, you might not realise this until you are actually being dropped. If, on the other hand, you allow the driver to open the conversation by asking where you're going, then the information you give him will be the basis for him to decide whether he thinks it's worth your while travelling with him. This is again very dangerous as his criteria could be way off the mark. He might think the illegal motorway junction just south of Mannheim is every hitcher's dream! So, to avoid ambiguity, always ask a driver for his destination. There are a large number of motorists who will refuse to play the game, on the basis that they may indeed be going to Stuttgart but do not wish to commit themselves to taking you all the way in case you turn out to be manic, smelly or the most boring person in the world. If this happens, you can only guess whether your potential host has sufficient awareness of hitching techniques to be relied upon to avoid miscellaneous illegal motorway junctions in the Mannheim area. Just don't get into a car until you're sure it's a lift you want to take. If in doubt, stay put.

As well as not fulfilling your minimum lift criteria, there are other reasons for not accepting a lift. A driver who looks dangerous, half asleep or totally drunk is not a good bet. If you suspect a driver of being a sexual or homicidal maniac, don't hesitate to turn him down. A very slow lorry might not be a good prospect. People have also been known to turn lifts down for the most trivial of reasons, like a bumper sticker supporting Real Madrid or the presence of a cat in the back seat. If you don't like a car's exterior trimmings or interior passengers, it is, of course, up to you.

Short Lifts. Perhaps most annoying of all is the situation in which you would gladly accept a lift of a mere five kilometers or so. You may be just a short distance from your final destination, or you may be five kilometers from the motorway exit you want to take, or you may simply be at a bad hitching spot just short of a busy service area. In this situation, you will be frustrated by the knowledge that nearly everyone going past is going as far as you want to. "Why don't they stop?" you ask yourself. Well, the answer is obvious. People have a built-in assumption that all hitch-hikers are seeking a lift of several hundred kilometers. Their short lifts have probably been turned down by previous hitch-hikers wanting something a bit longer. In cases such as these, many hitch-hikers would give up and walk, hoping, of course, that some driver will then have the insight to think: "Well, I may only be going five kilometers, but at least I can save him having to walk that far". But this theory does not seem to work in practice.

Do not despair, however: there are two things you can do. If the place you are going to has a name that might be recognised by the local drivers, make a sign. Otherwise, you have to psych the drivers into stopping. To do this, first get them to notice you and acknowledge your presence: stare them straight in the eye, but not too ferociously or you'll put them off. (This is actually a good principle whenever you're hitching, since it could just tip the scales with those drivers who approach with complete indifference as to whether or not they pick you up.) Having got the driver to notice you, he will either pass by impassively, or make some sort of reaction. The secret is to observe the reaction and react back. The commonest reaction is to indicate that they're only going about five kilometers. The gesture you will see are: pointing downwards ("I'm only going five kilometers, look at my number plates" or simply "I'm staying here"); pointing to the left or right ("I'm turning off this road in about five kilometers"); or a shrug of the shoulders ("Sorry, I can't help you, I'm only going five kilometers"). The meanings of other gestures will usually be all too obvious. The correct reaction is to nod your head violently (except in Balkan countries where you should shake your head) and wave your hand up and down motioning the driver to stop. The majority of drivers will still pass by and think you're mad, but the clever ones will catch on and stop.

Number Plates. Knowledge of the appearance and significance of cars' registration plates is of considerable importance to the hitch-hiker, both on international journeys and when travelling within one country. When standing by the road, it is useful to be able to see at a glance where are car comes from. If you see one that is going your way, you can wave frantically, point to the registration plate, and hope the driver gets the hint. In static situations, for instance at motorway service areas, you can instantly decide which drivers are worth approaching and asking for a lift. And number plates can help you to decide if your current location offers any hope at all. If you're at one of the more complex junctions outside Mannheim and the registration codes of the vehicles passing you are overwhelmingly local (which you can deduce from the lists provided in this book), you can safely dismiss any notion of reaching Stuttgart from that particular spot, and set about finding a better one.

Once you get a lift, some drivers join in the number plate game. Having learned that your final destination is Munich, they will chase and flash down any vehicle with *M* registration in order to ask the driver if he's willing to take you. At best this procedure can continue *ad infinitum* and you can travel the length of Germany with no further need to stand by the roadside.

Some words of warning, however, about the principles of registration spotting. First, the international registration disc is theoretically required on all vehicles that leave their home territory, but few countries seem to do anything about enforcing this. Hence the disc may well be absent. There is also the problem that the disc is invariably on the back of the car. To make life even more difficult, some vehicles are plastered with discs, the drivers collecting them as travel souvenirs. While it may be obligatory to display the disc of one's country of origin, there seems to be no internationally agreed convention about displaying additional discs. You may also come across some unofficial discs, often representing a small region of a country, like VL for Flanders.

Another point about identification of plates is that a car with registration plates from a particular town, region or country, is not necessarily going there. Thus, if you're hitching out of Frankfurt and heading south to Switzerland, you might assume that all Swiss cars going past are actually going to Switzerland; but a car could also belong to a Swiss businessman who is in Frankfurt for an international conference and is just returning to his hotel in a little village ten kilometers south of the city. Businessmen, students and holidaymakers are the most common groups within the category of people temporarily based away from home. There are also commercial travellers, whose day-to-day travels may take them on strange routes. So don't curse blindly at motorists who might apparently have provided an ideal lift. On the other hand, while the majority of locally registered traffic will be staying in the neighbourhood, there is always a small percentage setting off on a long journey.

The list below covers all the main countries in Europe, giving the current international registration codes, along with the new two-letter codes (where they differ from the current ones) that have been proposed—but not yet put into effect—by the International Standards Organisation in Geneva. The list also gives brief descriptions of the plates of all European countries. Only familiarity with the different typefaces used can lead to distinguishing between some of the more common designs. The question of regional identification of licence plates, where such systems exist, is dealt with separately under each country.

Albania (AL)—black on white; two letters, two pairs of numbers separated by dots; liberal sprinkling of red stars.

Andorra (AND/AD)—black numbers on white, to the right of the coat of arms and above the words *Principat d'Andorra*.

Austria (A/AT)—large white letters and numbers on black background.

Belgium (B/BE)—small red letters/figures (various combinations) on white background. If these colours are reversed (white symbols on red), the vehicle is registered at the Supreme Headquarters Allied Powers Europe (SHAPE) situated near Mons.

Bulgaria (BG)—mostly white on black; two Cyrillic letters then two hyphenated groups of numbers.

Czechoslovakia (CS)—black on white; two or three letters, a hyphen, then two hyphenated groups of numbers.

Denmark (DK)—two letters, four numerals; various colour schemes, mostly black on white, white on black or black on yellow.

Eire (IRL/IR)—as British plates but with red background on rear plate.

Finland (SF/FI)—three letters and three numbers separated by a hyphen; mostly black on white, but old ones are white on black.

France (F/FR)—white numbers/letters on black background. Being replaced by black on white (front) and black on yellow (rear).

West Germany (D/DE)—black letters/numbers on white; usually a hyphen after the first one, two or three letters.

East Germany (DDR/DD)—black letters/numerals on white (various combinations).

Gibraltar (GBZ/GI)—as British plates, but numbers only.

Greece (GR)—black on white; two letters, a hyphen, four numbers. Old ones have black numbers on white; rear plates also have a strip of light blue containing Greek or Roman letters, plus some numbers.

Hungary (H/HU)—front: white on black—six figures/letters in groups of two, separated by dots. Rear: black on white, no dots.

Iceland (IS)—white on black; one letter and up to five numerals.

Italy (I/IT)—front: white on black, letters/numbers only 4 cm. high. Rear: old ones are white on black, normal size, usually on square plates. New ones have the first two letters in orange, the rest in white, on black.

Liechtenstein (FL/LI)—as Swiss plates, but with the letters FL, the coat of arms and up to five numerals.

Luxembourg (L/LU)—one letter and four or five numbers, white on black or black on yellow.

Malta (M/MT)—as British plates but numerals only.

Monaco (MC)—blue on white, with red and blue coat of arms to left and the words *Principauté de Monaco* below.

Netherlands (NL)—six figures, in three groups of two, separated by dots; new ones are black on yellow, old ones white on black.

Norway (N/NO)—black on white; two letters and up to five numerals. Old ones have one letter and up to six numerals.

Poland (PL)—seven letters or numbers, various colour schemes. Old ones have two letters, then two pairs of numbers.

Portugal (P/PT)—white on black; two letters, two pairs of numbers.

Romania (R/RO)—black on white; one or two numbers, then two letters and up to four numbers.

San Marino (RSM/SM)—black on white, with the coat of arms on the left, and the letters RSM on the right.

Spain (E/ES)—black on white; one or two letters then five or six numbers or letters.

Sweden (S/SE)—black on white: three letters, three numbers.

Switzerland (CH)—black on white. On front plates, the first two letters are followed by a dot. On rear plates, the first two letters stand on a separate line, flanked on the left by the Swiss emblem (white cross on red shield), on the right by the cantonal of arms. CH stands for Confoederatio Helvetica.

Union of Soviet Socialist Republics (SU)—white on black; four figures followed or preceded by two or three Cyrillic letters.

Yugoslavia (YU)—white on black; first two letters followed by a red star and four to six figures in two hyphenated groups.

Cars from the British Isles all use the same typefaces for their licence plates, and currently use the following code letters:

	GB	Great Britain	
GBA	Alderney	GBJ	Jersey
GBG	Guernsey	GBM	Isle of Man

Vehicles from outside Europe also occasionally find their way on to European roads, and the more commonly seen international registration letters are listed below:

AUS	Australia	IL	Israel	RL	Lebanon
CDN	Canada	IND	India	SYR	Syria
CY	Cyprus	IR	Iran	TN	Tunisia
DZ	Algeria	IRQ	Iraq	TR	Turkey
ET	Egypt	MA	Morocco	USA	United States
HKJ	Jordan	NZ	New Zealand	ZA	South Africa

You may often find plates which have nothing in common with those described above. They will be on military, official or diplomatic vehicles, and their drivers (usually foreigners themselves) are often surprisingly eager to help. American servicement in Germany can be amazingly hospitable, the roads of Belgium are teeming with highly paid EEC and SHAPE officials in expensive cars, and the Gabonese Ambassador to France has been known to give lifts. Try extra hard when you see plates you don't recognise.

The Language Barrier. If you go abroad armed only with your native English and Grade F in CSE French, then you will certainly not enjoy your trip as much as a fluent polyglot. Although most European drivers will gallantly try to communicate in something approximating to English, an inability to reciprocate means that you may miss out on the main point of hitch-hiking, which is to establish contact with the people that pick you up.

Even if languages aren't your strong point, you are bound to pick up a few words on your trip, and one of the first will almost certainly be *autostop,* an internationally used term for hitch-hiking. There are regional variations, of course. The sport is known as *trampen* (pronounced "trempen") or *per Anhalter fahren* in Germany, *lifts* in the Netherlands, and *flaggin'* in Yorkshire. But once across the channel, the term *autostop* is universally understood.

More useful than being able to tell people what you're doing is the ability to avoid such hitch-hikers' nightmares as being dropped somewhere illegal or impossible, or even being taken hundreds of kilometers out of your way. The glossary below is designed to cover most such eventualities.

For signs:

English: Towards . . . please
French: Vers . . . S.V.P. (s'il vous plaît)
Italian: Verso . . . per favore
German: Richtung . . . bitte
Dutch: Naar . . . toe, S.V.P.
Portuguese: . . . por favor *(no word for towards)*
Spanish: Hasta . . . por favor
Swedish: Mot . . . var så god
Finnish: . . . suuntann, ole hyvä
Greek: Pros . . . parakalo
Czech: Směrem k . . . prosim

Chatting up:

GB: Where are you going?
F: Oú allez-vous?
I: Dove va?
D: Wo fahren Sie hin?
NL: Waar gaat U naar toe?
P: Para onde vai?
E: ¿Adonde va Ud?
S: Vart skall ni fara?
SF: Minne olette menossa?
GR: Poú páte?
CS: Kampak jedete?

GB: Are you going to (as far as) . . .?
F: Est-ce que vous allez à (jusqu'à) . . .?
I: Sta forse andando verso (fino a) . . .?
D: Fahren Sie nach (bis nach) . . .?
NL: Gaat U naar . . . toe (tot . . .)?
P: Passa por . . .?
E: ¿ Va Ud a . . .?
S: Far ni til (så långt som) . . .?
SF: Oletteko menossa . . . (asti)?
GR: **Páte** pros (méchri) . . .?
CS: Jedete až do . . .?

At the end of the ride:

GB: Stop! I want to get out here
F: Stop! Je veux descendre ici
I: Si fermi! Voglio scendere qua
D: Stop! Ich möchte hier aussteigen
NL: Stop! Ik wil hier eruistappen
P: Pare! Quero sair aqui
E: ¡Párase! Yo quiero bajar aqui
S: Stanna! Jag vill stiga av här
SF: Pysähykää! Haluan poistua **tässä**
GR: Stamatíste! Thélo na katevó ethó
CS: Zastavte! Ja chci vystoupit tady

GB: Thank you very much
F: Merci beaucoup
I: Molto grazie
D: Danke schön
NL: Dank U
P: Muito obrigado
E: Muchas gracias
S: Tack
SF: Kiitos
GR: Efcharistó polí
CS: **Děkuji** mockrat

Planned and Paid Lifts. Although not totally in keeping with the spirit of hitch-hiking, sharing petrol costs is nevertheless a safe and efficient form of travelling. Maybe you hear of someone driving your way and just get in touch with them; or you answer an advertisement on a college notice board or in a paper. Alternatively, you may find your chances of success higher if you use a lift agency. These are most useful if you live, or are temporarily based, nearby, since you may have to wait several days between signing on and getting your lift. Registration always involves payment, and this has to be made either by post or in person. Before registering, it is best to telephone to see if a lift is available in your direction. This saves the frustration of paying a registration fee and still not finding a suitable lift. Europe has a highly-developed system of lift agencies, and these are listed under each country.

Route Planning

Crossing the Channel. For reasons of cost, British hitchers have traditionally crossed to the Continent by sea. This remains the cheapest method (and can even be free), but air fares have come down to levels where a flight can be a realistic prospect to begin a hitch-hiking trip. If you know where to look, you can find real bargains, usually last-minute attempts to fill seats on charter flights. These are difficult to find at the height of summer, but widely advertised for the rest of the year. The best source of last-minute bargains is the London *Standard,* with the *Times* as a good alternative for those outside London. If you have access to Prestel or a television set with Oracle, these are also worth trying. In addition, any good travel agent should have a supply of cheap flights. Prices like £50 return from London to Malaga are not unknown. It is usually cheaper — despite the distance – to fly to holiday destinations like Alicante or Athens than to hop over to Brussels or Bordeaux. Charter flight tickets are invariably for return journeys, and must include some element of accommodation to meet regulations. The accommodation is usually fictitious or impractical (a bed in a barn 500 miles away, for example) to keep costs down. But Greece, and more recently Spain, are clamping down on these practices. Do not pay for a charter ticket to either country unless you are given a sufficiently genuine-looking accommodation voucher. Otherwise you may be sent back on the next flight or surcharged up to the normal economy fare.

Having bought a return ticket which you only intend to use one-way, you may be tempted to sell the return half, but since the name on the ticket can easily be checked against a passport, the buyer runs something of a risk. To avoid problems, go with the buyer to the airport, check in yourself, and hand over the boarding pass.

By sea there are a wide variety of routes to choose from, but most hitch-hikers use the shortest and cheapest routes from Dover, Folkestone or Ramsgate to Boulogne, Calais, Dunkerque, Ostend or Zeebrugge. Of these, Dover has the most sailings by far, and can be cheaply reached in a Hertz rental car from London. See *Great Britain: Planned and Paid Lifts* for details. The Continental ports of Boulogne (for Paris and the south) and Ostend (for Brussels and points south and east) offer the best prospects for onward hitching. But whichever route you choose, do not buy a one-way or ordinary return ticket. All ferry operators offer day-trip tickets for less than the single fare, and are unable to prevent you giving away the return half to some lucky soul on the other side. However, if you turn up at Dover bearing an overflowing rucksack, the clerk will decline to sell you a day ticket on the reasonable grounds that you're unlikely to return the same day — the regulations allow hand luggage only. Douglas Hutchinson is among the many hapless hitchers to be refused a cheap day return ticket after failing to conceal his baggage. Your best bet is to conceal any baggage before buying the ticket, or to buy a ticket in advance from a travel agent. Once you have a ticket, you're unlikely to be turned away.

On a day return ticket you can reach Dunkerque from Ramsgate for £8 on Sally the Viking Line, but it's worth investing a pound or two more to reach Boulogne or Ostend on P&O or Sealink. Hoverspeed charges more, but by joining the Hoverspeed Executive Club (membership free) you can treat yourself to free coffee and a newspaper before boarding the craft. You also get priority standby, useful in the height of summer. Write to Hoverspeed, International Hoverport, Dover, Kent for an Executive Club application form. Other high-speed hitchers wanting an early start in Belgium can pay the £6 jetfoil surcharge on a day return ticket from Dover to Ostend.

When you return from Europe, repeat the procedure; just make sure you have a good excuse ready when buying your day-return ticket to explain why you only want to spend a few hours in Britain.

The same ground rules apply to and from Ireland, and also on the longer Channel and North Sea crossings. These longer trips are most valuable for hitchers travelling from the west and north of Britain or those heading for western France or Scandinavia; details of services can be found in the *ABC Shipping Guide* or the *Thomas Cook Continental Timetable* at any library.

If you have a pathological objection to spending money on transport, it is still possible to get a free ride on commercial ferries. Most bookings for lorries allow for the driver and one passenger, so you may be lucky enough to find a lone lorry driver. The best places to look are both in London: around Smithfield Markct (tube to Farringdon) and at the Stratford International Freight Depot (tube to Stratford, then a long walk). Short of stowing away, the only other ways to get a free ride accross the channel are by latching on to private transport, e.g. sailing boats or private aircraft. For the former, try asking around at the marinas in Brighton, Dover or Walton-on-the-Naze. Offer to act as crew and claim years of sailing experience. Hitching a private aircraft is less easy unless you can cultivate contacts beforehand. Airport officials know the pilots personally and also know who's flying where, so try and get a friendly official on your side.

But if you're unable to convince anyone of your nautical or aeronautical prowess, you'll just have to join the masses on the cross channel ferries. Although you may be able to avoid the problems associated with hitching out of channel ports — crowds of hitchers and a hostile atmosphere — by arranging a lift with a driver on board, a port to port ticket may not represent the best value for money. It is usually better to start your trip by buying a through ticket by bus or train. The best rail bargains for anyone under 26 are those offered by Transalpino through many travel agents: London to Paris, or to any station in Belgium, for about £15; London to any Dutch station for £18 (day) or £20 (night). In Paris you are poised for all points south, while the other two tickets can take you right into Germany upon payment of the small additional fare across the border on the train (if they find you). The Belgian ticket is simply inscribed *Toute Gare Belge*, so you can stay on the train to Aachen. For the Dutch ticket you must name the station you wish to travel to. Oldenzaal is the station closest to the German border — stay on the train an extra 40 km over the border to the Rheine for the E8 to Hannover, Berlin and Scandinavia.

Over 26's can still qualify for special Sealink night fares to Paris or Brussels for £18 or so. And anyone can get a Magic Bus, Supabus or Euroways ticket to these cities for around £16. For a little more they'll take you further afield, but after a while hitching becomes just one of many preferable alternatives to sitting on a bus.

Finally, the introduction of Virgin Atlantic's low fare from Gatwick to Maastricht in southern Holland means that the jet-set hitcher can get off to a flying start for very little more than the cost of a train or bus ticket. Maastricht is ideally placed on the motorway network for the east and south of Europe. It is essential to reserve a seat early at any travel agency, or the Virgin Megastore in London's Oxford St, or by calling Crawley (0293) 38222.

Routes and Maps. There is no substitute for taking a long look at the map and choosing the fastest route to take before you set off on any journey. Even if you later change your plans to take advantage of a long lift on a slightly tangential course, an awareness of your general direction will stand you in good stead. The maps in this book are only useful as general guides, and you are advised to obtain route planning maps of all the countries you will pass through. These are always available free from the national tourist offices, although the quality and detail vary considerably from one country to another. It is well worth stocking up with free tourist office maps in London. A circumnavigation of every office listed takes a shade under two hours of foot, and will be rewarded with a rucksack-full of material, much of it in English.

A good free map of the whole of Europe (south of Gothenburg and west of Belgrade) is published each year by the Calais Chamber of Commerce. In England it is available from G. L. Treble Associates, 19 Hampstead Lane, London N6 4BR, and may be picked up at many travel agencies in Britain. On the reverse is a complete list of sailings from Dover to Calais. A more detailed planning map is Europe Overland (£2.95) published by Roger Lascelles, 47 York Road, Brentford, Middlesex TW8 0QP (tel: 01-847 0935). It is available from bookshops with a good foreign map section. Roger Lascelles also distributes a wide range of continental maps, including a new series covering every European country at £3.95 each.

Any self-respecting map, on whatever scale, should be able to tell you the difference between major and minor roads. However, there may still be occasions when you may have to rely on road signs alone. So under each country there is a brief guide to the road numbering systems. But remember that road numbers are allocated bureaucratically, so the routes chosen sometimes have little relevance to the quickest or shortest way between two points. This is especially true as more and more new motorways are built, reducing the importance of former trunk roads, and sometimes elevating a previously minor road into a vital and much travelled link route.

Bureaucratic principles have also appointed the international E-road numbers, which are widely used alongside national road numbers in several continental countries. In some cases, E-roads are no more than a bureaucratic way of dividing up the map, and the powers that decide the routes (the Inland Transport Committee of the UN Economic Commission for Europe) are often slow to realise when new motorways have been built. It can be fun to think that the E5 (which begins life as the A2 at the Elephant and Castle in London) goes right through to Istanbul and on into deepest Asia, but in fact the average traffic between London and Istanbul will probably choose to leave the E5 at Nuremburg, then go on the E6, E11, E14 and E94 before rejoining the E5 at Belgrade. East of Belgrade it splits into the E5N (north) and E5S, but the Bulgarians have chosen unilaterally to implement an entirely new and different system of E-numbering (see below). There is also an apparent bureaucratic horror of overlapping E-routes. The E3 and E4, for instance, both go from Lisbon to Helsinki, but they only meet for a brief kilometers around Stockholm. The policy of not overlapping has turned some E-roads into little more than jokes. The E7, an otherwise sensible road, crosses Italy from Udine to Rome. But, having taken the obvious *autostrada* route down as far as Bologna, it then inexplicably heads east to Forli and tackles the slow hilly road south to Rome via Perugia. Most people choose the *Autostrada del Sole,* E6.

In general, the lower the E-number, the more important it is. Numbers E1 to E27 are designated as "main international traffic arteries," the remainder as "branch and link roads." The longest come within the first twenty, and the top 27 are listed below. Note that some countries (e.g. Great Britain) choose to ignore the existence of E-roads, while those which pass through Bulgaria change numbers at the border.

E1: London – Southampton – Le Havre – Paris – Lyon – Nice – Livorno – Rome – Naples – Messina – Palermo

E2: London – Dover – Calais – Reims – Dijon – Lausanne – Simplon – Milan – Bologna – Ancona – Brindisi

E3: Helsinki – Turku – Stockholm – Gothenburg – Frederikshavn – Hamburg – Eindhoven – Paris – Tours – Bordeaux – Burgos – Valladolid – Coimbra – Lisbon

E4: Helsinki – Oulu – Sundsvall – Stockholm – Jönköping – Hälsingborg – Copenhagen – Rødby – Puttgarden – Hannover – Kassel – Frankfurt – Basel – Geneva – Chambéry – Nîmes – Perpignan – Madrid – Badajoz – Lisbon

E5: London – Dover – Ostend – Brussels – Cologne – Nuremburg – Linz – Vienna – Budapest – Szeged – Belgrade – Nis – Istanbul (E5N via Sofia, E5S via Skopje and Thessaloniki) – Ankara – Iskenderun

E6: Vollan – Trondheim – Oslo – Malmö – Trelleborg – Sassnitz – Berlin – Munich – Innsbruck – Bologna – Rome

E7: Warsaw – Krakow – Brno – Vienna – Villach – Udine – Bologna – Perugia – Rome

E8: London – Harwich – Hook of Holland – Utrecht – Hannover – Berlin – Poznan – Warsaw – Briest

E9: Amsterdam – Eindhoven – Liege – Metz – Strasbourg – Mulhouse – Lucerne – Como – Genoa

E10: Groningen – Amsterdam – Brussels – Paris

E11: Paris – Strasbourg – Stuttgart – Salzburg

E12: Paris – Saarbrücken – Nuremburg – Prague – Wroclaw – Warsaw – Bialystok

E13: Lyon – Turin – Milan – Venice

E14: Szczecin – Prague – Salzburg – Udine – Trieste

E15: Hamburg – Berlin – Prague – Bratislava – Budapest – Bucharest – Constanta

E16: Bratislava – Lodz – Gdynia

E17: Dijon – Basel – Zürich – Innsbruck – Salzburg

E18: Stavanger – Oslo – Örebro – Stockholm

E19: Igoumenitsa – Arta – Korinthos

E20: Florina – Thessaloniki – Sofia – Ruse – Bacau – Siret

E21: Savona – Turin – Aosta – Geneva (E21a via Grand St Bernard; E21b via Mont Blanc)

E22: Berlin – Wroclaw – Krakow – Przemysl

E23: Izmir – Ankara – Agri

E24: Kesan – Izmir – Adana – Gaziantep – Esendere

E25: Burgos – Madrid – Seville – Cadiz – Algeciras

E26: Barcelona – Valencia – Granada – Málaga – Algeciras

E27: Trieste – Split – Skopje – Sofia – Varna

This existing network first came into being with the *Declaration on the Construction of Main International Traffic Arteries*, dating from 1950. It has since been revised and new roads have been added, most notably at the Varna Conference in 1965, which introduced the whole of the south-east Europe into the system. The USSR and Albania have never participated.

The International Transport Committee of UNECE met again in Geneva on October 20th, 1975, and drew up a *European Agreement on Main International Traffic Arteries*. This will replace the existing network, but only when it has been agreed and signed by at least eight of the countries involved. If there ever seems any danger that this target will be reached, details of the scheme — which involves a complex grid system — will appear in future editions of this book.

Crossing Frontiers. Frontiers can be particularly effective time wasters. On the motorways, notice how traffic thins down after the last exit before the frontier. On other roads, note how traffic dwindles constantly over the last few kilometers. Some borders (notably between Spain and Portugal and in Eastern Europe) close at night, which can bring nocturnal hitching to an unceremonious halt. Always choose a main route, preferably a motorway, to negotiate frontier crossings. Many border posts nowadays have a whole host of side industries, like banks, haulage depots and tourist offices. On motorways, this makes pedestrians (therefore also hitch-hikers) legal, and there can actually be no better place to try your luck. Here you have all the long distance traffic forced to stop and channelled past your waiting thumb. On the other hand, if you get a lift going as far as the frontier, you have, in most cases, also got a lift going across the frontier, and you may prefer to get over this hurdle and well into the next country before you try for your next lift. So weigh up the volume and quality of traffic, as well as the possible reaction of the customs officers and border police, before you take the plunge. At motorway frontiers with very little banking and commercial activity, you could still be hitching illegally, and it might be worth asking the customs or immigration officials whether they would mind you hitching there before you get out of your current lift. If in doubt, drive on.

Borders are best crossed in private cars, since the only formality will be to check the validity of your passports. If it is established that you are a hitch-hiker (which isn't always obvious if your luggage is well tucked away), you may be asked the routine questions about how much money you have. If you envisage money problems, it's always worth sounding out the driver for a loan — just so you can wave something at the officials. Most border guards assume that all hitchers are students, and hence unlikely to be a permanent danger to their country. It's a good idea to ensure that the occupation shown in you passport confirms their beliefs. Many experienced travellers rely upon the title of 'student teacher,' which covers a multitude of sins. Even if you're actually a bus conductress or male model, there's no problem in describing yourself as a student teacher when applying for a passport. Remember that drivers may be carrying excess money, drugs or other naughty things, and may deliberately or accidentally implicate you if they are discovered by officials. So if you have any reason to suspect that your vehicle has tyres full of marijuana rather than air, or runs on whisky instead of petrol, then makes some excuse to get out before you cross the frontier.

Lorries and other commercial vehicles may sound like a good bet for international lifts, because they often cover such vast distances. But beware. They are also subject to vast amounts of paperwork. If you're offered a lift across a frontier in a truck, ask the driver if he expects a long wait to clear the paperwork. If in doubt, try to at least get some reassurance that you'll be allowed to get out and hitch at the frontier should he get held up. Drivers always know roughly how long they'll be, and usually within the EEC there is little problem (except when entering or leaving Italy). Switzerland can also usually provide clearance fairly quickly, and movement within the Nordic countries is tolerable. Elsewhere, expect a long wait: four hours is not uncommon, and some drivers allow a day for each border where they expect problems. At busy frontier crossings, the problem is often not the amount of paperwork for each lorry, nore the undue slowness or obstinacy of the officials. It simply boils down to a shortage of road space and the ensuing free-for-all that develops as the drivers and their vehicles try to fight their way through. In the attempt to save time, drivers merely obstruct each other and end up wasting everyone's time.

There are, of course, occasions when it's worth sitting out a four-hour frontier crossing. A very fast lorry going a very long way is one example. And if you're snowed up on the Brenner Pass in the middle of the night, there are certain advantages in sitting around in a nice warm cab.

Trains and Boats and Planes. The gentle art of hitching is not restricted to road transport, and some hints have already been given on ways of crossing the channel for free. Similar principles apply to most stretches of water, and, if you have the right contacts or persuasiveness, air hitching is theoretically possible from any airfield that carries private air traffic. Boats can also be hitched on canals — particularly in the Netherlands — and on such major waterways as the Rhine and the Danube. If you can claim to have nautical experience, then a free (or even paid) cruise in the Mediterranean is not completely unthinkable. Simply turn up at one of the ports on the French Riviera between Marseilles and Nice and extol your maritime expertise. *Work Your Way Around the World* (Vacation Work, £5.95) contains further information on earning a free passage.

If you fancy yourself as an American-style hobo in the Woody Guthrie and Jack Kerouac tradition, then the idea of jumping freight trains will undoubtedly appeal. Entry to most European stations and associated marshalling yards is completely uncontrolled. But containerisation has taken much of the fun out of riding freight trains. Comfortable old hay wagons with sliding doors are virtually extinct.

The Usual Warnings

Psychopaths. Everyone's mother worries about rapists, stranglers and unspecified maniacs, so it is worth commenting on the most common rational and irrational fears.

Girls, particularly single girls, are most at risk of sexual assault. Women should consider carefully the risks involved; if they choose to hitch alone, it is essential to take precautions. Always carry some device — a pepper pot, aerosol can or rape alarm — to give yourself time to get away. This is easier and safer than fighting back. Better still, turn down any offers of lifts which look as though they might cause problems. It is certainly true that aggressive males in the southern countries of Spain, Italy and Greece often make their intentions perfectly clear, and sometimes pursue them to the point of violence. Having been warned, you should try to avoid such characters and be prepared to defend yourself. Some single females have found that an expert command of curses in the vernacular is sufficient to ward off most unwanted approaches. An Australian girl who has survived many years of solo hitching in southern Europe has a neat solution. As soon as she gets into a vehicle, she takes out an apple and a knife. She peels the apple swiftly and deftly, and offers it to the driver. Having established her ability to defend herself, she travels without incidents. However, this trick requires skill and self-confidence if it is not to rebound on you.

A more serious warning is required about the hidden and unexpected danger that comes from the man who looks respectable or even fatherly. When he suddenly turns nasty, the surprise element makes this character twice as dangerous as the man who makes little attempt to conceal his intentions.

These warnings apply mainly to girls who insist on travelling alone despite what mother says. It can also be extended to girls hitching in pairs, and to a lesser degree to men who may be picked up by aggressive homosexuals. A sensible rule of thumb is to turn down offers of lifts in vehicles whose occupants outnumber yourselves. Adhering to this guideline, men should be able to fend for themselves, and a combination of a man and a girl, or two men together, should encounter no trouble of this nature. If a real psychopath (the type that uses shotguns, sharp knives and axes) picks you up, it doesn't really matter how many men you're travelling with.

Demon Drivers. If your main worry is getting picked up by someone trying to break the world land speed record over the Brenner Pass, then you will be choosy about the lifts you accept. Anyone who screeches to a halt and nearly knocks you over while stopping for you is not likely to appeal.

It is commonly thought that all drivers of Latin origin — from Calais to Brindisi — are suicidal speed merchants. This is partly true, but it is also true that the years of practice have made them highly skilled in the use of brakes and horns. Don't worry about Citröen 2CV drivers, either. They all claim that their cars are impossible to turn over, and will try to disprove this claim at every corner, hairpin bend or police road block. Few succeed. More dangerous than the speed kings are the slow dreamy drivers who are either drunk or just about to fall asleep.

Again, the blanket rule is to turn down anyone you suspect of being a dangerous driver. If you discover this only when you're in the car, then feigning sickness or suddenly announcing that you're going the wrong way are the most effective methods of getting out alive. It should not be necessary to warn that seat belts should be worn at all times as a protection against injury and the law.

Central Locking and Other Dangers. A serious threat has arisen from the central locking systems with which a driver can seal all the car doors at the touch of a switch. In the past, these were restricted to the more expensive makes — Jaguar, BMW and Mercedes — but they are now installed in large numbers of new vehicles. You could avoid the possibility of incarceration by sticking to beaten-up VW's, but few hitchers have sufficient willpower to turn down all modern cars. Keep alert, however safe you feel. Some central locking devices can be used to steal your luggage, since they operate the lock on the boot (or rear door on hatchbacks and estates). Travel insurance will cover your belongings should a driver misappropriate them, but this is poor compensation for a ruined trip. Protect your luggage by keeping it with you inside the car whenever possible. If this is not practical, then when you come to reclaim your pack from the boot try to keep at least one passenger door open until the operation is completed. This procedure is much more easily achieved by two people hitching together.

In vehicles not equipped with central locking, the driver usually has to get out or hand you the keys to open the boot. Wait for him to do so before getting out yourself. By following these rules, you should avoid a repeat of the fiasco on the *autostrada* near Rome a few summers ago, when a rogue driver made off with the goods and chattels of a dozen naive hitchers. Finally, keep your passport and funds close to your skin throughout your travels; disasters are slightly more bearable if you have some form of identification and finance.

Health. Staying fit and healthy is crucial to a hitch-hiking trip abroad. If you sprain your ankle running for a car, or contract a mysterious stomach complaint, you might as well give up and get the train. There's not much you can do to avoid injuries (except take care), but preventing stomach upsets is possible with a few sensible precautions. Wash all fresh fruit and vegetables, drink bottled water if the local tap variety seems dubious, and don't overindulge in cheap wine. Should you succumb, you'll have to rest up for a few days until you recover. Very few things are worse (for drivers and hitchers) than trying to hitch a long distance when you have to get out every hour and search for a highly unsanitary hole in the ground.

Insurance. If you follow all the recommendations above, there's no reason why, as a hitch-hiker, you're any more likely to come to grief than the average package tourist. Nevertheless, travelling abroad without insurance is most unwise. If you're British and pay full National Insurance contributions, form E111 (available from DHSS offices) will give partial medical cover within the EEC. Most non-EEC countries have more beneficial reciprocal agreements for reduced-rate treatment for British passport holders. However, the consequences of a serious accident could still be extremely costly. So you should also take out travel insurance covering yourself (in case of illness, injury or death) and your belongings (in case of theft, loss or damage). Any travel agent or insurance broker will sell you a policy. Pairs of hitchers should ensure that the cover extends to flying both back should one fall ill.

The Long Wait. After psychopaths, multi-car pile-ups and personal disasters, the next worry is the long wait. Although the advice in this book should reduce your waiting time, there is always the one unpredictable element — luck — that conspires against even the best of us, and the time will come when you simply get stuck. When this happens, take solace from reading the following paragraphs at hourly intervals.

At first, of course, you will not realise what is happening to you and your time will be spent trying to get a lift for maybe the first hour or two, carrying on in blissful optimism that the next car will stop. As your optimism wanes you will try all sorts of gimmicks, like dressing up in your spare gorilla costume. When this fails, you begin to feel a general malevolence towards your fellow man, and the symptoms of the long wait become apparent: optimism gives way to despair, and the task of securing a lift becomes an awful hardship. The timing of this depends on a lot of things and the most seasoned hitchers can stand for six hours or more without batting an eyelid. The speed of onset is directly related to the lack of traffic, location, weather and presence or absence of company, and also how much of a hurry you're in. Whenever the symptoms start — be it in half an hour or half a day — you will need something to occupy your mind.

If there are two of you, then passing the time is easy. I-spy and other trivial games can keep the spirits alive for hours. Or you can invent some game or form of betting that revolves around the business of hitching itself. Take turns at hitching and the one to get the lift wins a prize. Or bet on the colour of the next car to come along. If there's not much traffic, you might prefer to turn your thoughts on some totally different pursuit like snail racing or trying to catch lizards (you won't).

When you're alone, hitcher's depression is more severe and sudden. I-spy isn't much fun on your own, but singing is an occupation probably best undertaken alone if your musical abilities are those of the average hitch-hiker. It's not necessary to know all the words to a song, since you can always make up lyrics to fit your current plight: "In the Middle of Nowhere" becomes "In the Middle of Norway"; similarly "Thumb Kinda Wonderful" and "24 Hours from Tulse Hill." A radio is also useful to remind yourself you're not the only person in the world. The Sony Walkman type are light and easy to carry (and may also keep your ears warm in a blizzard) but Britons may prefer a portable which can pick up BBC Radio 4 (1500m/200kHz) and the World Service (463m/648kHz or short wave) in order to keep up with "Today in Parliament" or "News about Britain." Hand-held CB radio equipment is not recommended: British sets are incompatible with Continental rigs, their importation is prohibited by many countries, and double Dutch becomes a reality should you tune into the truckers' network in Holland. For similar technical and linguistic reasons, the flat TV sets produced by Sony and Sinclair do not form part of the solo hitcher's essential equipment.

When your radio batteries finally expire, and when you've written your memoirs up to date you can still invent some sort of game to keep your hopes up. Superstitious games can be fun, like trying to determine which car will stop. For example set a tin can on a gatepost and throw stones at it. If you hit it with, say, the seventh stone, that means the seventh car will stop. When the seventh car goes past, start throwing again.

Whatever happens, don't get caught in the vicious spiral that afflicts so many of the victims of the long wait. This trap is easy to fall into: you become progressively more miserable as the wait increases, in proportion to your distance from home and shortage of funds. Motorists are not inclined to pick up a hitcher who looks at though he's going to bemoan his misfortune for the duration of the ride, so fewer and fewer drivers even consider stopping for you. Hence you become miserable still, and so on.

You have to break out of the spiral. By now, you desperately need a lift — if only for a few kilometers — to reassure yourself that you're not the least desirable person on the face of the earth. So change your tactics. If you're displaying a sign for a rather hopeful and far-off destination, then get rid ot it. Better still, make a sign saying "20km". Its novelty value alone can entice drivers into stopping. Once inside the vehicle you're free to reveal that you're heading for Belgrade rather than Bruges and can negotiate accordingly. If you've strewn your belongings untidily by the roadside, manoeuvre them into the smallest possible space. Merely turning a rucksack so that the narrower side faces oncoming motorists can tilt the balance between a driver dismissing you as too much trouble or deciding to stop for you.

Some hitchers vent their frustration on road signs. Adding your contribution to the tales of woe on a motorway signpost is not recommended, since it gives the police something to book you for. But fellow sufferers' graffiti is often good to read. A sign on the A4 outside Strasbourg bears the following:

La patience est la loi du stop
Je veux retourner chez maman
This country is a real shit for hijackers (sic)

Finally, here are some ideas for when you run out of ideas — when you get really desperate for a car to stop:

Throw stones at passing traffic (someone will soon stop and beat you up).

Break a bottle and spread the glass liberally in the road (then offer to help change the wheel in exchange for a lift).

Stand, sit, kneel or lie down in the middle of the road (almost guarantees a lift in either an ambulance or a hearse).

Luck is such an essential part of hitching that it is advisable never to hitch against the clock or set yourself deadlines, as you could easily be disappointed. There is in fact an old hitcher's superstition that a deadline or time limit slows you down. This is known as Boo's Law, after an American girl who was hitching back from Greece to meet her parents off a plane at Heathrow. With 48 hours to go, she was picked up in a stolen car and arrested by the police in Milan. The twist in the story is that she made it back in time — luckily, her parents' flight was an hour late. But the moral is that deadlines are inadvisable. Even a vague thought like: "At this rate I should be in Paris by six o'clock tonight," can add hours on to your journey time.

Best and Worst in Europe

Worst. There are huge tracts of Europe where hitching can be very slow and a thoroughly miserable affair: for example southern Spain, most of Yugoslavia, and northern Scandinavia in winter. But each of the three blackspots below is a place where hitchers are frequently abandoned to an almost hopeless fate. Do not accept any lift which could leave you at any of the following:

1. **Lyon,** trying to hitch on the the A6 north or A7 south. Most of the interchanges are in built-up squalor clogged with local traffic, and because the waiting times are so long most junctions are crawling with rival hitchers.

2. **Nimes-Ouest** (heading east) and **Nimes-Est** (heading west) on the A9 in the south of France. It is always difficult to get a lift in the required direction from a motorway junction on the 'wrong' side of the town. Nowhere is this principle better illustrated than at these dismal autoroute junctions. The only possible remedy (apart from going into Nimes then out again) is to hitch the other way: back down the A9 to the nearest service area, then cross the autoroute to change direction and start again.

3. **Salzburg,** going east on the E11 towards Munich. It is never easy to hitch across impending frontiers, but the virtual impossibility of getting a ride over the Austro-German border from this tourist-infested city has reduced lifelong hitchers to taking the train (to Traunstein in Germany). Only Salzburg-Mitte and the Kasern service area offer any hope at all. The local drivers realise the problems for hitchers to the extent that they routinely demand money before picking you up. If you can negotiate a lift as far as the border for around 50 schillings, it would seem like a good investment under the circumstances.

Best. The criteria for the top three places involves not only how quickly you get a lift, but how good the lift is likely to be. The very best hitching spot in Europe used to be Bentheim on the E8 in western Germany, close to the Dutch border and hence cheaply reached on Transalpino ticket from London. All the international traffic was channeled past the lucky hitcher's thumb on a single carriageway road equipped with traffic lights and laybys.

Unfortunately, to coincide with the new edition of this book, a new stretch of autobahn is due to bypass Bentheim in 1985. But Germany still provides the winner.

1. **Dreilinden frontier post, West Berlin,** heading south or west. This spot is always crowded with a motley assortment of hitchers plus their offspring, pets and possessions; the city authorities have erected barriers to prevent hitchers from blocking the road entirely. But such is the siege mentality in West Berlin that around half the available vehicles stop. And because of the regulation that you have to get a lift straight through to West Germany, West Berlin is the one place in Europe where you're guaranteed a minimum lift of 200km. The only cloud on the horizon is that the hitching spot is technically part of the motorway, so West Berlin could lose the title overnight at the whim of the authorities.

2. **Krakow,** Poland heading north on the E7. Any westerner is guaranteed easy lifts in Poland, particularly during the official summer hitching season. The road to Warsaw is often crowded but the hitching is consistently good, at least during the hours of daylight.

3. **M5/A40** junction between Cheltenham and Gloucester. Of the many excellent hitching spots in Britain, this is the quickest.

Author's note: The winners in both best and worst categories have been arrived at as a result of my own experiences and in consultation with many other hitch-hikers. Readers are warmly invited to suggest other contenders for either category.

Hitching out of Towns

From the northern channel ports it is easy to plan all-motorway routes as far as Denmark, Poland, Vienna, the toe or heel of Italy or the Costa Blanca in Spain. The main thing about travelling the motorways is that you never need to delve into the towns on your route, although in some cases — London, Paris and Munich spring to mind — there are towns that generate so much of their own traffic that it may be worth going into them and starting again on the other side. Otherwise, the general rule is that, as long as there's a satisfactory motorway going past the town, you should get out at a busy service area or slip road before you reach the town (shown on the motorway maps in each country section) then wait till you get a lift past it.

Despite this, there will be occasions when you plan to visit a particular town before moving on. The problems come when you want to leave, but the basic principles are quite simple. Find a map of the town and work out where the traffic is routed in your direction. If the town is close to a motorway, select the best motorway slip road for your purposes, and aim for that. On the map, pick yourself a good looking location to stand: the motorway slip road if it's close enough, otherwise a promising looking junction on the edge of town.

Reckoning that every kilometer represents a brisk ten-minute walk, and considering such factors as the amount of luggage you're carrying, how much of a rush you're in, decide whether your selected location is within walking distance. If so, off you go. If not, accost some likely looking native and ask which bus or tram to take to get there. Because maps can often be deceptive (not to say inaccurate), this method is partly trial and error. If you can't afford the error, try to find someone who looks as if they might know about hitching from first hand, in order to confirm the best place to stand.

A general principle about any town is that the further you go from the town centre, the more pleasant and effective the hitching becomes. It is possible, for instance, to hitch from the Place de la Concorde in Paris, but you're unlikely to get a lift going further than the suburbs. It is also an unpleasant place to stand because of the high density of pedestrians and the sheer volume of traffic, 99% of which is very local. Going north, it is also possible to hitch at the Porte de la Chapelle. Pedestrians are less of a problem here, because you're at the start of the *Autoroute du Nord,* but many other hitch-hikers know of the place so you're likely to be one of the dozen or more; and the volume of traffic is still too heavy to make life easy for the drivers who would otherwise like to stop and pick you up.

For real style, why not invest in the bus fare to an outer suburb like Le Bourget, where the slip road has a respectable flow of traffic, you only need a 20km lift to the first major service area, the pace of life is slow enough to allow you to stand unimpeded by pedestrians and other hitch-hikers, and where the volume of traffic is low enough to allow drivers to stop if they want to. After waiting an hour at Porte de la Chapelle, this might be where you get dropped in any case!

Any town is a headache to get out of, but the headaches can be reduced to a minimum if you select a good place to stand, with the above criteria in mind. Remember particularly that a heavy flow of traffic is not, in itself, a good thing. Hordes of local cars prevent each other from stopping — if indeed they even see you all — and make it impossible for you to pick out the long distance ones. A three-hour wait at a very busy exit from a large town is one of the most depressing, frustrating and exhausting experiences on record. Too much traffic is, if anything, worse than too little.

In general, the worst towns to get out of are those that have complex motorway networks extending well into the city centre. Although you won't have to go far to find a hitching point, you will invariably find that you can hardly move for local traffic. The worst culprits are Lyon, Dusseldorf, Cologne and Hamburg — towns which you should bypass at all costs.

To help you get out of Europe's biggest, most difficult and most frequently visited towns, we offer a *Town Guide* for each country. The abbreviations and symbols used are as follows:

N:	north	L:	left
W:	west	R:	right
S:	south	jn:	junction
E:	east	rdbt:	roundabout
St:	Street or Saint	Str:	Straat/Strasse
Rd:	Road	Ave: Avenue/Avenida	Blvd:	Boulevard

⊞ :	walk	⊞ :	bus	⚏ :	train
⚓ :	boat/ferry	⊖ :	underground	⬚ :	tram

The ⊖ symbol is used for all types of metropolitan railway, eg underground in London; *metro* in Paris, Barcelona, Rome, etc; *U-Bahn* in Germany and Austria; *T-Bana* in Stockholm; etc. Urban networks that more closely resemble railways than undergrounds are awarded the symbol, followed by the name of the system (eg S-Bahn) in parentheses.

While train and metro services are normally easy to use, buses and trams can present problems. Before you pay for a bus or tram, check with the driver that he's going your way. Show him the entry from the *Town Guide* in this book. Just mention "autostop" and you'll probably be inundated with advice.

Information on routes, and destinations and hitching points is presented as in the following example:

Starting point (and native version —————	**GENOA (Genova)**
of town name if English is	
different)	
Road number(s): Destination(s) ———	**A12: La Spezia, Rome (A11, A1)**
	A10: Ventimiglia; A7: Milan
Directions to hitching points from ——	⊞ 1.5km: from the main station W
town centre	along Via S. Benedetto, Via Buozzi
	and Via A. Cantore to motorway
Star rating (see below) —————————	entrance. Sign pref.***

On the route/destination line, more than one route is sometimes given. Numbers separated by a stroke (/) are alternative numbers for the same road (eg national/E numbers). Numbers following a comma (,) are branch roads off the previous road given. Numbers in parentheses are branch routes to the last named town only. Routes out of towns are given in clockwise order, usually starting with the busiest.

The star ratings give an indication of the quality of the hitching place referred to. This, of course, is very hard to specify and depends on many factors. Some of them are straightforward, like the quantity and direction of the traffic. Others are less obvious: for example, hitching outside a police station increases your waiting time. But as a very rough guide, the maximum time that a single male (or a male and female) might expect to wait during business hours are given below for each of the star ratings.

        *   2 hours or more
        **   1-2 hours
        ***   30 minutes-1 hour
        **** 30 minutes or less

Motorway Hitching

It is universally illegal to hitch on motorways. Many hitchers openly flaunt the law, and spot-fines are rare in proportion to the number of offences. But on most stretches of motorway — where traffic is going much too fast to think of stopping for you — hitching is impractical, frustrating and dangerous. The Germans are particularly strict about their theory that motorways begin at the beginning of the slip road, and they may send you back on to the main road. But in most other countries you can in practice stand on the slip road, which is after all the safest place for drivers to pull in. Anders Sterner survived a long hitching career and numerous brushes with the law by using a simple motto: always be obsequious. He recommends appearing neat rather than looking like a menace to society, and being polite and deferential. In this way he has often earned lifts from the police, and has not received a single ticket.

A growing menace to the hitch-hiker's freedom of movement lies with "semi-motorways", denoted by a sign showing the front view of a car in white on a background of green or blue. These *autoschnellwegs* and *superstradas* suffer from roughly the same rules as motorways but are not up to so high a quality. So the slip roads may not have hard shoulders, and there won't be service areas every few kilometers as there are on real motorways. These roads are best avoided.

If you're aiming for speed, then stick to motorway hitching as much as possible. Once on a motorway, use the diagrammatic maps (under each country) to choose where to get out and try for your next lift. If you're on one of the less important motorways that isn't covered by this book, the general principle is to hop from one service area to the next. Alternatively, choose exits that look busy on the map, i.e. close to a big town, or serving a route that otherwise carries fairly heavy traffic.

If you get out at a motorway slip road serving a large town, be careful how you choose the slip road. Most traffic leaving towns to go west will use a slip road to the west of the town, so don't get dropped at the one to the east of the town (as is likely to happen if you're coming from the east). In this case, get out at an earlier service area or a busier junction.

If you're lucky enough to have a map with details of all the service areas marked, then follow the principle of the larger the better. This principle breaks down where two of fairly equal size are close together. In such cases, the first one is usually busier than the second. There are interesting variations, too, as you approach frontiers, where the busiest services will be just inside the country where petrol is cheaper. Belgium, Finland and

Switzerland sell petrol for less than their neighbours. Service areas with nothing more than petrol stations are usually pretty deserted, where as those with restaurants (a knife and fork on the road signs) are generally busy. Service areas usually stay open and well lit at night so are better than slip roads for 24 hours of the day. Avoid all picnic areas and the like, since their only visitors are cars filled with families. They are not shown on the motorway maps, as you should never allow a driver to drop you off at one (unless you actually want a picnic).

In this book, a fair amount of space is devoted to diagrammatic maps of the main international motorways. The purpose of these maps is to indicate the best places to get lifts. The junctions and service areas marked with an arrow (▲ or ▼) are good places to hitch in the direction of the arrow. A diamond, or double arrow (◆) indicates good hitching in both directions. This information is comparative rather than absolute: the arrows merely indicate the best places on that particular stretch of motorway, and some of these may still be pretty bad. The places without arrows are notably worse.

The interpretation of the maps should otherwise be pretty clear. Motorways are shown as double lines, and with text in **bold print**; other roads are shown as single lines, with text in medium print. Services are marked as short thick lines alongside the main motorway, and with text in *italics*. The method of naming or numbering junctions varies from country to country, but the names and numbers given on the maps will reflect what you will see on road signs. Some junctions only allow access to the motorway in one direction, and this can cause huge problems if you're going the other way. Such junctions are marked in the map with an 'x' on the carriageway to which access is not possible. The other major hazard is the all-motorway junction where two motorways meet and the entire interchange is subject to motorway regulations. These junctions are clearly marked **illegal**. You should try to persuade drivers not to drop you off at an offending interchange, for instance by pointing out that the regulations do not allow cars to stop. If this fails, you have a choice between leaving the junction by the shortest available route for another road, or hitching illegally. If you choose the latter, be warned that the police are always on the lookout for stray hitchers at such places.

Austria

Austrian drivers regard hitchers as a necessary hazard of being at the crossroads of Europe, and some of them are fairly happy to pick you up. But if they don't feel in the mood, they are Europe's greatest exponents of driving past without noticing you. Nothing is more calculated to raise hitchers' tempers and lower their spirits than being totally ignored. You will get a lift eventually, usually totally out of the blue.

Rules of Thumb

Getting In. Austria has always claimed to be a country "where East meets West"; no less than seven other countries share her borders. The complexities of political alliance and geographical location mean that crossing into Austria can present problems to all nationalities. Searches are unlikely, however. It is more probable that you will have to prove that you are able to support yourself. If all you possess is 50 pfennigs and some sandwiches, you're out of luck. But the border guards seem remarkably impressed by credit cards and bundles of low denomination travellers cheques.

The Law. You get the feeling that Austrian police are sick of hitchers, and they make their feelings known by a fair amount of harrassment. For instance, you may thing that you're behaving quite legally, standing on the right side of a motorway sign, but the police seem to get almost sadistic pleasure from sending you 200 yards down the road to a hopeless hitching spot. Motorway law is the same as the rest of Europe, and very strictly enforced, so don't deliberately hitch from anywhere illegal. The police are particularly 'efficient' in the province of Oberösterreich. If you do get into trouble, Austrian jails are some of the worst in Europe.

Two of Austria's provinces — Vorarlberg and Styria — actually forbid hitching by young people under 16. Whatever you feel about such arbitrary discrimination, avoid hitching in either province until you're old enough. The frequency of police checks means that detection is likely. A letter from your parents permitting you to hitch-hike may soften their range a little, but it's just not worth the trouble getting caught. Fortunately, it's possible to travel through Austria without encroaching on these two forbidden provinces.

Route Planning. Apart from the motorways, which are numbered with the prefix A, Austrian road numbering falls into three classes. Minor roads are unnumbered, more important highways are numbered (sometimes with the prefix B, for *Bundesstrasse*) but are sub-divided into those without right of way (signposted by yellow circles) and those with right of way (signposted with blue squares). The E-route numbering system is also found on maps and signs.

Fortunately, most motorway junctions are fairly well used and many service stations (*Rastplätze*) are located by junctions, which is an ideal arrangement for hitching: you get all the normal slip road traffic plus the vehicles using the service station.

Maps. The free map issued by the Austrian Government Tourist Office, 30 St George St, London W1, is pretty basic, but city tourist offices generally tend to produce detailed and accurate street plans of the main cities. Detailed maps of the country will have to be paid for, but the western part of the country (as far as the Brenner motorway) is covered on the free map of Switzerland given away by the Union Bank of Switzerland or Swiss National Tourist Offices.

Place Names. The only possible confusion about place names may arise from Vienna (officially Wien, Wenen in Dutch, Vienne to the French) and the provinces of Styria (officially Steiermark) and Carinthia (Kärnten).

Number Plates. The town or province of origin is indicated by the first one or two letters of the number plates. The subsequent numbers reveal more about the precise locality of origin, but for hitching purposes the main letter codes, given below, should be sufficient.

B	Burgenland	N	Niederösterreich	T	Tirol
G	Graz	O	Oberösterreich	V	Vorarlberg
K	Kärnten	S	Salzburg	W	Wein
L	Linz	St	Steiermark		

Winter Hitching. Most main roads stay open in the winter, but the following passes are likely to be closed at least from December to April:

Gerlos   Silvretta   Loibl
Hochkrumbachsattel Würzner   Plöcken

Planned and Paid Lifts. The *Mitfahr* idea has spread from Germany to Austria. In Vienna, call 564174 or drop in at Franzengasse 11; in Innsbruck, call 32343.

Town Guide

(for key and explanation, see the introduction)

GRAZ

A9/E93 (north): Bruck, Salzburg (B113, B145, B158) Linz (B113, B138, A1)
⊞ 2km: N from station along Bahnhofgurtel, Wienerstr and over bridge to start of A9 approach road.**

B65: Gleisdorf, Budapest (8), Vienna (B54, A2)
⊞ 1km: NE along Elizabethstr to Leonhardtdplatz. Stand by cemetery on Riesstr (B65).**
🚌 1 to above jn.

A2 (east): Vienna, Budapest (B308, 8)
⊞ 3km: SE along Conrad von Hötzendorf-Str, L along Liechtensteingasse, R along Liebenauer Hauptstr to 200m past police station. Sign pref.*
🚌 4 along Hötzendorf-Str then ⊞ to above jn.

A9/E93 (south): Maribor (B67), Klagenfurt (A2 west, B70)
⊞ 1.5km: S along Kärtnerstr to start of A9. Sign pref.**

The 🚃 from Graz across the Yugoslav border to Sentilj costs about 50 Schillings.

INNSBRUCK

A12/E17 (west): Feldkirch, Munich (E6)
⊞ 2km: SW along Innrain and Volser Str to Innsbruck West motorway jn. Stand on A12 slip road. Sign pref.**

A12/E17 (east): Kufstein, Munich (E86, E11), Salzburg (B312)
⊞ 2km: SE along Amraser Str (or E along Burgerlandstr) and Amraser See Str to Innsbruck Ost motorway jn. Stand on A12 slip road. Sign pref.**

A13/E6: Brenner, Bolzano
⊞ to start of Brenner Str (B182) just east of Stubaitalbahnhof. Stand at lights on B182.** If there is any competition then ⊞ 2km up B182 to wide layby just beyond sharp left hand bend.***

Since tolls are charged on the Brenner Autobahn (A13), a lot of traffic uses the parallel B182. Hitch before the roads split to catch all the traffic.

LINZ

A7/E14 (south): Vienna (A1/E5), Salzburg (A1/E14), Nuremberg (E5)
⊞ to start of motorway on Unionstr, 300m south of Hauptbahnhof. Stand on slip road. Sign pref.***
🚌 14, 15 to above jn.

A7/E14 (north): Prague
⊞ as above. Sign pref.*
⊞ 1km: NE from Nibelungen Brücke along Untere Donaulände and Hafenstr to A7 jn (Linz-Hafen Str).

Stand on northbound slip road. Sign
pref.**
🚌 22 to above jn.

SALZBURG

A1/E14 (east): Linz, Vienna (E5)
🚶 3km: W from Lehener Brücke
along Ignaz Harrer Str and
Münchner Bundesstr to Salzburg
Mitte motorway jn. Stand on
eastbound slip road.***
🚌 4 to above jn.

🚌 S under airport to where bus turns
off at Himmelreich then 🚶 500m S
along Innsbrucker Bundesstr to
Salzburg West motorway jn. Stand
on eastbound slip road.**
🚌 G to Salzburg Nord motorway jn.
Stand on either eastbound slip
road.*

A1/E11 (west): Munich
🚌 G to Landstr/Samstr jn 200m
before motorway jn, then 🚶 300m E
along Samstr, L on Ruprechterstr for
100m, R down lane, under
motorway and across field to
Raststätte Kasern (services). Sign
pref.*
🚶 🚌 as for A1/E14 (east) above to
Salzburg Mitte, but stand on
westbound slip road. Sign pref.*

A10/E14 (south): Villach
🚌 3 to terminus then 🚶 S along
Alpenstr to A10 jn. Stand on slip
road.***
🚶 🚌 as for A1/E14 (east) above to
Salzburg Mitte, but stand on

westbound slip road. Sign pref.*
🚌 🚶 to Raststätte Kasern as for
A1/E11 (west) above. Sign pref.**

B1/E17: Innsbruck
🚌 🚶 as for A1/E14 (east) above to
Salzburg Mitte motorway jn. Stand
on B1**

VIENNA (Wien)

A1/E5 (west): Linz, Salzburg (E14)
🚌 49 or ⊖ 4 to Hutteldorf and 🚶
100m S to A1.** Or 🚶 1km to service
station*** or 500m more to start of
A1 proper opposite Novotel.****
🚶 from Camping-West 1km S to A1.

B2/E84: Stockerau, Prague (38,2)
🚌 32 to Prager Str (B2)/Nord
Autobahn/Gebauergasse jn.**

B7/E7 (north): Brno (52)
🚌 31 to Brunner Str (B7)/
Gerasdorferstr jn.**

B9: Bratislava
🚌 to Schwechat-Flughafen Wien.
Stand outside airport on B9.***

B10/E5 (east): Bruck, Budapest (1, M1)
🚌 72 to terminus at Schwechat then
🚶 500m E along B10 to jn with B9.**

A2/E7 (south): Graz, Klagenfurt
🚌 67 to Altes Landgut rdbt on
Favoritenstr, 6km S of city centre.
Stand on motorway slip road. Sign
pref.**

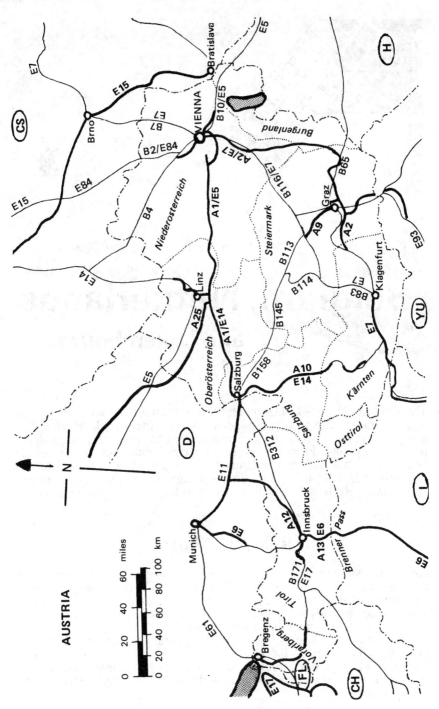

AUSTRIA

Belgium, Netherlands
and Luxembourg

The Low Countries — Belgium and the Netherlands — have among the highest traffic densities of any countries in the world. Hitch-hiking prospects are therefore quite encouraging, especially on the through routes to Germany and France. In general, the volume of traffic in the Netherlands and northern Belgium is far higher than in the south and Luxembourg, but to counteract this advantage the roads around Amsterdam, Rotterdam and Brussels are often choked with hitch-hikers.

Rules of Thumb

Getting In. No matter where you arrive from, Belgian and Luxembourgois customs are unlikely to offer much resistance. Dutch frontier officials sometimes express an interest in your funds, but rarely turn travellers away. Once inside Benelux, the constituent nations form a single economic unit and customs and immigration control has virtually ceased along common frontiers. You are more likely to meet the customs man if you enter from Germany or the UK, but the border posts on the north-east French frontier are often unmanned. If your passport is inspected and it is noticed that you have recently been in Turkey or Morocco, expect to be searched for drugs.

The Law. You are not allowed to hitch on motorways, and transgressions are likely to result in an on-the-spot fine. In Belgium, the police may stop you and enquire whether you are an international terrorist: the procedure usually involves holding on to your passport for ten minutes while they check your credentials over the radio. Drivers have been known to wait behind the police car and pick you up as soon as you've been cleared. The Dutch police have a more benevolent attitude to foreign hitch-hikers, and have been known to give lifts.

Road Strategy. Off the motorways, it's largely a question of finding a reasonable place to stand, and biding your time. On the motorways you will move quickly if you select your hitching points with care. Motorway service areas are not used as extensively as in Italy or Germany, so the best points are the access roads outside large towns. If you get a lift turning off to some remote village, get out at an earlier exit that serves a larger town. Wherever possible, choose a motorway route in preference to cross-country roads, even if it means doing two sides of a triangle. Most drivers do exactly the same. There are many all-motorway junctions to avoid, so using a sign becomes a virtual necessity.

Route Planning. Although there is a perfectly adequate system of numbering roads at a national level (A for *autoroute* or *autosnelweg*, N for *route nationale*), the E-numbers are much more widely used where they exist, i.e. most of the motorways. City ring roads in Belgium have the prefix R. R0 is Brussels, R1 Antwerp, etc.

Maps. If you want a decent road map of the Netherlands you'll have to pay for it. The map put out by the National Tourist Office, 143 New Bond St, London W1, is rather short on detail. Some local tourist offices (*VVV*) in the Netherlands make a charge for town maps: a much better plan is to visit the London office where they have been known to photocopy the required maps for you. If you're doing a lot of hitching in the eastern half of the Netherlands (east of Hilversum/Utrecht/Eindhoven), you will find this area covered in excellent detail on the free map of Germany issued by the German National Tourist office.

The Belgian Tourist Office map (free from 38 Dover St, London W1) is adequate. The town plans on the reverse are as good as any you can get free from local tourist offices. Better Belgian road maps and town plans are those published by Girault Gilbert and Recta Foldex, available from Roger Lascelles. The free map of Luxembourg available from the tourist office at 36 Piccadilly, London W1, is hardly worth bothering with.

Place Names. Being a bi-lingual country, there are many Belgian towns that have both French and Dutch names. The list below should aid your identification, and may avoid trouble: some people get very touchy if you use the wrong one. French speakers hate having Mons called Bergen, and so on. Apart from Brussels, for which both versions are "official", the official, i.e. native, version is given first. When composing signs, you may wish to use both Dutch and French names to avoid offence to speakers of either language. However, you may end up offending both.

French	Dutch		Dutch	French
Bruxelles	Brussel		Aalst	Alost
Arlon	Aarlen		Antwerpen	Anvers
Bastogne	Bastenaken		Brugge	Bruges
Gembloux	Gemblers		Dendermonde	Termonde
Huy	Hoei		Gent	Gand
Lessines	Lessen		Ieper	Ypres
Liège	Luik		Kortrijk	Courtrai
Mons	Bergen		Leuven	Louvain
Namur	Namen		Mechelen	Malines
Nivelles	Nijvel		Oostende	Ostende
Soignies	Zinnik		Roeselaere	Roulers
Tournai	Doornik		Tienen	Tirlemont
Waremme	Borgworm		Tongeren	Tongres
Wavre	Waver		Veurne	Furnes

Apart from Brussels, Antwerp, Ghent and Ostend, English versions of Belgian towns are faithful to one of the originals. German versions tend to be close to the Dutch, but most important variation is Liège (Lüttich).

As for the Netherlands, the British persist in callling Vlissingen Flushing. The Hook of Holland is called Hoek van Holland in Dutch, and the Hague is either den Haag or 's Gravenhage. In French, two towns are singled out for special treatment — the Hague (la Haye) and 's Hertogenbosch (Bois le Duc). In German, Arnhem is Arnheim and Nijmegen is Nimwegen.

Planned and Paid Lifts. The French system of hitch-hiking agencies is beginning to catch on in Belgium, and the main agency is *Taxi-Stop*, which has offices at Onderbergen 51, Gent, tel: 23.80.73; 6 place des Brabançons, 1340 Louvain-la-Neuve, tel: 41.81.99; and 31 rue de Bruxelles, 1300 Wavre, tel: 22.75.75. Otherwise, try university newspapers or notice boards, or the notices in *Info-Jeugd* or *Infor-Jeunes* offices.

Lift Service of Amsterdam operate only on behalf of people living in the Netherlands. All payments and lift arrangements must be made by post and telephone, and they have a two-week waiting list in summer. They can be contacted at Postbus 8310, 1005AH Amsterdam (tel: 020-84 67 30). An alternative — not restricted to Dutch residents — is to call Eindhoven (040) 555539.

Town Guide

(for key and explanation, see the introduction)

Belgium and Luxembourg

ANTWERP (Antwerpen, Anvers)

A1/E10 (south): Brussels
🚌 32 or 🚋 7, 15 to Grote Steenweg/ Elizabethlaan jn at Berchem. Stand on Elisabethlaan.**

A12: Brussels
🚌 25, 27 or 🚋 2 to Jan de Voslei/Jan van Rijswijcklaan jn. Stand at start of Boomsesteenweg.***
🚌 6, 13, 34 to Bolivarplaats. Stand on slip road leading to Jan de

Voslei.***
🚌 4, 12, 24, to K Silvertopstr just
south of Antwerp Zuid Station.
Stand on Jan de Voslei.***

A14/E3 (west): Ghent, Ostend (A10/ E5)

🚌 6, 13, 34 to Bolivarplaats. Stand
on westbound slip road to A14.***

A14/E3 (east): Liège (E39)

🚌 10 to Turnhoutsebaan at
Borgerhout. Stand at start of
motorway. Sign pref.***

A1/E10 (north): Rotterdam

🚌 63-67 to Breda Baan/A1 jn at
Merksem.**

BRUGES (Brugge)

A10/E5 (east): Ghent, Brussels

🚶 to start of Koning Albertlaan, just
behind station.**
🚌 7 to Jagersstr at St-Michiels, 🚶
along Jagersstr to Koning Albertlaan
and then S to Expressweg jn. Stand
on southbound slip road.***

A10/E5 (west): Ostend

🚶 to Koning Albertlaan, just behind
station. Sign pref.**
🚌 66b to motorway jn just before
Loppem. Stand on westbound slip
road.***

N71: Zeebrugge, Blankenberge

🚌 13 to Kasteel Rustenburg, then 🚶
500m along Oostendse Steenweg to
Expressweg jn. Stand on
northbound slip road.**

BRUSSELS (Brussel/Bruxelles)

A10/E5 (west): Ghent, Ostend

🚌 85 or 🚌 62 or 🚋 to start of A10 at
Berchem-St-Agathe. Stand on rdbt
(illegal).**** Or on approach road,
with sign (legal).***

A12: Antwerp, Amsterdam

🚌 52, 92 to start of A12 at Gros
Tilleul, just north of Laken Park.***

A1/E10 (north): Antwerp, Amsterdam

🚋 or 🚌 59, 63, 65 to start of A1 at

Bordet. Sign pref.***

A3/E5 (east): Liège, Aachen

⊖ 5 to Diamant Station. Stand on
approach road to A3.**

A4/E40: Namur, Luxembourg

⊖ 1 to Beaulieu Station. Stand at
start of A4.***

A7/E10 (south): Mons, Paris

🚌 50 from Gare du Midi/Zuid
Station to Stallestr/A7 jn at
Ruisbroek. Stand on A7 slip road.**

GHENT (Gent, Gand)

A10/E5 (east): Brussels
A14/E3 (south): Kortrijk, Lille
N58: Oudenaarde, Ronse

🚶 800m: S from Cathedral/Stadhuis
along Limburgstr, Vlaanderenstr
and Frére Orbanlaan. Stand on
approach road to motorway flyover.
Sign pref.***
🚋 1, 21, 22 or 🚌 70, 71 to above jn.
🚶 2km: S from St-Pieters Station
along Voskenslaan and
Oudenaardsesteenweg (N58) to
motorway jn. For A10 (east) stand
on eastbound slip road.*** For A14
(south) and N58 stand on N58
beyond motorway jn.**
🚌 86 to above jn.

A10/E5 (west): Bruges, Ostend

🚶 2km: S along Voskenslaan and
Kortrijksesteenweg to motorway jn.
Stand on westbound slip road.***
🚌 81, 83, 85 to above jn.

A14/E3 (north): Antwerp, Eindhoven Amsterdam (A1/E10)

🚋 21 or 🚌 9 to motorway jn on
Brusselsesteenweg. Stand on
northbound slip road.***

LIEGE (Luik)

A3/E5 (west): Brussels, Ostend (A10)
A15/E41: Namur, Charleroi

🚶 1.3km: SW along Blvd D'Avroy,
R along Rue Ste-Marie and stand on
approach road to motorway. Sign
pref.***
🚌 1, 4, 9, 25, 27, 30 to above jn by
Parc d'Avroy.

A13: Antwerp (E39)

🚶 500m: W from Place St-Lambert along Rue de Bruxelles then bear L along Rue de l'Academie to Place Hocheporte. Stand on Rue de Campine.*

🚌 1099 to start of Blvd Fossé Crahay (just beyond Radio Liège building) then 🚶 100m to start of motorway.***

A25/E9 (north): Maastricht, Amsterdam
A3/E5 (east): Aachen, Cologne

🚶 1.5km E from Place St-Lambert along Rue Léopold then continue along either side of the Meuse, R over Pont de l'Atlas V and stand at start of motorway.**

🚌 1079, 1108 to above jn.

N15/E9 (south): Bastogne, Luxembourg (N4)

🚶 2km: S from Pont de Longdoz along E bank of Meuse Dérivation to start of Quai des Ardennes.**

🚌 4, 25, 30, 48, 1085, 1134 to above jn by Pont de Fétinne.

When heading north, east or south of Liège, you can get a lift from any slip road leading on to the highway which runs along the east bank of the Meuse Dérivation. Stand on the northbound slip road for the north or east, or the southbound slip road for the south, and use a sign.

LUXEMBOURG

N6/E9 (west): Arlon, Liège (N15), Brussels (N4/E40)

🚶 1km: W along Grand' Rue and Ave Emile Reuter to Place de l'Etoile. Stand on Route d'Arlon.**

🚌 3, 7, 8, 11, 12 to above jn.

N1: Trier, Koblenz

🚶 1km: N along Ave de le Porte Neuve to Rondpoint Schumann. Stand at start of Pont G-D Charlotte.**

🚌 3, 4, 9A, E to above jn.

N2/E42: Remich, Saarbrücken

🚶 1.5km: S from Place du St Esprit over viaduct, L along Blvd d'Avranches to start of Blvd du Général Patton.**

🚌 15, 18 to above jn.

N3/E9 (south): Metz, Nancy, Strasbourg

🚶 to start of Route de Thionville just SE of station.**.

🚌 6 to Ronnen Eck on Route de Thionville.**

N5: Longwy, Reims

🚶 1km: W along Ave Monterey to start of Ave du 10 Septembre.**

Buses in Luxembourg sometimes charge the adult fare for rucksacks.

OSTEND (Oostende/Ostende)

A10/E5: Brussels, Antwerp (A14/E3)

🚶 800m: W from Station along Leopold III Laan to Vuurkruisenplein and stand at rdbt on Verenigde Natieslaan. Often crowded in summer, otherwise****

🚌 14 to near Rondpunt Kennedy. Stand at start of A10.***

ZEEBRUGGE

N71: Bruges, Brussels (A10/E5)

🚶 from Zeedijk up Pieter Troostlaan and stand just beyond Kustlaan.**

N72: Ostend (south), Knokke (north)

🚶 as above and stand on Kustlaan in the appropriate direction.* Or take 🚌 1 to Knokke, 🚌 2 to Ostend.

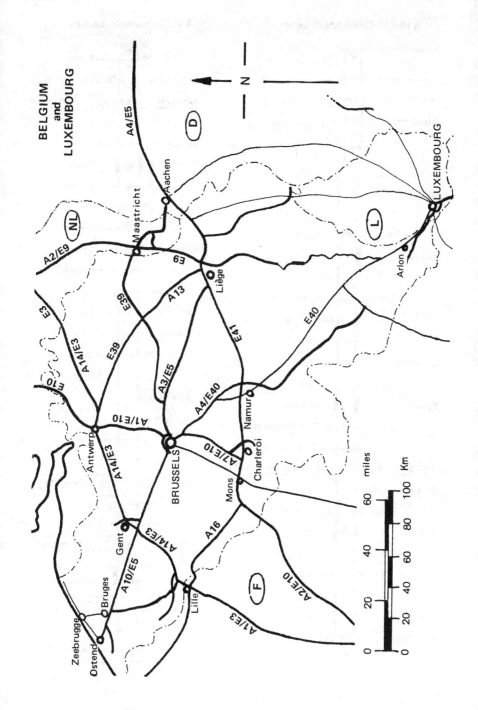

BELGIUM and LUXEMBOURG

A10/E5: Oostende-Brussels

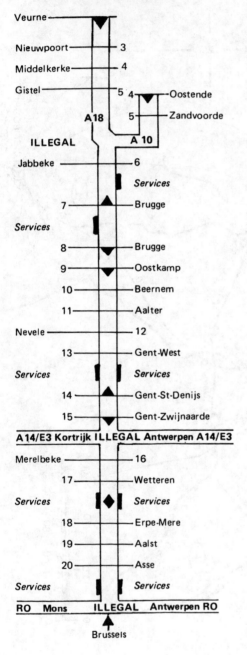

A3/E5: Brussels-Aachen

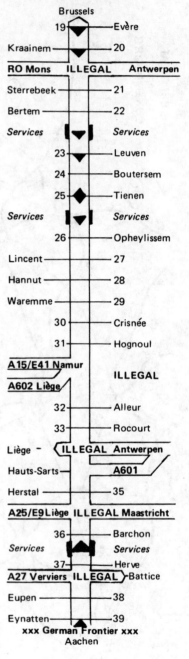

46

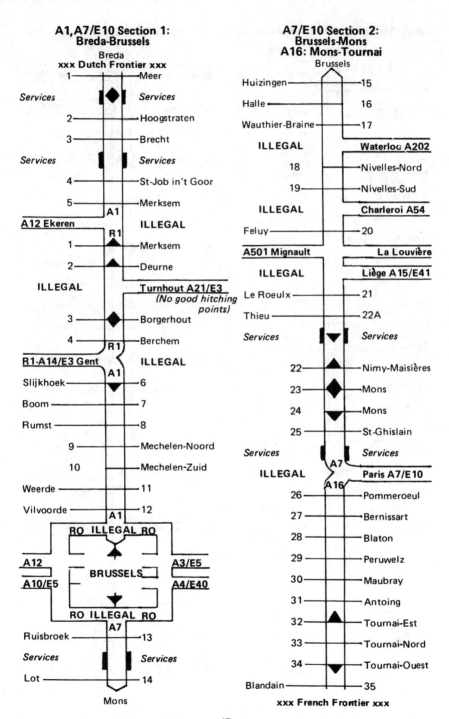

A1, A7/E10 Section 1:
Breda-Brussels

Breda
xxx Dutch Frontier xxx

1	Meer
Services ◆ *Services*	
2	Hoogstraten
3	Brecht
Services ▮ *Services*	
4	St-Job in't Goor
5	Merksem

A1

A12 Ekeren — **ILLEGAL**

R1

1 ▲	Merksem
2 ▲	Deurne

ILLEGAL — **Turnhout A21/E3**
(No good hitching points)

3 ◆	Borgerhout
4	Berchem

R1

R1-A14/E3 Gent — **ILLEGAL**

A1 ▼

Slijkhoek	6
Boom	7
Rumst	8
9	Mechelen-Noord
10	Mechelen-Zuid
Weerde	11
Vilvoorde	12

A1

RO ILLEGAL RO
▼

A12	A3/E5
BRUSSELS	
A10/E5	A4/E40

RO ILLEGAL RO
▼

A7

Ruisbroek	13
Services ▮ *Services*	
Lot	14

Mons

A7/E10 Section 2:
Brussels-Mons
A16: Mons-Tournai

Brussels

Huizingen	15
Halle	16
Wauthier-Braine	17

ILLEGAL — **Waterloo A202**

18	Nivelles-Nord
19	Nivelles-Sud

ILLEGAL — **Charleroi A54**

Feluy	20

A501 Mignault — **La Louvière**

ILLEGAL — **Liège A15/E41**

Le Roeulx	21
Thieu	22A

Services ▼ *Services*

22 ▲	Nimy-Maisières
23 ◆	Mons
24 ▼	Mons
25	St-Ghislain

Services ▮ *Services*

A7

ILLEGAL — **Paris A7/E10**

A16

26	Pommeroeul
27	Bernissart
28	Blaton
29	Peruwelz
30	Maubray
31	Antoing
32 ▲	Tournai-Est
33	Tournai-Nord
34 ▼	Tournai-Ouest
Blandain	35

xxx French Frontier xxx

47

R1, A14/E3: Antwerpen-Kortrijk

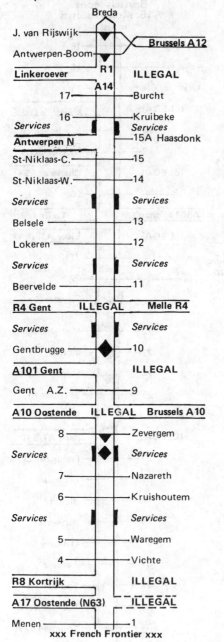

Breda

J. van Rijswijk

Brussels A12

Antwerpen-Boom

Linkeroever   R1   ILLEGAL

A14

17 — Burcht

16 — Kruibeke

Services   *Services*

Antwerpen N   15A Haasdonk

St-Niklaas-C. — 15

St-Niklaas-W. — 14

Services   *Services*

Belsele — 13

Lokeren — 12

Services   *Services*

Beervelde — 11

R4 Gent   ILLEGAL   Melle R4

Services   *Services*

Gentbrugge — 10

A101 Gent   ILLEGAL

Gent   A.Z. — 9

A10 Oostende   ILLEGAL   Brussels A10

8 — Zevergem

Services   *Services*

7 — Nazareth

6 — Kruishoutem

Services   *Services*

5 — Waregem

4 — Vichte

R8 Kortrijk   ILLEGAL

A17 Oostende (N63)   ILLEGAL

Menen — 1

xxx French Frontier xxx

A15/E41: Liège-Mons

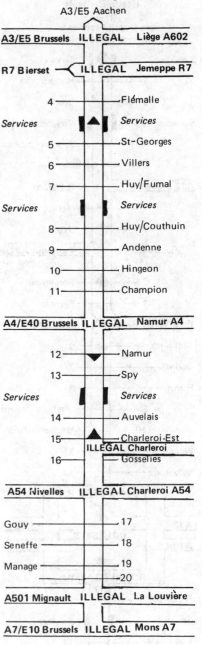

A3/E5 Aachen

A3/E5 Brussels   ILLEGAL   Liège A602

R7 Bierset   ILLEGAL   Jemeppe R7

4 — Flémalle

Services   *Services*

5 — St-Georges

6 — Villers

7 — Huy/Fumal

Services   *Services*

8 — Huy/Couthuin

9 — Andenne

10 — Hingeon

11 — Champion

A4/E40 Brussels   ILLEGAL   Namur A4

12 — Namur

13 — Spy

Services   *Services*

14 — Auvelais

15 — Charleroi-Est

ILLEGAL Charleroi

16 — Gosselies

A54 Nivelles   ILLEGAL Charleroi A54

Gouy — 17

Seneffe — 18

Manage — 19

— 20

A501 Mignault   ILLEGAL   La Louvière

A7/E10 Brussels   ILLEGAL   Mons A7

Netherlands

If you buy a *Strippenkaart* of public transport tickets, they are valid on all ⊖ 🚌 and 🚋 services throughout the Netherlands.

AMSTERDAM

A2/E9: Utrecht, Arnhem (A12/E36), Breda (A27/E37)
🚋 25 to terminus by Europabrug. Often crowded, otherwise.*** If crowded, 🚶 300m along A2 to services.***

A4/E10 (south): The Hague, Rotterdam (A13)
🚌 36 or 🚋 1 to Lelylaan. Stand on southbound motorway slip road.*** 🚋 6, 16, 24, or 🚌 15, 23, 60 to Olympic Stadium and 🚶 S along Amstelveenseweg. Stand on westbound motorway slip road.*** 🚋 4 or 🚌 8, 60 to RAI station. Stand at Europa Blvd jn on westbound motorway slip road.***

A7/E10 (north): Hoorn, Groningen
🚌 31, 32, 33, 34, 35 to north end of Ij Tunnel.** 🚋 13 or 🚌 18, 19, 36 to Bos en Lommerplein. Stand on northbound slip road.***

A1/E35: Amersfoort, Enschede (E8), Groningen (A28)
🚋 12 or 🚌 8, 15, 56 or 🚌 or ⊖ to Amstel Station. Stand at rdbt by station.**

ARNHEM

A12/E36 (west): Utrecht, The Hague (E8), Rotterdam (A20), Amsterdam (A2/E9)
A50: 's-Hertogenbosch
🚌 8 (direction Schaarsbergen) to Amsterdamseweg between Hijenoordseweg and Hoogkamp. Stand on Amsterdamseweg. (Take the first lift to the motorway).***

N50: Apeldoorn, Enschede (A1/E8)
🚌 4 (direction Geitenkamp) to Apeldoornseweg (N50)/Kluizeweg jn. Stand on N50.*** Or 🚶 on 1.5km to motorway jn. Stand on N50.***

A48: Zutphen
A12/E36 (west): Emmerich, Oberhausen
🚌 8 to Presikhaaf. Stand on Lange Water, with sign.*** Or 🚶 along Lange Water to rdbt (Europa Circuit) and stand at start of appropriate motorway (illegal).****

A52: Nijmegen
🚌 3 (direction Duifje) or 5 (direction Holthuizen) to De Monchyplein. Stand on Nijmegseweg.***

GRONINGEN

A7/E35 (east): Winschoten, Oldenburg, Bremen
A28/E35 (south): Zwolle, Amersfoort, Amsterdam (A1), Utrecht (E8)
N7, A7 (west): Sneek, Amsterdam (E10)
🚶 1.5km: E from station along Stationsweg, on S bank of canal, R along Europaweg to rdbt at Europaplein.****

E10: Leeuwarden
🚶 2km: W from station along Emmasingel and Eeldersingel and across Eendrachtsburg. Then follow the canal round and turn R up to Friesestraatweg. Stand 600m up opposite Sportpark at jn with Westelijke Ringweg.***

THE HAGUE ('s Gravenhage, Den Haag)

A4/E10 (north): Amsterdam A12/E8 (east): Utrecht, Arnhem (E36), Enschede (A28, A1)
🚶 to Utrechtse Baan (A12/E8)/Juliana van Stolberglaan jn 300m NE of Centraal Station. Sign pref.***

A13/E10 (south): Rotterdam, Breda (A16)
🚌 11, 21 or 🚃 1 to Haag Straat Weg and stand at jn with Nassaukade.***

E8 (west): Hook of Holland
🚌 51, 53 to start of Monsterseweg at Ockenburgh.***

HOOK OF HOLLAND
(Hoek van Holland)

E8: The Hague, Utrecht (A12), Amsterdam (A4/E10)
⊞ 500m: N from station along Rietdijkweg and Harwichweg. Stand at start of 's Gravenzandscheweg.**

E36: Rotterdam (A20), Utrecht (A20, A12)
⊞ as above, but continue for 500m along 's Gravenzandscheweg, turn R and stand on the main road (by the big *Rotterdam* sign).**

MAASTRICHT

A2/E9 (north): Eindhoven, Amsterdam, Aachen (A76/E39)
⊞ 1km: E from station to President Roosevelt Laan, then L to start of A2/E9.***

N78: Aachen; A2/E9 (south): Liège
🚌 5, 7 to Akerpoort. Stand on eastbound slip road just E of Kennedybrug.***
🚌 4, 5, 14 to Waldeck Bastion. Stand by rdbt at start of Prins Bisschofsingel.***

N40: Tongeren, Brussels (E5)
🚌 4, 5, 14 as above but stand on Tongerseweg.**
🚌 3 to terminus at Vroenhoven. Stand on main road.***

N2: Hasselt, Antwerp (E39)
⊞ 1km: W along Brusselse-Straat and St Annalaan to Ziekenhuis (hospital). Stand at rdbt at start of Via Regia.**
🚌 4, 8 to Brusselse Poort. Stand at rdbt on Via Regia.***

ROTTERDAM

A20/E36 (west): Hook of Holland
🚌 5 to Schieplein. Stand on westbound slip road.***

A13/E10 (north): The Hague, Amsterdam (A4)
🚌 32, 33 to Kleinpolderplein. Stand on sliproad. Sign pref.**
🚌 3 to Blijdorp. Stand on Stadhoudersweg.***

A20/E36 (east): Gouda, Utrecht (A12/E8)
🚌 5 to Schieplein. Stand on eastbound slip road.***

A16/E10 (south): Breda, Brussels, Nijmegen (A15)
🚌 34, 48 to Kralingseplein, 6km E of centre. Stand on southbound slip road.***
🚌 48, 75 from Zuidplein ⊖ to Ijsselmondseplein. Stand on southbound slip road.***

A29: Bergen op Zoom, Flushing (A58)
⊖ 🚌 40, 42 to Zuidplein. Stand on Vaanweg, 200m SW of station.**

UTRECHT

A2/E9 (north): Amsterdam
🚌 14, 40, 47, 48, 64, 96 to Lage Weide motorway jn on Verlengde Vleutenseweg. Stand just beyond rail bridge on northbound slip road.***

A27: Hilversum
🚌 9, 10, 20 to Darwindreef. Then ⊞ to Robert Kochplein and stand at start of Einthovendreef. Sign pref.****

A28/E8 (east): Amersfoort, Groningen (E35), Apeldoorn (A1)
🚌 14 to rdbt at end of Bilt Str. Stand at start of Bilt Straatweg at Bere Kuil.***

A12/E36 (east): Arnhem, Oberhausen
🚌 5 to 't Goy Plein. Stand on southbound motorway slip road.

Sign pref.***
🚌 25, 26, 28, 29, 30, 32 to just
beyond A12 on Europalaan. Stand
on eastbound motorway slip
road.***

A2/E9 (south): 's-Hertogenbosch,

Eindhoven, Breda (A27/E37)
A12/E8/E36 (west): The Hague,
Rotterdam (A20/E36)
🚌 as above to Europalaan but get
off before A12. Stand on westbound
slip road. Sign pref.***

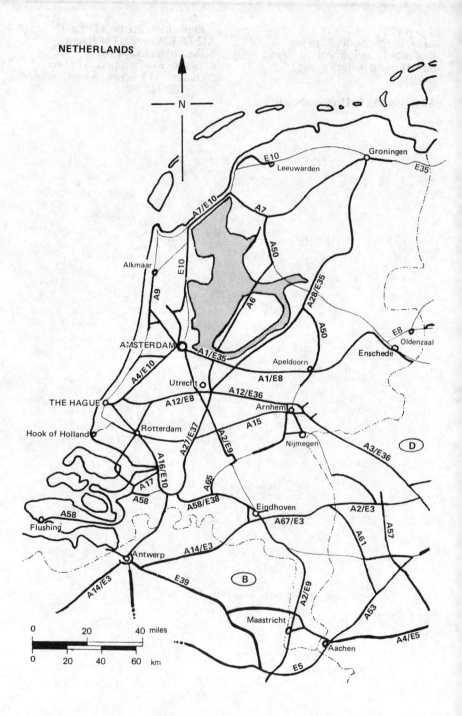

NETHERLANDS

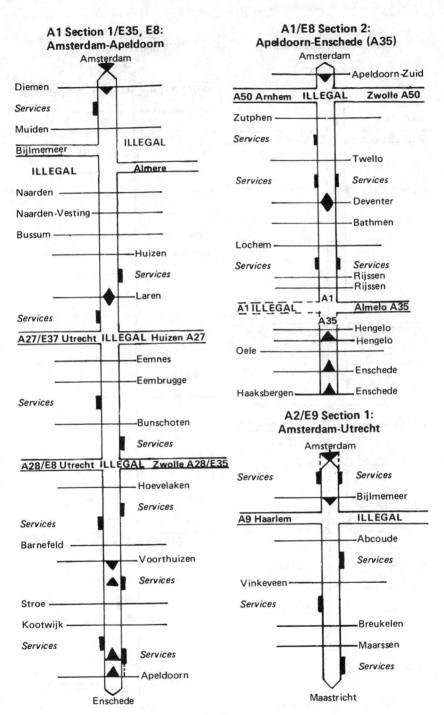

A1 Section 1/E35, E8:
Amsterdam-Apeldoorn

Amsterdam

Diemen

Services

Muiden

Bijlmemeer

ILLEGAL

ILLEGAL

Almere

Naarden

Naarden-Vesting

Bussum

Huizen

Services

Laren

Services

A27/E37 Utrecht ILLEGAL Huizen A27

Eemnes

Eembrugge

Services

Bunschoten

Services

A28/E8 Utrecht ILLEGAL Zwolle A28/E35

Hoevelaken

Services

Services

Barnefeld

Voorthuizen

Services

Stroe

Kootwijk

Services

Services

Apeldoorn

Enschede

A1/E8 Section 2:
Apeldoorn-Enschede (A35)

Amsterdam

Apeldoorn-Zuid

A50 Arnhem ILLEGAL Zwolle A50

Zutphen

Services

Twello

Services *Services*

Deventer

Bathmen

Lochem

Services *Services*

Rijssen

Rijssen

A1

A1 ILLEGAL Almelo A35

A35

Hengelo

Hengelo

Oele

Enschede

Haaksbergen Enschede

A2/E9 Section 1:
Amsterdam-Utrecht

Amsterdam

Services *Services*

Bijlmemeer

A9 Haarlem ILLEGAL

Abcoude

Services

Vinkeveen

Services

Breukelen

Maarssen

Services

Maastricht

53

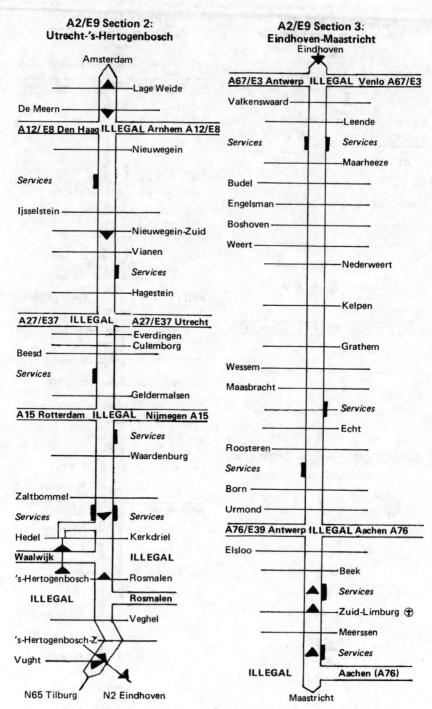

A2/E9 Section 2:
Utrecht-'s-Hertogenbosch

Amsterdam

— Lage Weide

De Meern —

A12/ E8 Den Haag ILLEGAL Arnhem A12/E8

— Nieuwegein

Services

Ijsselstein —

— Nieuwegein-Zuid

— Vianen

Services

— Hagestein

A27/E37 ILLEGAL A27/E37 Utrecht

— Everdingen
— Culemborg

Beesd —

Services

— Geldermalsen

A15 Rotterdam ILLEGAL Nijmegen A15

Services

— Waardenburg

Zaltbommel —

Services   *Services*

Hedel —   — Kerkdriel

Waalwijk   **ILLEGAL**

's-Hertogenbosch —   — Rosmalen

ILLEGAL   **Rosmalen**

— Veghel

's-Hertogenbosch-Z —

Vught —

N65 Tilburg   N2 Eindhoven

A2/E9 Section 3:
Eindhoven-Maastricht
Eindhoven

A67/E3 Antwerp ILLEGAL Venlo A67/E3

Valkenswaard —

— Leende

Services   *Services*

— Maarheeze

Budel —

Engelsman —

Boshoven —

Weert —

— Nederweert

— Kelpen

— Grathem

Wessem —

Maasbracht —

— *Services*

— Echt

Roosteren —

Services

Born —

Urmond —

A76/E39 Antwerp ILLEGAL Aachen A76

Elsloo —

— Beek

— *Services*

— Zuid-Limburg ⊕

— Meerssen

— *Services*

ILLEGAL   **Aachen (A76)**

Maastricht

54

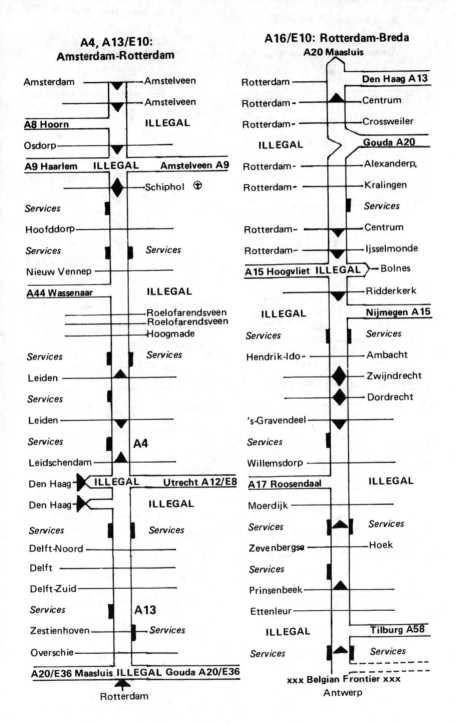

A4, A13/E10: Amsterdam-Rotterdam

Amsterdam	Amstelveen
	Amstelveen
A8 Hoorn	**ILLEGAL**
Osdorp	
A9 Haarlem **ILLEGAL**	**Amstelveen A9**
	Schiphol ✈
Services	
Hoofddorp	
Services	*Services*
Nieuw Vennep	
A44 Wassenaar	**ILLEGAL**
	Roelofarendsveen
	Roelofarendsveen
	Hoogmade
Services	*Services*
Leiden	
Services	
Leiden	
Services	**A4**
Leidschendam	
Den Haag **ILLEGAL**	**Utrecht A12/E8**
Den Haag	**ILLEGAL**
Services	*Services*
Delft-Noord	
Delft	
Delft-Zuid	
Services	**A13**
Zestienhoven	*Services*
Overschie	

A20/E36 Maasluis ILLEGAL Gouda A20/E36

Rotterdam

A16/E10: Rotterdam-Breda
A20 Maasluis

Rotterdam	**Den Haag A13**
Rotterdam	Centrum
Rotterdam	Crossweiler
ILLEGAL	**Gouda A20**
Rotterdam	Alexanderp.
Rotterdam	Kralingen
Services	*Services*
Rotterdam	Centrum
Rotterdam	Ijsselmonde
A15 Hoogvliet ILLEGAL	Bolnes
	Ridderkerk
ILLEGAL	**Nijmegen A15**
Services	*Services*
Hendrik-Ido-	Ambacht
	Zwijndrecht
	Dordrecht
's-Gravendeel	
Services	
Willemsdorp	
A17 Roosendaal	**ILLEGAL**
Moerdijk	
Services	*Services*
Zevenbergse	Hoek
Services	
Prinsenbeek	
Ettenleur	
ILLEGAL	**Tilburg A58**
Services	*Services*

xxx Belgian Frontier xxx
Antwerp

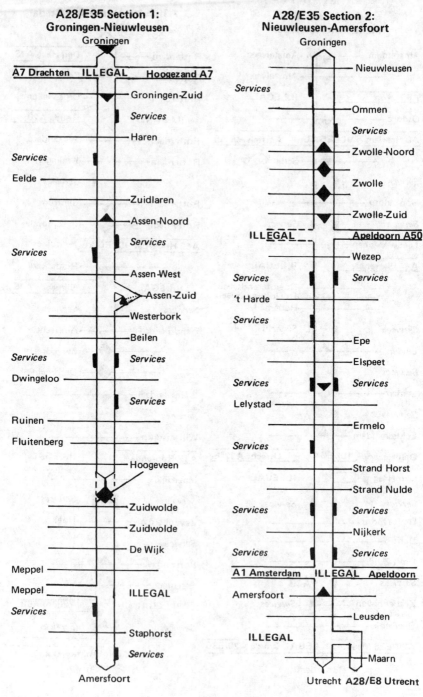

A28/E35 Section 1: Groningen-Nieuwleusen

Groningen

A7 Drachten   ILLEGAL   Hoogezand A7

Groningen-Zuid

Services

Haren

Services

Eelde

Zuidlaren

Assen-Noord

Services

Services

Assen-West

Assen-Zuid

Westerbork

Beilen

Services   *Services*

Dwingeloo

Services

Ruinen

Fluitenberg

Hoogeveen

Zuidwolde

Zuidwolde

De Wijk

Meppel

Meppel   ILLEGAL

Services

Staphorst

Services

Amersfoort

A28/E35 Section 2: Nieuwleusen-Amersfoort

Groningen

Nieuwleusen

Services

Ommen

Services

Zwolle-Noord

Zwolle

Zwolle-Zuid

ILLEGAL   Apeldoorn A50

Wezep

Services   *Services*

't Harde

Services

Epe

Elspeet

Services   *Services*

Lelystad

Ermelo

Services

Strand Horst

Strand Nulde

Services   *Services*

Nijkerk

Services   *Services*

A1 Amsterdam   ILLEGAL   Apeldoorn

Amersfoort

Leusden

ILLEGAL

Maarn

Utrecht   A28/E8 Utrecht

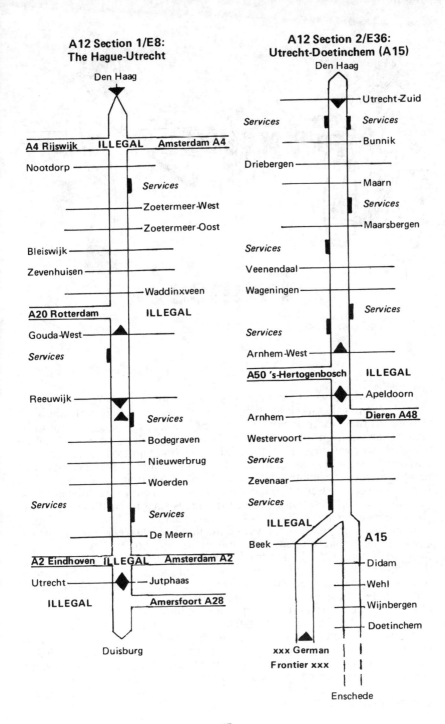

A12 Section 1/E8:
The Hague-Utrecht

Den Haag

A4 Rijswijk   ILLEGAL   Amsterdam A4

Nootdorp

Services

Zoetermeer-West

Zoetermeer-Oost

Bleiswijk

Zevenhuisen

Waddinxveen

A20 Rotterdam   ILLEGAL

Gouda-West

Services

Reeuwijk

Services

Bodegraven

Nieuwerbrug

Woerden

Services

Services

De Meern

A2 Eindhoven   ILLEGAL   Amsterdam A2

Utrecht   Jutphaas

ILLEGAL   Amersfoort A28

Duisburg

A12 Section 2/E36:
Utrecht-Doetinchem (A15)

Den Haag

Utrecht-Zuid

Services   Services

Bunnik

Driebergen

Maarn

Services

Maarsbergen

Services

Veenendaal

Wageningen

Services

Services

Arnhem-West

A50 's-Hertogenbosch   ILLEGAL

Apeldoorn

Arnhem   Dieren A48

Westervoort

Services

Zevenaar

Services

ILLEGAL   A15

Beek

Didam

Wehl

Wijnbergen

Doetinchem

xxx German
Frontier xxx

Enschede

57

France

Two of the three worst hitching spots in Europe are in France. But you should not infer that hitching throughout the country is uniformly abysmal. Among all the nations in Europe, France is where it is most critical to be standing in the right place at the right time. In a good spot, you can be whisked away within minutes for a ride of several hundred kilometers; at a bad one, you could waste entire days hitching fruitlessly in the company of many other unfortunates. The widely-held poor opinion of hitching in France is usually based upon bad experiences in notoriously difficult areas: near the channel ports, in isolated rural areas such as Brittany, or on the *Autoroute du Soleil* which is crawling with rival hitchers and police. Timing is also crucial; on public holidays and the first and last weekends in August, even in the unlikely event that you get a lift, you'll make very slow progress. There was a 170km traffic jam on the autoroute through Lyon in the summer of 1980. The secret of successful hitching in France is careful route planning combined with good timing. Decide on a sensible route and choose a few strategic intermediate points, then don't deviate from the plan without good reason — such as a long lift at a slight tangent to your intended course. And don't try hitching after dark in rural areas (because there won't be any traffic) or on the autoroutes at peak weekends in summer (there will be too many cars, all of them full up, and a great deal of competition). The lifts you get won't necessarily be from the usual single males. Families of eight plus dog sometimes cram hitchers in next to the kids, and liberated single women have no hesitation in offering lifts halfway across the country.

Rules of Thumb

Getting In. You are likely to have no trouble unless you come by sea direct from North Africa or you have recent Asian or North African stamps in your passport: then you will be searched for drugs. You can similarly expect to be thoroughly searched for excess alcohol if you enter from Andorra.

The Law. As everywhere else, hitching is not allowed on motorways, but France goes one step further and also forbids hitching at motorway service areas. Expect a warning the first time, a fine if they catch you again. There may be a law against hitch-hiking, but no law has yet been devised that prohibits pedestrians at service areas or prevents you from asking the drivers for lifts.

You will find French hitch-hikers quite blatant about standing at toll booths on the motorway and also at all-motorway junctions. If you ever get thrown out of a car at one of these places, you will see their point. Cars will screech to a halt in the rush to whisk you away before you are caught by *les flics*. As a deliberate strategy, this is too risky and nerve-racking to be recommended.

France also has a law restricting hitch-hiking among the under-18 age group. If you are under 18, you must have a letter from your parents permitting you to hitch-hike. Make this look as official as possible and keep it with your passport. Whatever your age, everyone needs to be someone in France. Take your passport with you everywhere. The police will ask to see it at least once a day.

Road Strategy. Be warned against being dropped on one of those long straight stretches of road that French drivers use for speed trials. At least make sure you can be dropped at a village (where cars *might* slow down) or at a junction where some traffic will be turning on to your road. Garages are also worth trying, as well as roadside restaurants — the French take food very seriously and will interrupt the most urgent journey to eat. Best of all, find a roadhouse run by the *Prévention Routière*. These supply free coffee even to hitchers, free maps and a rest. Look out for the *Bison Futé* symbol, a green buffalo cartoon character.

One advantage of hitching in France is that almost every *autoroute* runs parallel to a well-used *route nationale* (RN). Tolls are charged on all autoroutes (except for short urban sections) and many drivers prefer to use the free but slower RNs. The consequences for hitchers are good: if you get stuck at a lousy motorway junction, or get picked up by police on the autoroute for the twentieth time, you can switch to a route nationale, where travel is slower but surer. The extremes of hitching occur on autoroutes: either you wait at a junction for days, or you travel the length of France in a few hours. So if you want a more sedate, predictable journey, stick to RNs. In Corsica, do not hitch with your thumb as this may be misinterpreted as a rude gesture. Use your open palm instead. On the coast road do not hitch in an anti-clockwise direction. You'll spend the time clinging to precipices.

Route Planning. On paper the French road numbering system is quite simple — A or B for *autoroutes*, N or RN for *routes nationales*, and D for *chemins départementaux*. But the simplicity is deceptive: some N roads (like the N5 between Dijon and Geneva) actually carry little more traffic than the average country lane. The system also has built-in complexities like the "bis" roads. Two roughly parallel roads will have the same N or D number, but one — not necessarily the less important — will be relegated to "bis". Add this to the fact that many French roads are currently being renumbered every two or three years and the average road map is rendered comparatively useless. When in doubt, just follow town names on road signs. Above all, don't prejudge the hitching quality of minor roads, which can be surprisingly good: if the first car doesn't stop, the second will. But you may have to wait a long time for the first car.

Although the first four E roads pass through France, the E numbering system has not gained as wide acceptance as in most neighbouring countries. One final warning: at the last count there were twenty separate stretches of *autoroute* around Paris, so wait for a lift well clear of the metropolis. Alternatively, invest in a train ride of 80km or so from the capital.

Maps. Large scale road maps are not easy to come by unless you're prepared to pay, but the French Government Tourist Office's free map (from 179 Piccadilly, London W1) is all right for main routes. You should never get lost in any French town because the streets of even the smallest town will be cluttered with maps on walls or stands. There's a free map of Paris (including the *métro*) in almost every Paris hotel lobby. Street plans are also handed out free by city tourist offices. The best town plans — the Guide Blay series — are available from Roger Lascelles, who also stocks the 15-sheet Recta Foldex regional maps and a back-to-back national. To do battle with the motorway system, spend 25F on the Michelin *Autoroutes* book, no. 400.

Place Names. Few French towns have English variations, and these are usually only minor variations in spelling, e.g. Marseille(s) and Lyon(s). Dunkirk is spelt Dunkerque in French. There are, however, a number of German versions, especially in the German-speaking section of France along the border opposite Saarbrücken. Strasbourg is spelt Strassburg; Sarreguemines is Saargemünd; and so on. The reason for this is that the two regions of Alsace (*Elsass* in German) and Lorraine (*Lothringen*) have changed hands so many times that they now experience a split personality.

Dutch variations are equally unremarkable (Paris is Parijs, for instance), and the use of Rijsel for Lille is restricted in any case to Flemish (not Netherlands Dutch). Of the Italian deviations, Nizza (Nice), being close to the border is probably the most common.

Number Plates. French registration plates look superficially uninformative, but in fact the last two digits represent the *département* or origin — so you can tell the probable origin or destination of any vehicle. The *départements* are numbered alphabetically (except the last six, which were afterthoughts), but since few people will know the names of the *départements*, the list names the main towns, along with a geographical clue (eg SC = south central).

01	EC	Bourg	33	SW	Bordeaux	65	SW	Tarbes	
02	NE	Laon	34	SC	Montpellier	66	SC	Perpignan	
03	C	Moulins	35	NW	Rennes	67	NE	Strasbourg	
04	SE	Digne	36	C	Châteauroux	68	NE	Colmar	
05	SE	Gap	37	WC	Tours	69	SE	Lyon	
06	SE	Nice	38	SE	Grenoble	70	EC	Vésoul	
07	SE	Privas	39	EC	Lons	71	EC	Mâcon	
08	NE	Mézières	40	SW	Biarritz	72	NW	Le Mans	
09	SC	Foix	41	C	Blois	73	SE	Chambéry	
10	C	Troyes	42	SE	St-Etienne	74	SE	Annecy	
11	SC	Carcassonne	43	SC	Le Puy	75	NC	Paris—N	
12	SC	Rodez	44	WC	Nantes	76	NC	Rouen	
13	SE	Marseille	45	C	Orléans	77	NC	Paris—E	
14	NW	Caen	46	SC	Cahors	78	NC	Paris—W	
15	SC	Aurillac	47	SW	Agen	79	WC	Niort	
16	SW	Angoulême	48	SC	Mende	80	NC	Amiens	
17	WC	La Rochelle	49	WC	Angers	81	SC	Albi	
18	C	Bourges	50	NW	Cherbourg	82	SC	Montauban	
19	SC	Tulle	51	EC	Châlons	83	SE	Toulon	
20	SE	Corsica	52	NE	Chaumont	84	SE	Avignon	
21	EC	Dijon	53	NW	Laval	85	WC	La Roche	
22	NW	St-Malo	54	NE	Nancy	86	WC	Poitiers	
23	C	Guéret	55	NE	Bar-le-Duc	87	SC	Limoges	
24	SW	Périgueux	56	NW	Vannes	88	NE	Epinal	
25	EC	Besançon	57	NE	Metz	89	C	Auxerre	
26	SE	Valence	58	C	Nevers	90	EC	Belfort	
27	NC	Evreux	59	NC	Lille	91	NC	Paris—S	
28	NC	Chartres	60	NC	Beauvais	92	NC	Paris—S	
29	NW	Brest	61	NW	Alençon	93	NC	Paris—E	
30	SE	Nîmes	62	NC	Calais	94	NC	Paris—E	
31	SC	Toulouse	63	SC	Clermont—F	95	NC	Paris—N	
32	SW	Auch	64	SW	Pau				

Winter Hitching. The following passes are guaranteed to be closed every winter, often right through from October to June.

Alps: Allos, Aravis, la Bouette, la Cayolle, Croix de Fer, Galibier, Glandon, l'Iséran, Izoard, Mont Cénis and Petit St. Bernard.
Pyrenees: Aspin, Aubisque, Jau, le Pourtalet, le Tournalet.
Massif Central: Pas de Peyrol.

In these three areas, and in the Jura, other roads are liable to be temporarily blocked during the winter. Apart from blockages, traffic is always greatly reduced in these areas whenever there is snow about.

Planned and Paid Lifts. There is a well-organised system of car-sharing agencies, most of which are members of the *Allostop* federation. All are licenced by the Ministry for Sport and Youth. If you wish to make only a single journey, the cost of registration is 35F. Alternatively, you can register for a year for 130F. The federation recommends registering a day or two in advance of the date you wish to travel; however, this is not always practical for hitch-hikers. If your time is limited, make sure of a suitable lift before handing over the registration fee. The driver can charge a share of the petrol costs up to a maximum of 15 centimes per kilometer. As he makes no "profit" from this deal, you are covered by his mandatory passenger insurance. The following agencies are members of Allostop: although opening hours vary, most are open each afternoon from 3pm-6pm.

> Angers: CAD, 43 place Grégoire Bordillon 49000 (41-88 93 33)
> Angoulême: 10 rempart de l'Est 16000 (45-92 98 99)
> Bordeaux: 13 cours de la Somme 33000 (56-94 58 49)
> Cannes: MJC Picaud, 23 Ave Raymond Picaud 06400 (93-38 60 88)
> Cholet: Office de Tourisme, Place de Rougé 49300 (41-62 22 35)
> Grenoble: 9 rue Barginet, Quartier St Bruno 38000 (76-96 72 99)
> La Rochelle: CDIJ, 14 rue des Gentilhommes 17007 (46-41 16 99)
> Lille: Office de Tourisme, Palais Rihour 59800 (20-57 96 69)
> Lyon: 8 rue de la Bombarde 69005 (7-842 38 29)
> Nantes: CRIJ, 10 rue Lafayette 44000 (40-89 04 85)
> Paris: 65 passage Brady 75010 (1-246 00 66)
> Rennes: CIJ Bretagne, Maison du Champs de Mars 35043 (99-30 98 87)
> Strasbourg: 5 rue du Général Zimmer 67000 (88-37 13 13)
> Toulouse: Oc' Stop, 1 ter, rue du Languedoc 31000 (61-53 82 92)

There are four other agencies which are not members of Allostop, but which offer a free service:

> Le Havre: Info-Jeunesse, 177 blvd de Strasbourg 76600 (35-22 63 02)
> Limoges: CIJ, 3 rue de Jules Guesdes 87000 (55-77 53 53)
> Nancy: Maison des Jeunes, rue de Lorraine 54512 (8-355 23 64)
> Poitiers: CIJ, 64 rue Gambetta 86000 (49-88 64 37).

Some of the Allostop agencies also operate the *Allostop-Dormir* service, which provides low-cost accomodation.

Alternatively, you could have your request for a lift broadcast on Radio Télé-Luxembourg (236m MW) by dialling Paris (1) 720.22.11 between 9 and 12 am Monday-Saturday and talking to Max Meynier, the presenter of the programme *Fréquence-Max*. You may see bumper stickers advertising this programme, which has a wide following among lorry drivers and other long-distance travellers. It's worth writing in for a sticker (*un auto-collant*) to RTL, 22 rue Bayard, 75608 Paris and attaching it to your rucksack.

Town Guide

(for key and explanation, see the introduction)

BORDEAUX

A62: Paris (A10)
🚌 29 (direction Lormont) to start of A62 just south of 'Le Lac'. Stand at start of motorway. Sign pref.***

N10 (north): Paris
🚌 4 to Ave Carnot (N89)/Ave Cassagne (N10) jn. Stand on N10.**

🚶 from Camping CES 200m N along Ave Cassagne to above jn.

N89: Périgueux
🚌🚶 as above but stand on N89.**

A62 or N113: Toulouse
🚌 B, L to motorway jn on Route de Toulouse in Villenave. Stand on N113 or on motorway slip road. Sign pref.**

A63, N10 (south): Bayonne
🚌 G to A63/N10 jn at le Bijou.
Stand on N10 or on A63 slip road.**
🚌 DU to University Village No 4.
Stand on approach road to A63.**

BOULOGNE

N1 (south): Amiens, Paris
🚶 3km: E from harbour over Pont
Marquet, R along Blvd de la Poste,
Blvd Diderot and Blvd d'Alembert
to jn with N1.**
🚌 17 to above jn.

N42: St-Omer, Lille (A25)
🚶 2km: E from harbour over Pont de
l'Entente Cordiale (southernmost
bridge) along Rue de la Lampe,
Grande Rue, L along Blvd Mariette
(around old town) and L at Porte de
Calais to Ave Charles de Gaulle
(N1)/Route de St-Omer (N42) jn.**
🚌 4, 5, to above jn.

N1 (north): Calais, Dunkerque
🚶 🚌 as above but stand on N1.**

*For best results on arrival ferries, try
the vehicle exit from the west docks/
hoverport, and use a sign.*

CALAIS

*For each of the buses listed, you
should first take the free bus into town
from the car ferry terminal or
hoverport.*

N1 (south): Boulogne, Paris
🚌 1 (westbound) along Boulevard
Leon Gambetta (N1) to bus turn-off.
Stand on N1.*

N1 (east): Dunkerque, Ostend (N72)
🚌 1 (eastbound) along Ave de St-
Exupery (N1) to bus turn-off. Stand
on N1.*

N43: St-Omer, Lille (N42, A25),
  Paris (A26, A1)
🚌 3 to turn-off on Route de St-Omer
(N43).*

DIEPPE

N27: Rouen, Paris (A13)
🚶 1km: W from Avant-Port along
Grande Rue and Rue de la Barre, L
along Rue Gambetta (N27) to jn
with Ave Jean Jaures (D925). Stand
on N27.**

DUNKERQUE

N1 (east): De Panne, Ostend
🚌 6 to Rue Félix Coquelle/Route de
Furnes (N1) jn at Chapeau Rouge.
Stand on N1.*

A25: Lille, Paris (A1)
🚌 1 to A25/N1 jn at St-Nicolas.
Stand at start of A25.**

N1 (west): Calais, Boulogne
🚌 2 to Voie Express rdbt just past
Rue de Cassel. Stand on Voie
Express.**

*All buses start from or pass
Dunkerque–Ville Station. If you
arrive at Dunkerque-Ouest, hitch
outside the dock gates or take the bus
into town.*

LE HAVRE

N15: Rouen, Paris (N14)
🚌 9 to Harfleur. Stand at N15/Route
Pont de Tancarville (N182) jn on
N136.**

N182: Paris (A13)
🚌 9 as above but stand on N182.**

LILLE

A1 (south): Arras, Paris
🚶 500m: S from Gare along Rue de
Tournai to start of dual carriageway.
Sign pref.**
🚌 3 to Rue d'Arras/A25 jn. Stand
on southbound slip road. Sign
pref.**
🚌 2 to Boulevard de la Moselle then
🚶 500m N to A25 jn. Stand on
southbound slip road. Sign pref.**

A27: Mons, Aachen
⊠ ⊕ as above. Sign pref.*

A25: Dunkerque, Calais (N42)
⊠ ⊕ to A25 rdbt above. Stand on
westbound slip road. Sign pref.**

**A1 (north), A14/E3: Ghent,
   Antwerp, Brussels (A10/E5)**
⊕ ELRT to Ave de la Marne/A1
jn.**

LYON

A6: Paris; A7: Avignon
⊠ ⊕ ⊖ to west bank of Pont
Galliéni, 250m E of Gare de
Perrache, S of city centre. Locate
and stand on appropriate slip road.*
⊕ 5, 72 to Ave Victor Hugo/A6 jn
near Pont d'Ecully, N of city centre.
Stand on slip road. Sign pref.
Paris**, Avignon*
⊕ 19 to A6 jn 300m N of Stade
Municipal, 7km NW of city. Stand
on slip road. Sign pref. Paris**,
Avignon*
⊕ 15, 43 to Blvd de l'Europe/Rue
Jules Guesde jn in Pierre Bénite,
8km S of city, then ⊠ 200m S to A7
approach road. Stand at start of
approach road. Sign pref.*
⊕ 21 to N6/Route du Puy d'Or jn
10km NW of city, then ⊠ 1km N
along N6 to A6 jn. Stand on A6 slip
road. Sign pref.* (Warning: there is
a gendarmerie next to this jn.)
⊠ 300m N from Camping Porte de
Lyon to above jn.

N6 (north): Paris
⊕ ⊠ as above to N6/A6 jn. Stand on
N6.**

**N83: Bourg, Strasbourg, Geneva
   (N84)**
⊕ 8, 40B, 41, 58, 59, 71 to start of
Route de Strasbourg (N83) at St-
Clair. Sign pref.*
⊠ to Gare St-Clair by above jn.
⊕ 58, 71 to N83/N84 jn by Collége
d'Enseignement Technique. Stand
on N83: Bourg, Strasbourg**; or
N84: Geneva.**

A43: Chambéry, Grenoble (A48)
⊠ ⊕ ⊖ to east bank of Pont Galliéni,

300m E of Gare de Perrache, S of
city centre. Stand on Ave Berthelet.
Sign pref.*
⊕ 23, 34, 38, 39 to Place du 11
Novembre 1918. Stand on Ave Jean
Mermoz. Sign pref.**

**N6 (east): Chambéry, Grenoble
   (N85)**
⊕ 1, 24, 65 to Ave Rockefeller/Blvd
Pinel/Ave Franklin Roosevelt (N6)
rdbt. Stand on N6. Sign pref.**

N7 (south): Avignon
⊕ 13, 18, 32 to Square Galtier (by
Abattoirs Municipaux, 4km S of
city) then ⊠ 700m E along Ave Jules
Carterest to start of Blvd Chambaud
de la Bruyèe (LY1). Stand on LY1.
Sign pref.**

D42: St-Etienne (A47)
⊕ 10, 43 to Place Joffre in St-Genis
Laval (10km S of Lyon). Stand at
start of Ave Maréchal Foch (D42).**

N7 (north): Roanne, Paris
⊕ 55 to Place des 3 Renards, 5km W
of city. Stand on N7.**

MARSEILLE

**A7: Lyon, Aix (A51), Paris (A46),
   Cannes (A51, A8)**
⊠ to Place Jules Guesde in city
centre. Stand at start of A7. Sign
pref.**
⊕ 15-18, 26-30 to Place Jules
Guesde as above.
⊖ to Colbert then ⊠ 200m to above
jn.
⊖ to Rue St-Lazare/A7 jn in city
centre. Stand on A7 slip road. Sign
pref.**

**A50: Aubagne, Toulon, Cannes
   (N560, A8)**
⊠ 2km: S from Croix St-Louis along
Rue de Rome, bear L at Place
Castellane along Ave Jule Cantini to
jn with Blvd V Delpeuch. Stand on
Blvd V Delpeuch. Sign pref.**
⊕ 24 to above jn by Gare du Prado.
⊖ to Castellane then ⊠ 700m along
Ave Jules Cantini to above jn.

N559: Cassis, Toulon
🚌 23, 245, 72 to Rond-Point du Prado. Stand at start of Michelet. **

NANTES

N23: Le Mans, Paris (A11)
🚌 21, 23, 61, 70, 95 to 'Paris', then 🚌 85 to Bel Air. Stand on N23. **

N137 (south): Bordeaux
🚌 32, 34, 38, R to La Carrée (3km S of Loire) then 🚶 500m S along N137. **

N165: Quimper
🚌 80, 90 to Le Croisy, then 🚶 500m W to N165 jn. **
🚌 32 to terminus at Bout des Landes, then 🚶 200m W by stadium to N137. Stand at start of motorway. ***

N137 (north): Rennes, St-Malo
🚌 32 to Bout des Landes, then 🚶 as above. Stand on Route de Rennes (N137). **

NICE

A8 (west): Aix, Marseille (A51), Paris (A7)
🚌 9, 10 to Les Moulins, Route de Grenoble. Stand at motorway entrance. Sign pref. **

A8 (east): Monaco, Ventimiglia
🚌 9, 10 to above jn. Sign pref. *
🚌 3, 6, 16 to Nice-L'Ariane motorway jn. 🚶 200m N to Route Levens and stand on motorway slip road. **

PARIS

A1: Lille, Dunkirk (A25), Calais (A26, N43) Brussels (A2/E10)
Ø 12 to terminus at Porte de la Chapelle, then 🚶 500m S along Rue de la Chapelle to rdbt at jn with Rue Bourcry. *
🚌 350 from Gare du Nord to A1 slip road at Le Bourget. ***

A3, N3: Meaux, Chalons, Metz
Ø 3 (direction Galliéni) to Porte de Bagnolet, then 🚶 across Place de Bagnolet and bear R along Ave Cartell to A3 slip road. **

A4:Reims, Metz, Strasbourg (A32, A34), Nancy (N4 or A31)
🚶 or Ø to Quai de la Rapée/Blvd Diderot jn on north bank of Seine, between Gare d'Austerlitz and Gare de Lyon. Stand on Quai de la Rapée. Sign pref. *
Despite the one-star rating, traffic congestion at this point often peforms the near-impossible in reducing Parisian hitching to a personal level.
🚌 24, PC to Boulevard Poniatowski/ Quai de Bercy jn, just north of Pont National. Stand on A4 slip road. **
Ø 8 (direction Créteil) to Porte de Charenton, then 🚶 500m S to above jn.

A6: Lyon, Marseille (A7), Nice (A7, A8), Perpignan (A7, A9)
Ø 7 (direction Mairie d'Ivry) to Porte d'Italie (not Place d'Italie) then 🚶 300m S to motorway slip road. Sign pref. **

A10: Tours, Bordeaux, Le Mans (A11)
Ø 🚶 as for A6 above. Sign pref. *
🚇 (RER) B4 to Orsay. Stand on N306 (leading to A10). Sign pref. **

A13: Rouen, Caen, Le Havre (N182)
Ø 10 (direction Boulogne) to Porte d'Auteil, then 🚶 200m E to A13 slip road. **

N14: Rouen, Dieppe (N27), Le Havre
Ø 13 (direction St-Denis) to St-Denis-Porte de Paris. Stand at N14/ N1 jn on N14. **

N1: Boulogne, Calais, Amiens (N16)
Ø as above but stand on N1. Sign pref. **

PERPIGNAN

N9 (south): Le Perthus, Barcelona (A9/E4)
🚌 11 (direction Porte d'Espagne) to Centre Commercial. Stand by entrance to Centre on N9. **

N116: Andorra (N20)

🚶 2km: W along Ave M Leclerc, Ave de Grande Bretagne and Ave de Prades to jn with Ave de la Massane. Stand on N116.**

N9 (north): Narbonne, Nîmes (A9)

🚶 1km: N over Pont Argo along Pénétrante (N9) to jn 400 m N of bridge (ignore "no pedestrian" signs). Stand on N9.**
🚌 5 (direction Languedoc) to Rue J Perrin/Ave de Languedoc (N9) jn. Stand on N9.**

STRASBOURG

N4 (east): Kehl, Basel (A5 south), Frankfurt (A5 north)

🚌 21 to east bank of Rhine (or 🚌 11, 32 to west bank then 🚶 across Pont de l'Europe). Stand on dual carriageway (leading to A5). Sign pref.***

A35, N83: Colmar, Basel (N422), Besançon (A36)

🚶 1km: SW from station along Rue de Mülheim, under rail bridge and flyover to A35 slip road.**
🚌 13, 23, 38 to above jn.
🚌 16 to Route de Strasbourg/Route du Rhin jn at Place du Calvaire.**
🚶 1km: south from Camping Baggersee along Route de Strasbourg to above jn.

N4 (west): Nancy, Paris

🚶 500m: W from Place de la Porte Blanche along Rue de Koenigshoffen (N4) under rail bridge to motorway jn.**
🚌 12, 22 along Route de Wasselonne (N4) to jn with Ave de Général de Gaulle on edge of city.***

A34: Metz (A32), Paris (A32, A4)

🚶 to Place de Haguenau, 500m north of city centre. Stand on A34 slip road.**

TOULOUSE

N20 (north): Paris, Bordeaux (A62)

🚶 2km: from Place Arnaud-Bernard N along Ave H Serres, over Canal du Midi and along Ave des Minimes to Barrière de Paris. Stand at start of Ave des Etats-Unis. Sign pref.**
🚌 10, 14 to above jn.
🚌 P to Ave des Etats-Unis/Chemin du Pont de Rupe jn. Stand on N20.**
🚶 500m: from Camping Municipal de Rupe E along Chemin du Port de Rupe to above jn.

A61: Carcassonne, Narbonne

🚶 3km: S from Place Lafourcade along Grande-Rue St-Michel, Ave de l'URSS and Ave Jules Julien, over bridge to start of Route de Narbonne (N113).*
🚌 2 to above jn.
🚌 62 to Route de Narbonne/Ave Pierre Georges Latecoere jn by Ecole Nationale d'Apprentissage at La Bourdette. Stand on N113.**

N20 (south): Pamiers, Andorra

🚶 2.5km: S from Place du Fer-à-Cheval along Ave de Muret, L along Route d'Espagne to rdbt under rail bridges. Stand on N20.**
🚌 K to above rdbt.

N125, N117: Tarbes, Bayonne

🚶 3km: S from Place du Fer-à-Cheval along Ave de Muret and Route de Seysses to jn with Ave du Corps-Franc Pomies. Stand on N125 slip road. Sign pref.**
🚌 144 to above jn.

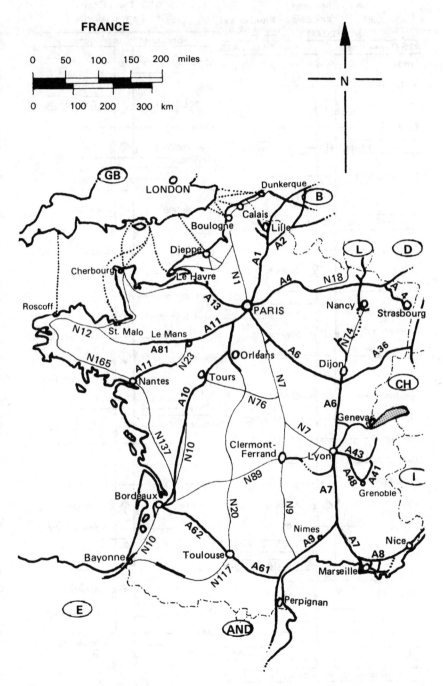

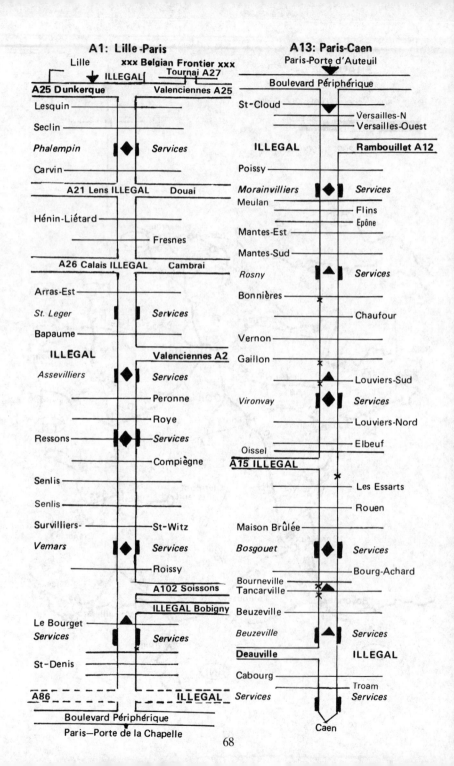

A1: Lille-Paris

Lille — xxx Belgian Frontier xxx
ILLEGAL — Tournai A27

A25 Dunkerque — Valenciennes A25

Lesquin
Seclin
Phalempin — Services
Carvin

A21 Lens ILLEGAL — Douai

Hénin-Liétard
— Fresnes

A26 Calais ILLEGAL — Cambrai

Arras-Est
St. Leger — Services
Bapaume

ILLEGAL — **Valenciennes A2**

Assevilliers — Services
— Peronne
— Roye
Ressons — Services
— Compiègne
Senlis
Senlis
Survilliers- — St-Witz
Vemars — Services
— Roissy

A102 Soissons
ILLEGAL Bobigny

Le Bourget
Services — Services

St-Denis

A86 — — — **ILLEGAL**
Boulevard Périphérique
Paris—Porte de la Chapelle

A13: Paris-Caen

Paris-Porte d'Auteuil
Boulevard Périphérique

St-Cloud
— Versailles-N
— Versailles-Ouest

ILLEGAL — **Rambouillet A12**

Poissy
Morainvilliers — Services
Meulan
— Flins
— Epône
Mantes-Est
Mantes-Sud

Rosny — Services
Bonnières
— Chaufour
Vernon
Gaillon
— Louviers-Sud
Vironvay — Services
— Louviers-Nord
— Elbeuf
Oissel
A15 ILLEGAL
— Les Essarts
— Rouen
Maison Brûlée
Bosgouet — Services
— Bourg-Achard
Bourneville
Tancarville
Beuzeville
Beuzeville — Services

Deauville — **ILLEGAL**
Cabourg
— Troam
Services — Services

Caen

68

A10 Section 1: Paris-Poitiers

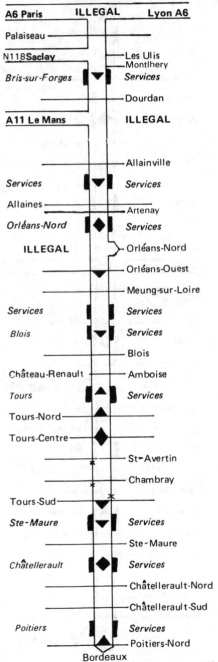

A6 Paris — ILLEGAL — Lyon A6
Palaiseau
N118 Saclay — Les Ulis
Bris-sur-Forges — Montlhery / *Services*
Dourdan
A11 Le Mans — ILLEGAL
Allainville
Services / *Services*
Allaines — Artenay
Orléans-Nord / *Services*
ILLEGAL — Orléans-Nord
Orléans-Ouest
Meung-sur-Loire
Services / *Services*
Blois / *Services*
Blois
Château-Renault — Amboise
Tours / *Services*
Tours-Nord
Tours-Centre
St-Avertin
Chambray
Tours-Sud
Ste-Maure / *Services*
Ste-Maure
Châtellerault / *Services*
Châtellerault-Nord
Châtellerault-Sud
Poitiers / *Services*
Poitiers-Nord
Bordeaux

A10 Section 2: Poitiers - Bordeaux

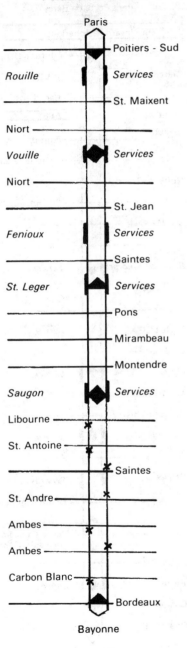

Paris
Poitiers - Sud
Rouille / *Services*
St. Maixent
Niort
Vouille / *Services*
Niort
St. Jean
Fenioux / *Services*
Saintes
St. Leger / *Services*
Pons
Mirambeau
Montendre
Saugon / *Services*
Libourne
St. Antoine
Saintes
St. Andre
Ambes
Ambes
Carbon Blanc
Bordeaux
Bayonne

69

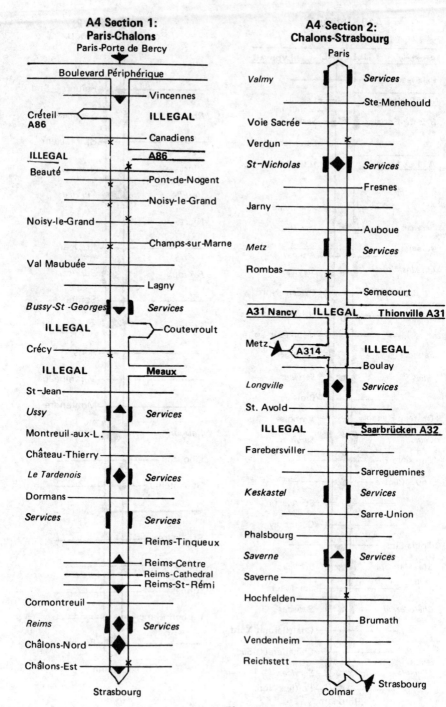

A4 Section 1: Paris-Chalons

Paris-Porte de Bercy

Boulevard Périphérique

Vincennes

Créteil A86

ILLEGAL

Canadiens

ILLEGAL — A86

Beauté

Pont-de-Nogent

Noisy-le-Grand

Noisy-le-Grand

Champs-sur-Marne

Val Maubuée

Lagny

Bussy-St-Georges — *Services*

ILLEGAL

Coutevroult

Crécy

ILLEGAL — Meaux

St-Jean

Ussy — *Services*

Montreuil-aux-L.

Château-Thierry

Le Tardenois — *Services*

Dormans

Services — *Services*

Reims-Tinqueux

Reims-Centre

Reims-Cathedral

Reims-St-Rémi

Cormontreuil

Reims — *Services*

Châlons-Nord

Châlons-Est

Strasbourg

A4 Section 2: Chalons-Strasbourg

Paris

Valmy — *Services*

Ste-Menehould

Voie Sacrée

Verdun

St-Nicholas — *Services*

Fresnes

Jarny

Auboue

Metz — *Services*

Rombas

Semecourt

A31 Nancy **ILLEGAL** **Thionville A31**

Metz — A314 — **ILLEGAL**

Boulay

Longville — *Services*

St. Avold

ILLEGAL — **Saarbrücken A32**

Farebersviller

Sarreguemines

Keskastel — *Services*

Sarre-Union

Phalsbourg

Saverne — *Services*

Saverne

Hochfelden

Brumath

Vendenheim

Reichstett

Strasbourg

Colmar

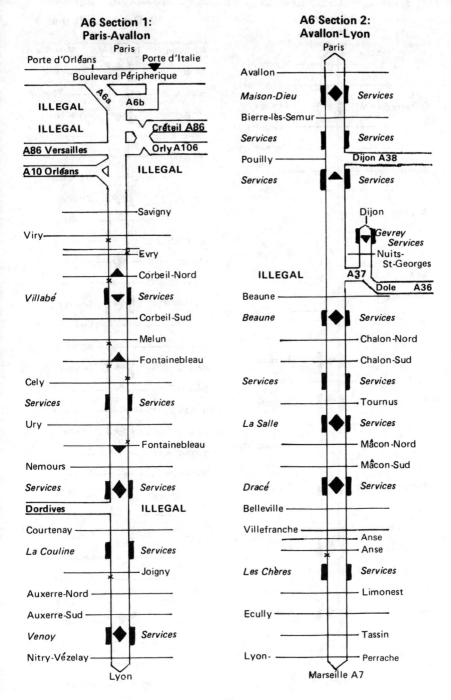

A6 Section 1: Paris-Avallon

Paris

Porte d'Orléans — Porte d'Italie

Boulevard Péripherique

A6a — A6b

ILLEGAL

ILLEGAL — Créteil A86

A86 Versailles — Orly A106

A10 Orléans — ILLEGAL

Savigny

Viry

Evry

Corbeil-Nord

Villabé — Services

Corbeil-Sud

Melun

Fontainebleau

Cely

Services — Services

Ury

Fontainebleau

Nemours

Services — Services

Dordives — ILLEGAL

Courtenay

La Couline — Services

Joigny

Auxerre-Nord

Auxerre-Sud

Venoy — Services

Nitry-Vézelay

Lyon

A6 Section 2: Avallon-Lyon

Paris

Avallon

Maison-Dieu — Services

Bierre-lès-Semur

Services — Services

Pouilly — Dijon A38

Services — Services

Dijon

Gevrey Services

Nuits-St-Georges

ILLEGAL — A37

Dole — A36

Beaune

Beaune — Services

Chalon-Nord

Chalon-Sud

Services — Services

Tournus

La Salle — Services

Mâcon-Nord

Mâcon-Sud

Dracé — Services

Belleville

Villefranche

Anse

Anse

Les Chères — Services

Limonest

Ecully

Tassin

Lyon- — Perrache

Marseille A7

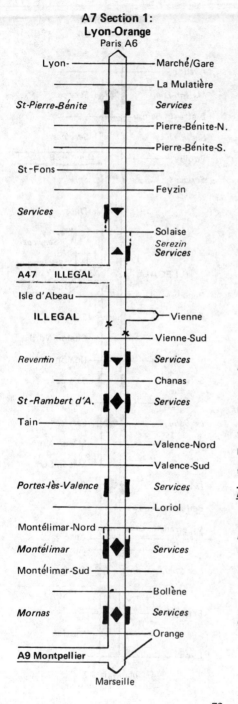

A7 Section 1:
Lyon-Orange

Paris A6

Lyon- — Marché/Gare
La Mulatière
St-Pierre-Bénite — Services
Pierre-Bénite-N.
Pierre-Bénite-S.
St-Fons
Feyzin
Services
Solaise
Serezin
Services
A47 ILLEGAL
Isle d'Abeau
ILLEGAL — Vienne
Vienne-Sud
Reventin — Services
Chanas
St-Rambert d'A. — Services
Tain
Valence-Nord
Valence-Sud
Portes-lès-Valence — Services
Loriol
Montélimar-Nord
Montélimar — Services
Montélimar-Sud
Bollène
Mornas — Services
Orange
A9 Montpellier
Marseille

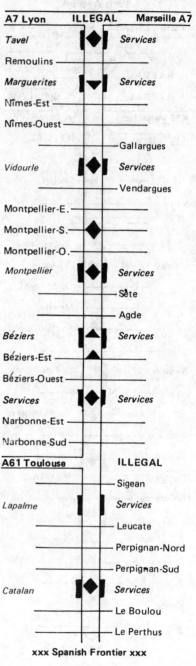

A9: Orange-Le Perthus

A7 Lyon — ILLEGAL — Marseille A7
Tavel — Services
Remoulins
Marguerites — Services
Nîmes-Est
Nîmes-Ouest
Gallargues
Vidourle — Services
Vendargues
Montpellier-E.
Montpellier-S.
Montpellier-O.
Montpellier — Services
Sète
Agde
Béziers — Services
Béziers-Est
Béziers-Ouest
Services — Services
Narbonne-Est
Narbonne-Sud
A61 Toulouse — ILLEGAL
Sigean
Lapalme — Services
Leucate
Perpignan-Nord
Perpignan-Sud
Catalan — Services
Le Boulou
Le Perthus
xxx Spanish Frontier xxx

72

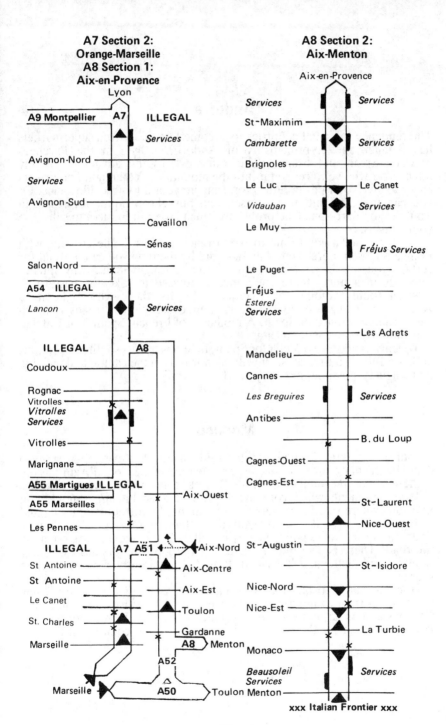

**A7 Section 2:
Orange-Marseille
A8 Section 1:
Aix-en-Provence**

Lyon

A9 Montpellier | A7 | ILLEGAL

Services

Avignon-Nord

Services

Avignon-Sud

Cavaillon

Sénas

Salon-Nord

A54   ILLEGAL

Lancon   *Services*

ILLEGAL   A8

Coudoux

Rognac
Vitrolles
*Vitrolles
Services*

Vitrolles

Marignane

A55 Martigues ILLEGAL

A55 Marseilles

Les Pennes

ILLEGAL   A7   A51   Aix-Nord

St Antoine

St Antoine   Aix-Centre

Le Canet   Aix-Est

St. Charles   Toulon

Marseille   Gardanne

A8   Menton

A52

Marseille   A50   Toulon Menton

**A8 Section 2:
Aix-Menton**

Aix-en-Provence

Services   *Services*

St-Maximim

Cambarette   *Services*

Brignoles

Le Luc   Le Canet

Vidauban   *Services*

Le Muy

Fréjus Services

Le Puget

Fréjus

*Esterel
Services*

Les Adrets

Mandelieu

Cannes

Les Breguires   *Services*

Antibes

B. du Loup

Cagnes-Ouest

Cagnes-Est

St-Laurent

Nice-Ouest

St-Augustin   St-Isidore

Nice-Nord

Nice-Est

La Turbie

Monaco

*Beausoleil
Services*   *Services*

xxx Italian Frontier xxx

73

Andorra

The tendency for small countries to become large duty-free supermarkets has befallen the co-principality of Andorra, lodged in the Pyrenees between Spain and France. This can work to the advantage of any hitch-hiker who ventures so far into the mountains. You might find drivers eager to give you rides in return for using up your duty-free allowance. Or you can take the initiative yourself and buy cheap liquor for resale in Toulouse or Barcelona (the profits are much larger in France) to subsidise your travels.

Winter is not a good time to try to reach Andorra. The crossing with France is closed more often than not, and by the time you can find out for certain you are faced with a long detour through Spain. Any hitcher remotely in a hurry to reach France is advised to take the eastern or western route avoiding the Pyrenees. But for those who make it to Andorra, hitching around the fairly limited selection of roads is much easier than in France or Spain. A modicum of French, Spanish or Catalan will help you to communicate.

To leave Andorra La Vella for Spain, take bus 6 to its southern terminus at Santa Julia. To France, start walking north from the capital and pick the first vaguely possible spot beyond Les Escaldes.

Monaco

If your sole ambition in life is to hitch a ride in a Rolls-Royce, then Monaco could be the place for you: this tiny principality on the Cote d'Azur has the **highest *per capita* number of Rolls-Royces in the world. But it also has** several ingredients which combine to produce lousy hitching. Should you find somewhere safe for drivers to stop among the tortuously curving and sloping roads, you'll rapidly gain the attention of one of the many underemployed traffic policemen, who will delight in moving you on along the road. There is also the problem that the local drivers are extremely wealthy and share a collective distaste for apparently poverty-stricken tourists.

Hitching out is so bad that you may well be tempted to invest a few francs for a train to nearby Nice or Menton. If you insist upon hitching, take bus 2 to its terminus on Avenue Hector Otto for the west, or bus 1 to Place St-Roman for the east. Better still, bypass the country on the A8.

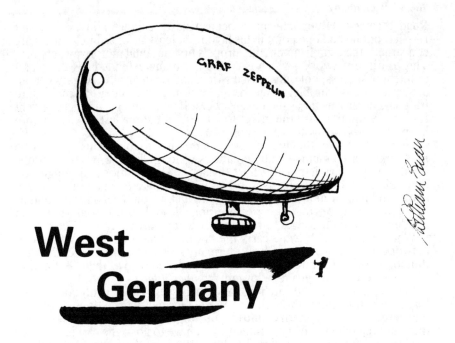

West Germany

Hitching in West Germany is probably the best that you will ever experience. The sheer speed, ease and comfort of hitching around the birthplace of the automobile and the autobahn will amaze you. Germany is the land of *wanderlust*. Despite political unrest and residual worries about terrorism, German motorists are very generous givers of lifts. Life goes on around the clock, so an overnight trip the length of Germany from Hamburg to Munich is a perfectly feasible prospect.

Rules of Thumb

Getting In. There is a general paranoia of anything vaguely left wing among German officialdom, and frontier guards are no exception. If your hair is long, your means of support unclear, you have Eastern European stamps in your passport or they generally don't like your face, they may well search you and photocopy your passport. Arriving from Eastern Europe or overland from West Berlin, you could be searched for excess duty free goods.

The Law. Hitch-hiking is illegal on motorways and will probably get you an instant fine. Expect frequent police checks amongst hitch-hikers at motorway services areas. If your hair isn't too long and you have your passport ready you shouldn't be detained more than a few seconds.

Road Strategy. Hitler may have been a nasty character in every other respect, but he had one point in his favour, at least as far as hitch-hikers are concerned: the establishment of Europe's first national motorway network. This toll-free network—which is constantly being extended—is the secret of hitching success, but only if used wisely and strategically. Always get out at service areas, the bigger the better. Before accepting a lift, make sure it's going at least as far as the next services. If you don't get a lift going right to your destination, ask the driver to put you out at the last services before he parts company with your motorway.

Once you leave the motorways, you're in trouble. This is because hitch-hikers are assumed to be creatures of long distance, whereas traffic off the motorways is mostly short distance. The solution—although you may still have a long wait—is to set your sights on a town about 50–60km ahead and make out a sign for it. If you're lucky, you'll get a lift beyond it, but don't count on that. Lorries are not allowed to use some roads on Sundays, but then lorries rarely pick you up anyway.

Wherever you are, always carry the raw materials for a sign. With a road network as complicated as West Germany's, a sign can be essential as a thumb. Most native hitchers use only the code letter(s) of their destination on signs; these are given below in *Number Plates*.

Finally, a word about hitching to West Berlin. There is no law against foreigners travelling through in West German cars, or in vehicles registered in other western countries. But while West German drivers have their visa fee paid by the government, you have to go to the cashier's booth to pay DM5 for a one-way visa. The best routes are the E6 (try Münchberg Services) and E8 (try Helmstedt Services), and a *Berlin* or *B* sign will help. The one stipulation is that you must get a lift going all the way. On a transit visa to West Berlin you are not allowed to stand and hitch in East Germany. *Do not accept a lift that is not going all the way.*

Route Planning and Maps. Stick to the motorways as much as possible and you won't go far wrong. The Autohansa map, free from the German National Tourist Office, 61 Conduit St, London W1, is excellent. For a detailed analysis of German motorways—including the locations, facilities (including showers) and size of every service area, write off for the booklet *Autobahn Service,* free from the *Gesellschaft für Nebenbetriebe der Bundesautobahnen m.b.H.,* 5300 Bonn 1, Poppelsdorfer Allee 24. If you want to get decent local or regional maps, expect to pay dearly for them. Fortunately many German drivers transport veritable libraries of atlases in their vehicles, so you may reasonably rely upon consulting your hosts collection.

There is a two-tier road numbering system. Motorways are prefixed A (*Autobahn*). Other main roads are theoretically prefixed B (*Bundesstrasse*). In reality, e.g. on maps, just the number will be used—without a prefix—and the distinction will be made by either different colours or different styles of depicting the two types of road. The E numbers are widely used.

Place Names. There are a few towns that have English names (or variations in spelling), though some—like Brunswick and Coblence—are fairly archaic and hardly used any more.

Braunschweig	Brunswick	Koblenz	Coblence
Hannover	Hanover	Konstanz	Constance
Hameln	Hamelin	München	Munich
Köln	Cologne	Nürnberg	Nuremburg

In addition, you may come across versions of towns in other languages: Munich is Monaco in Italian; in Dutch, Aachen is Aken, Cologne is Keulen, Nuremburg is Neurenberg and Braunschweig is Bruenswijk; in French, Aachen is Aix-la-Chapelle, Frankfurt is Francfort, Köln is Cologne, Mainz is Mayence and Trier is Trèves.

Number Plates. Germany is the country *par excellence* to be driven crazy trying to work out whether the car that just went past was going anywhere near your destination. The first one, two or three letters on the registration plate are an abbreviation of the district or town of origin: the shorter the abbreviation, the larger the town.

Since many of the smaller towns will not mean much to the average traveller, the list of codes gives the names of only the better known towns. As a geographical reference, the list is divided to correspond with the eight postal zones of West Germany. The number of the zone will also be the first number of each town's postal code within that zone. Zone 1 is West Berlin (B on number plates). The other seven zones are numbered approximately north to south. Zone 8 (Munich) is so large that it is divided into three sections.

Zone 2: Hamburg

Principal Towns		*Codes for Smaller Towns*						
FL	Flensburg	AUR	ECK	JEV	NOR	PI	SL	WL
HB	Bremen	BRA	EMD	LER	OD	PLÖ	STD	WST
HH	Hamburg	BRV	EUT	MED	OH	RD	SY	WTM
HL	Lübeck	CUX	HEI	NF	OHZ	ROW	TÖN	
KI	Kiel	BEL	HUS	NIB	OLD	RZ	VEC	
OL	Oldenburg	DH	IZ	NMS	OTT	SE	WHV	

Zone 3: Hanover

Principal Towns		*Codes for Smaller Towns*						
BS	Braunschweig	ALF	ESW	HMÜ	NOM	SZ	WOH	
GÖ	Göttingen	BID	FAL	HOG	NRÜ	UE	ZIG	
H	Hannover	BRL	FKB	HOL	OHA	VER		
HE	Helmstedt	CE	FZ	HX	PE	WAR		
HM	Hameln	CLZ	GAN	KB	RI	WEM		
KS	Kassel	DAN	GF	MEG	ROH	WF		
L	Lahntal	DUD	GS	MR	SOL	WIZ		
LG	Lüneburg	EIN	HI	NI	SPR	WOB		

Zone 4: Düsseldorf

Principal Towns		*Codes for Smaller Towns*						
BI	Bielefeld	AH	CLP	HER	LÜN	OB	WAT	
BO	Bochum	ASD	COE	HR	ME	RE	WD	
D	Düsseldorf	BE	DIN	HW	MEL	RY	WES	
DO	Dortmund	BF	DT	KK	MEP	SO	WTL	
DU	Duisburg	BOH	GE	KLE	MG	STH		
E	Essen	BOR	GEL	LE	MH	TE		

KR	Krefeld	BOT	GLA	LH	MI	UN
MS	Münster	BSB	GT	LIN	MO	VIE
OS	Osnabrück	BÜR	GV	LK	NE	WAF
PB	Paderborn	CAS	HAM	LP	NOH	WAN

Zone 5: Köln (Cologne)

Principal Towns		Codes for Smaller Towns				
AC	Aachen	AK	BRI	GK	JUL	NR	SU
BN	Bonn	AL	COC	GL	LEV	OP	WEB
K	Köln	AR	DAU	GM	LS	PRÜ	WIL
KO	Koblenz	AW	DN	GOA	LÜD	RH	WIT
OE	Olpe	BIT	EMS	GOH	MES	RS	
SG	Solingen	BKS	EN	HA	MON	SAB	
TR	Trier	BLB	ERK	HS	MT	SI	
W	Wuppertal	BM	EU	IS	MY	SLE	

Zone 6: Frankfurt am Main

Principal Towns		Codes for Smaller Towns					
DA	Darmstadt	ALS	DÜW	HOM	LM	ROF	USI
F	Frankfurt	AZ	ERB	HP	MGH	ROK	VK
FD	Fulda	BCH	FB	HU	MOS	RÜD	WEL
GI	Giessen	BIN	FH	HÜN	MZG	SIM	WND
HD	Heidelberg	BIR	FT	IGB	NH	SLS	WO
LU	Ludwigshafen	BÜD	GER	KH	NK	SLÜ	WZ
MA	Mannheim	BZA	GG	KIB	NW	SNH	ZW
MZ	Mainz	DI	GN	KL	OF	SP	
SB	Saarbrücken	DIL	HEF	KUS	OTW	SWA	
WI	Wiesbaden	DIZ	HG	LAT	PS	TBB	

Zone 7: Stuttgart

Principal Towns		Codes for Smaller Towns						
BAD	Baden-Baden	AA	CW	GRI	LÖ	RA	STO	WN
FR	Freiburg	BB	DS	HCH	LR	RT	TT	WOL
HN	Heilbronn	BC	EHI	HDH	MÜL	RV	TUT	
KA	Karlsruhe	BH	EM	HOR	MÜN	RW	UB	
KN	Konstanz	BK	ES	ILL	NEU	SAK	VAI	
OG	Offenburg	BL	FDS	KEL	NT	SHA	VL	
S	Stuttgart	BR	FN	KÜN	NU	SIG	VS	
TÜ	Tübingen	BÜS	GD	LB	ÖHR	SLG	WG	
UL	Ulm	CR	GP	LEO	PF	ST	WL	

Zone 8: München (Munich)

Principal Towns		North:			Centre:			South:	
A	Augsburg								
AB	Aschaffenburg	AM	KT	SAN	AIC	MAL	VOF	AIB	MB
BA	Bamberg	AN	KU	SEL	ALZ	NAB	WER	AÖ	MM
BT	Bayreuth	BRK	LAU	STE	BEI	ND	WOS	BGD	MN
CO	Coburg	EBN	LIF	SUL	BOG	NEN	WÜM	BGL	MOD
ER	Erlangen	EBS	LOH	TIR	BUL	NM	WUG	DAH	MÜ
FÜ	Fürth	FO	MAK	UFF	CHA	NÖ		DGF	PAN
GAP	Garmisch-P.	GEM	MAR	VOH	DEG	OBB		EBE	REI
HO	Hof	GEO	MET	WEN	DKB	OVI		ED	SF
IN	Ingolstadt	HAB	MIL	WUN	DLG	PAF		EG	SMÜ
KE	Kempten	HAS	MÜB		DON	PAR		FDB	SOG
LA	Landshut	HER	NAI		EIH	REG		FFB	STA

LI	Lindau	HIP	NEA	ESB	RID	FS	TÖL
M	München	HOH	NEC	FEU	ROD	FÜS	TS
N	Nürnberg	HÖS	NES	FRG	ROL	GRA	VIB
PA	Passau	KAR	NEW	GUN	SAD	KF	WEG
R	Regensburg	KC	OCH	GZ	SC	KRU	WM
RO	Rosenheim	KEM	PEG	KEH	SOB	LAN	WOR
SW	Schweinfurt	KG	REH	KÖZ	SR	LF	WS
WÜ	Würzburg	KÖN	ROT	MAI	VIT	LL	

Planned and Paid Lifts. There is a nationwide association of lift-matching agencies called *Interessengemeinschaft Mitfahrzentralen Bundesrepublik*, or *MFZ-Mitfahrzentrale* for short. As a reflection of the amount of business they do, many are housed in plush offices in city centres. The best plan is to call them a few days before you plan to travel, then, if they have a suitable lift, go to the office to pay your insurance premium and thus book your ride. They operate set prices of around DM10 per 100 kilometers including insurance and registration fees. Example: Freiburg-Hannover, DM61. The addresses are:

Aachen: Roermonderstr 4 (0241-155400)
Berlin: Arndtstr 42 (030-6936095)
Berlin: Kufürstendamm 227 (030-8827606)
Bielefeld: Viktoriastr 53 (0521-68978)
Braunschweig Rudolfplatz 9 (0531-506363)
Bremen: Humboldtstr 6 (0421-72001)
Darmstadt: Rheinstr 40 (06151-33696)
Dortmund: Westerbleichstr 27 (0231-822067)
Düsseldorf: Kolnerstr 212 (0211-774011)
Erlangen: Neuestr 10 (09131-27917)
Essen: Heinickestr 33 (0201-221018)
Frankfurt: Baselerstr 7 (0611-236444)
Freiburg: Belfortstr 13 (0761-37315)
Göttingen: Obere-Masch-Str 18 (0551-44004)
Hamburg: Hogerdamm 26A (040-231823)
Hannover: Weissekreuzstr 18 (0511-312021)
Heidelberg: Hauptstr 118 (06221-161111)
Hildesheim: Leunisstr 10 (05121-56085)
Karlsruhe: Rankestr 14 (0721-33666)
Kassel: Frankfurterstr 153 (0561-27033)
Kiel: Holstenbrucke 25 (0431-96001)
Koblenz: Rheinstr 34 (0261-17433)
Köln: Saarstr 22 (0221-233464)
Krefeld: St-Anton-Str 240 (02151-771313)
Mainz: Bonifaziusplatz 6 (06131-612828)
Mannheim: Quadrat N 4, 19 (0621-22733)
Mühlheim: Hansastr 16 (0208-52282)
München: Amalienstr 87 (089-286015)
Münster: Papenburgerstr 6 (0251-661006)
Nürnberg: Allersbergerstr 31A (0911-436913)
Oldenburg: Zeughausstr 42 (0441-76610)
Ravensburg: Untere Breite 19 (0751-26574)
Recklinghausen: Dortmundstr 63 (02361-44519)
Regensburg: Steinweg 26 (0941-85959)

Saarsbrücken: Rosenstr 31 (0681 67981)
Schwebheim: Untere Heide 16 (09723-2568)
Siegen: Freudenberger Str 15 (0271-2998)
Stuttgart: Lerchenstr 68 (0711-297691)
Ulm: Zinglerstr 35 (0731-62242)
Wiesbaden: Rudesheimerstr 29 (06121-444179)
Wuppertal: Luisenstr 27-29 (0202-450316)
Würzburg: Am Zinkhof 1 (0931-14904)

Town Guide

(for key and explanation, see the introduction)

AACHEN

**A4/E5 (west): Cologne, Düsseldorf
(A44, A46)**
⊞ 2km: from main station R along
Römestr, L on Wilhelmstr and
Heinrichsallee, R along Jülicher Str
then bear R at Blücherplatz to
Europaplatz at start of motorway.
Sign pref.****
⇔ 43 to above jn.

A44/E5 (west): Liège, Brussels
⊞ ⇔ as above. Sign pref.*
⇔ 1, 11 to Lichtenbusch motorway
jn just before Lichtenbusch village.*
*If this jn is too quiet, walk along
motorway and stand at the services at
the frontier post.*****

**A4/E39 (west): Maastricht, Antwerp,
Eindhoven (E9)**
⊞ 700m: from Rathaus along Pontstr
to Ponttor and stand at start of
Roermonder Str.*
⇔ 7, 17, 44, 47 to Wildbach then ⊞
600m E along Schlossparkstr, L
along Kohlscheider Str to Aachen
motorway jn. Stand on westbound
slip road.***
⇔ 51 to Strangenhäuschen
motorway jn. Stand on westbound
slip road.***

BERLIN

E15: Hamburg
⇔ (S-Bahn) to Staaken, then ⊞ 1km
S to Heerstr frontier post.****
⇔ 97 to Staaken frontier post.

**E6: Munich, Hannover (E8 west),
Hamburg (E15)**
⊖ (U-bahn) 2 to Oskar-Helene
Heim, then ⇔ 18 from outside
station to stop beyond motorway jn.
Cross road and follow E6/E8 signs to
Dreilinden frontier post. Stand by
hitchers' railings. Invariably
crowded. Sign pref.***

**E8 (east): Poznan, Wroclaw (E22),
Prague (E15)**
⊖ ⇔ as for E6 above. Sign pref.* (or
less)

*Do not accept a lift that is not going
all the way through to West
Germany, Poland or
Czechoslovakia. Non-residents of
West Berlin or West Germany must
pay 5DM for a transit visa through
East Germany.*

BONN

**A555: Cologne, Aachen (A4/E5),
Essen (A3/E36), Dortmund (A1/
E73), Düsseldorf (A562, A59)**
⊞ 1km: NW from Berliner Platz
along Max Str and Vorgebirgstr to
rdbt at start of A555. Sign pref.****

B9: Andernach, Koblenz
⇔ to Bonn-Mehlem Station. Stand at
start of B9 dual carriageway just past
Austr.***

A565, A61: Koblenz, Mannheim
⊞ 2km: as for A555 above but bear L
along Lievelingsweg to Bonn-

Tannenbusch motorway jn. Stand on southbound slip road.***
🚌 10, 14, 20 to above jn.
Ⓧ 1km: W from station along Herwarthstr and Endenicher Str to Bonn-Endenich motorway jn. Stand on southbound slip road.***
🚌 23, 31, 34, 35, 37, 38, 43–45, 47 to above jn.

BREMEN

A1/E3 (south): Osnabrück
🚌 1 to Niedersachsen Damm then 🚌 53 along Kattenturmer Heerstr to motorway approach road, then Ⓧ 800m S to motorway slip road.***

A28/E35: Oldenburg
Ⓧ 2km: SW from Burgermeister-Smidt-Brucke along Langemarckstr and Duckwitzstr to jn with Oldenburgerstr. Stand on approach road.**
🚌 6 to above jn.

A27/E71 (north): Bremerhaven
🚌 26, 29 to rdbt at jn with Utbremen Ring. Stand on Autobahnzubringer Freihafen. Sign pref.***

A1/E3 (north): Hamburg, Kiel (A7), Lübeck (E4)
🚌 as above. Sign pref.**
🚌 2, 10 to terminus at start of Heerstr, then 🚌 36 along Osterholzer Heerstr to terminus, then Ⓧ 100m to motorway slip road. Sign pref.***

A27/E71 (south): Hannover (A7/E4)
🚌 2, 10 then 🚌 36 as above. Sign pref.***

COLOGNE (Köln)

A57: Neuss, Mönchengladbach (A52)
🚌 5 to Subbelrather/Innere Kanalstr jn. Stand at entrance to motorway off Innere Kanalstr.***
🚌 5 to Nussbaumer Str/Parkgürtel jn at Neu Ehrenfeld. Then Ⓧ NE along Parkgürtel to motorway jn and stand on northbound slip road.***

A1/E73 (north): Dortmund, Düsseldorf (A59), Duisburg (A3/ E36)
🚌 to either of above jns.***
Θ 4, 11, 16 to Wiener Platz, near Mulheim. Stand at start of Clevischer Ring.***
🚌 4 to Rixdorfer Str. Ⓧ back along Berliner Str, R to end of Tiefentalstr and stand at start of Mülheimer Zubringer.***

A4 (east): Olpe, Giessen (A45)
Θ 11, 16 to Reichensperger Platz. Ⓧ along Riehler Str to motorway jn. Stand on eastbound slip road.**
🚌 1, 3, 4 to Deutz Justinian Str. then Ⓧ N along Deutz-Mülheimer Str to Messe Kreisel. Stand on eastbound motorway slip road off Pfälzischer Ring.***
Θ 4, 11, 16 to Wiener Platz then 🚌 143, 152 along Frankfurter Str to motorway jn. Stand on eastbound slip road.***

A3/E5 (south): Frankfurt
Θ 🚌 🚌 Ⓧ as for A4 (east) above or A59 (south) below.

A59 (south): Bonn
🚌 1, 3, 4, to Deutz Justinian Str. Ⓧ along Deutz-Kalker Str and stand at start of motorway.***

A555: Bonn, Koblenz (A565, A61)
🚌 132 to rdbt at end of Bonner Str. Stand at start of motorway.***

A553, B51, A1 (south)/E42: Euskirchen, Trier
🚌 133 to Raderthal. Stand on Brühler Str just past Militärringstr jn.**
🚌 20 (from Neumarkt) to Frechen motorway jn. Stand on southbound slip road.***

A4/E5 (west): Aachen
🚌 132 as for A555 above.
🚌 151 (from Friesenplatz) to Köln-Lövenich motorway jn. Stand on southbound slip road.***

In the above directions, 🚌 *also signifies* **S-Bahn.**

Because of Cologne's complex motorway network, a sign is required at all the above hitching points.

DÜSSELDORF

A46 (east): Wuppertal, Dortmund (A1/E73), Cologne (A59 or A3/ E36)
⚐ 2km: S along Berliner Allee, Corneliusstr, Erasmusstr and Mecumstr to jn with Süd Ring and stand at start of Witzelstr.**
🚌 4 to above jn.

A46 (west): Aachen (A44), Cologne (A57)
⚐ 2km: W along Haroldstr and L along Voklinger Str to jn with Süd Ring.**

A52 (west): Mönchengladbach, Krefeld (A57), Venlo (A61)
⚐ 1.5km: W over Oberkasseler Brücke, along Lügallee then bear L to slip road to A52.**
⚐ 700m: S along Berliner Allee and Corneliusstr, L along Herzog Str and stand at start of motorway.**
⚐ 2.5km: N along Kaiserstr, Fischerstr and Kennedy Damm to motorway jn. Stand on westbound slip road.**
🚐 (S-bahn) to Derensdorf by above jn.
🚌 11, 18 to above motorway jn at Kennedy Damm.

A52 (north): Essen, Duisburg (A3/ E36)
⚐ 🚌 🚐 as above to Kennedy Damm, but stand on eastbound slip road.**
🚌 8 to Brehmstr/Grashofstr jn. Stand at start of Nördlicher Zubringer.**

FRANKFURT am MAIN

A5/E4 (south): Heidelberg, Karlsruhe
🚌 61 to end of Mörfelder Landstr just beyond stadium. Stand at first rdbt on westbound slip road.****
🚐 S-Bahn 15 to Flughafen, then ⚐ 300m E to eastbound slip road.****

A3/E5 (west): Wiesbaden, Cologne
🚌 61 as above to Mörfelder Landstr.****
🚐 as above to Flughafen but ⚐ 300m E then under motorway to westbound slip road.****
See also A66 below.

A66: Wiesbaden, Cologne (A3/E5)
🚌 33, 34, 50 to Opel Rondell rdbt at end of Theordo-Heuss-Allee. Stand on slip road.***

A5/E4 (north): Giessen, Kassel (A48, A7), Dortmund (A45)
🚌 as A66 above.***
🚌 39 to A661/Hugelstr jn at Eckenheim.***

A3/E5 (east): Würzburg, Nuremburg
🚌 61 to end of Mörfelder Landstr. Stand on eastbound slip road (second rdbt).***
🚐 S-Bahn 15 to Flughafen then ⚐ 300m E to eastbound slip road.***

A sign is required on all the above roads.

HAMBURG

A24/E15: Berlin
A1/E4 (north): Lübeck, Puttgarden
Ө 3 to Horner Rennbahn, then ⚐ 800m W along Sievekingsallee to rdbt at start of A24.***
🚌 31, 39, 160, 161, 260 to above rdbt.

A7/E4 (south): Hannover, Kassel
A1/E3 (south): Bremen, Dortmund
🚐 (S-Bahn) 1, 2, 4 or Ө 2, 3 to Berliner Tor, then ⚐ 1.2km S along Heidenkampsweg to Amsinckstr jn. Stand on any of the approach roads to the Neue Elbbrücke.**
🚐 (S-Bahn) 3 or 🚌 34, 105, 106, 252, 254 to Veddel and stand at start of motorway.***

*If hassled by police, ⚐ S along Reichstr, R along Niedergeorgsweder Deich, and take the first road R past the rail bridge to Georgsweder motorway jn. Stand on southbound slip road.***

From the above points take any southbound lift. If it's going the wrong way get out at Stillhorn Services and use a sign.

🚋 (S-Bahn) 3 to Harburg then 🚌 141, 240 to motorway jn Hamburg-Heimfeld. Sign pref.**
🚋 (S-Bahn) 3 to Harburg then 🚌 143 to terminus by Harburger Berge motorway service station. Sign pref.***

B73: Stade, Bremerhaven (74, 71)
🚋 (S-Bahn) 3 to Neugraben or 🚌 240, 340 to terminus at Neu Wulmstorf. Stand on Cuxhavener Str.**

A7/E3 (north): Flensburg, Itzehoe (A23), Kiel (A215)
🚌 34, 39 along Kieler Str to jn with A7/E3. Stand on northbound slip road.***

HANNOVER

A2/E8 (west): Dortmund, Osnabrück (A30)
🚶 1km: W from main station along Kurt-Schumacher Str, across Goseriede and along Lange Laube and Brühlstr to Königsworther Platz. Stand on Bremer Damm.***
🚌 5, 16 to above jn.
🚌 1, 14 to Ungerstr. Stand on northbound slip road to Westschnellweg.** Or 🚶 500m N over River Leine to Schwanenburg-Kreisel. Stand on Westchnellweg.***
🚌 17 to Berliner Platz (terminus). Stand on either westbound slip road at Langenhagen motorway jn.***

A7/E4 (north): Hamburg, Bremen (A27/E71)
🚌 5, 6, 14 to Clausewitzstr.
🚶 along Hans-Böckler-Allee to Pferdeturm. Stand on Messe-Schnellweg, heading north**
🚋 (S-Bahn) 3 to terminus at Lahe and 🚶 to Buchholz motorway jn. Stand on B3.**

If offered a lift to Celle, accept and get out at Kirchhorst motorway jn.

*Stand on northbound slip road.***
🚌 17 to Langenhagen motorway jn at Berliner Platz. Stand on B552 (signposted *Flughafen*).***
*If offered a lift to the airport, accept and get out at A352 motorway jn. Stand on northbound slip road.***

A2/E8 (east): Braunschweig, Berlin
🚌🚶 as above to Pferdeturm.**
🚌🚶 as above to Langenhagen or Buchholz motorway jns, but in each case stand on eastbound slip road. From Langenhagen**, from Bucholz.***

B6: Hildesheim, Kassel (A7/E4 south)
🚌🚶 as above to Pferdeturm but stand on Messe-Schnellweg heading south.***
🚌 5, 14 to Tierärzliche Hochschule at Braunschweig Platz. Stand on Bischofsholer Damm.***
🚌 1, 11 to Laatzen-Sud, then 🚶 500m E along Wulferoder Str and down embankment to A7 approach road.***

MUNICH (München)

A8/E11 (west): Stuttgart
⊖ 1 to Rotkreuzplatz, then tram 12 to Amalienburgstr, then 🚌 73, 75 to start of A8 at Blutenberg.***

A9/E6 (north): Nürnberg, Berlin
⊖ 6 to Studentenstadt, then walk 500m N to A9 jn at Frankfurter Ring.*** If hassled by police, move 200m back to truck stop.

A8/E11 (east): Salzburg, Vienna
⊖ 1, 8 to Karl-Preis-Platz then walk 500m SE to start of A8.***

A95/E6 (south): Garmisch-P, Innsbruck
⊖ 3, 6 to Westpark then walk 500m S to start of A95.***

A96/E61: Lindau, Kempten
⊖ 3, 6 to Westpark then walk 400m N to start of A96.***

NUREMBURG (Nürnberg)

A3/E5 (west): Würzburg, Frankfurt, Kassel (A7/E70)
🚋 1, 21 to motorway entrance on Fürther Str. Stand on westbound slip road.***
🚋 4, 9 to Thon, then 🚌 30 to Tennenlohe motorway jn. Stand on westbound slip road.***

A9/E6 (north): Bayreuth, Berlin B14/E12 (east): Sulzbach, Prague
🚋 8 to terminus at Erlenstegen. Stand on Erlenstegenstr. Sign pref.***

A9/E6 (south): Munich
🚶 1.5km: from station along Bahnhofstr and Regensburger Str. Stand at jn with Hainstr.**
🚌 44 to terminus. Stand on Regensburgerstr.**
🚋 12 to terminus. Stand on Munchnerstr.***
⊖ 1 to Langwasser Süd, then 🚌 59 to Fischbach Station and 🚶 2km S to Fischbach motorway jn. Stand on southbound slip road.***

A6 (west): Mannheim (E12), Stuttgart (A81/E70), Basel (A5/E4)
🚶 🚋 as A9/E6 (south) above, but stand on Hainstr.***
⊖ 🚌 🚶 as A9/E6 (south) above to Fischbach.***
⊖ 1, 11 or 🚋 8 to Frankenstr/Südring jn then 🚌 52, 59 just over railway to Trierer Str. Stand on Münchener Str.***

SAARBRÜCKEN

A6/E12 (east): Mannheim, Nuremburg, Frankfurt (A67/E4), Basel (A5/E4), Stuttgart (A5/E4, A8/E11)
🚶 to southern end of either Wilhelmheinrichbrücke or Bismarckbrücke and stand on eastbound slip road to Stadtautobahn at either rdbt.***

A620/E42 (north): Saarlouis, Luxembourg (B406, N2)
🚶 as above but stand on westbound slip road at either rdbt.***

A6, A34/E12 (west): Metz, Paris (A4), Nancy (A31)
🚶 S along Viktoriastr, Eisenbahnstr, R along Vorstadtstr, L up Forbacher Str and Metzer Str.** Or 🚶 3km along Metzer Str to motorway jn.***

STUTTGART

A81 (south): Schwenningen, Konstanz (B33)
🚌 93 to rdbt at end of Leonberger Str. Stand S of rdbt on road to Vaihingen. Sign pref.**

A8/E11 (west): Karlsruhe, Basel (A5/ E4 south), Frankfurt (A5/E4 north)
🚌 as above. Sign pref.**
⊖ to Marienplatz then 🚌 93 to Leonberg motorway jn. Stand on southbound slip road.***
🚌 77 to Degerloch motorway jn. Stand on westbound slip road off rdbt (illegal).*** Or on southbound approach road to rdbt (legal). Sign pref.**

A81/E70 (north): Heilbronn, Würzburg, Nuremburg (A6), Kassel (A7/E4)
🚌 99 to Zuffenhausen motorway jn at Kallenberg. Stand on northbound slip road.***

A8/E11 (east): Munich, Salzburg
🚌 77 to Degerloch motorway jn. Stand on eastbound slip road off rdbt (illegal).*** Or 🚶 W along service road to Stuttgart service area.***

B27/E70 (south): Tübingen
🚌 77 to Degerloch motorway jn. Stand on southbound slip road off rdbt or on B27 itself.***

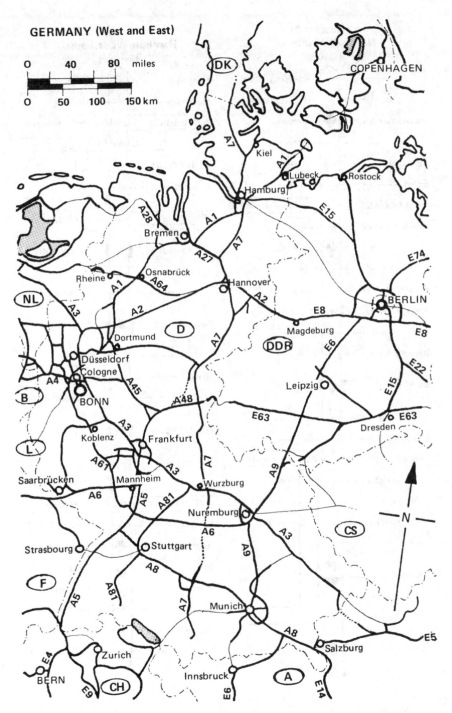

GERMANY (West and East)

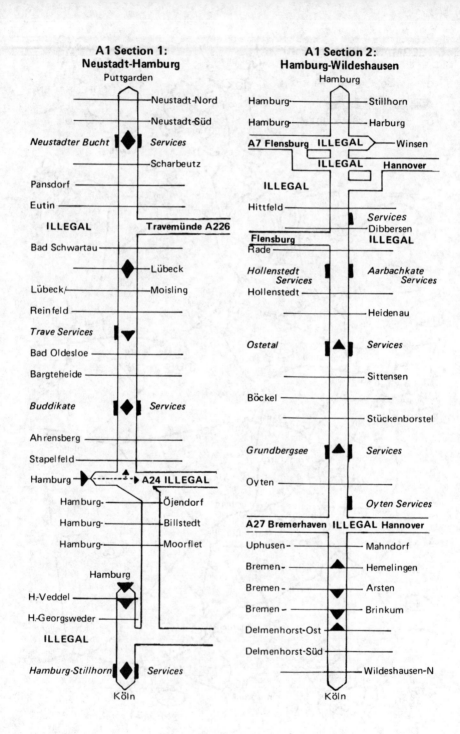

A1 Section 1:
Neustadt–Hamburg
Puttgarden

Neustadt-Nord
Neustadt-Süd
Neustadter Bucht | *Services*
Scharbeutz
Pansdorf
Eutin
ILLEGAL | Travemünde A226
Bad Schwartau
Lübeck
Lübeck/ | Moisling
Reinfeld
Trave Services
Bad Oldesloe
Bargteheide
Buddikate | *Services*
Ahrensberg
Stapelfeld
Hamburg | A24 **ILLEGAL**
Hamburg- | Öjendorf
Hamburg- | Billstedt
Hamburg- | Moorflet
Hamburg
H.-Veddel
H.-Georgsweder
ILLEGAL
Hamburg-Stillhorn | *Services*
Köln

A1 Section 2:
Hamburg–Wildeshausen
Hamburg

Hamburg- | Stillhorn
Hamburg- | Harburg
A7 Flensburg **ILLEGAL** | Winsen
ILLEGAL | **Hannover**
ILLEGAL
Hittfeld
Services
Dibbersen
Flensburg | **ILLEGAL**
Rade
Hollenstedt | *Aarbachkate*
Services | *Services*
Hollenstedt
Heidenau
Ostetal | *Services*
Sittensen
Böckel
Stückenborstel
Grundbergsee | *Services*
Oyten
Oyten Services
A27 Bremerhaven **ILLEGAL** **Hannover**
Uphusen- | Mahndorf
Bremen- | Hemelingen
Bremen- | Arsten
Bremen- | Brinkum
Delmenhorst-Ost
Delmenhorst-Süd
Wildeshausen-N
Köln

86

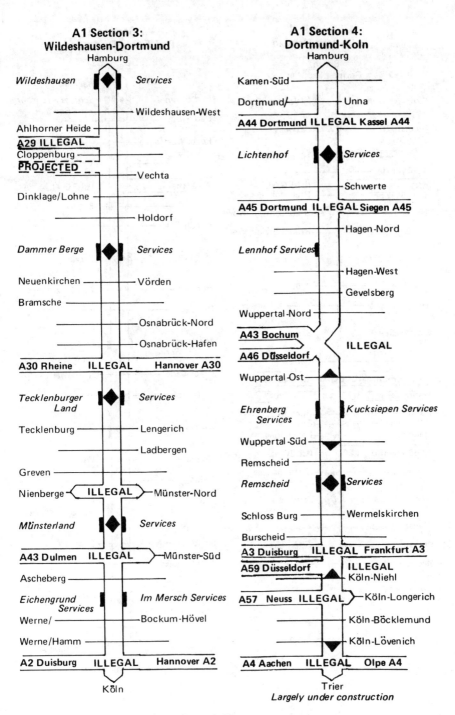

A1 Section 3:
Wildeshausen-Dortmund
Hamburg

Wildeshausen — Services

Wildeshausen-West

Ahlhorner Heide

A29 ILLEGAL
Cloppenburg
PROJECTED

Vechta

Dinklage/Lohne

Holdorf

Dammer Berge — Services

Neuenkirchen — Vörden

Bramsche

Osnabrück-Nord

Osnabrück-Hafen

A30 Rheine ILLEGAL Hannover A30

Tecklenburger Land — Services

Tecklenburg — Lengerich

Ladbergen

Greven

Nienberge — ILLEGAL — Münster-Nord

Münsterland — Services

A43 Dulmen ILLEGAL — Münster-Süd

Ascheberg

Eichengrund Services — Im Mersch Services

Werne/ — Bockum-Hövel

Werne/Hamm

A2 Duisburg ILLEGAL Hannover A2

Köln

A1 Section 4:
Dortmund-Koln
Hamburg

Kamen-Süd

Dortmund/ — Unna

A44 Dortmund ILLEGAL Kassel A44

Lichtenhof — Services

Schwerte

A45 Dortmund ILLEGAL Siegen A45

Hagen-Nord

Lennhof Services

Hagen-West

Gevelsberg

Wuppertal-Nord

A43 Bochum

A46 Düsseldorf — ILLEGAL

Wuppertal-Ost

Ehrenberg Services — Kucksiepen Services

Wuppertal-Süd

Remscheid

Remscheid — Services

Schloss Burg — Wermelskirchen

Burscheid

A3 Duisburg ILLEGAL Frankfurt A3

A59 Düsseldorf ILLEGAL
Köln-Niehl

A57 Neuss ILLEGAL — Köln-Longerich

Köln-Böcklemund

Köln-Lövenich

A4 Aachen ILLEGAL Olpe A4

Trier
Largely under construction

87

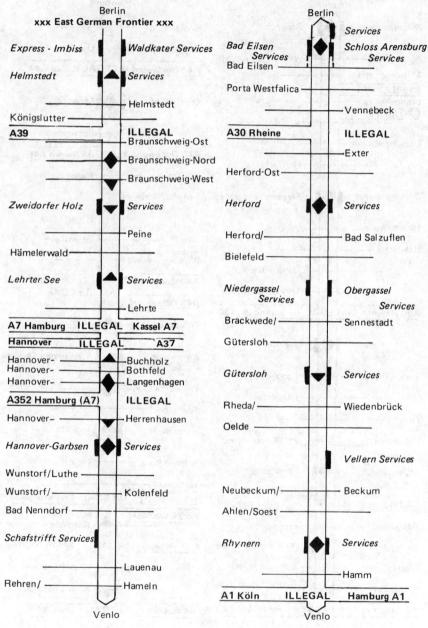

A2 Section 1:
Helmstedt-Hameln

Berlin
xxx East German Frontier xxx

Express - Imbiss — Waldkater Services

Helmstedt — Services

Helmstedt

Königslutter

A39 — **ILLEGAL**
Braunschweig-Ost

Braunschweig-Nord

Braunschweig-West

Zweidorfer Holz — Services

Peine

Hämelerwald

Lehrter See — Services

Lehrte

A7 Hamburg **ILLEGAL** **Kassel A7**

Hannover **ILLEGAL** **A37**

Hannover- — Buchholz
Hannover- — Bothfeld
Hannover- — Langenhagen

A352 Hamburg (A7) **ILLEGAL**

Hannover- — Herrenhausen

Hannover-Garbsen — Services

Wunstorf/Luthe

Wunstorf/ — Kolenfeld

Bad Nenndorf

Schafstrifft Services

Lauenau

Rehren/ — Hameln

Venlo

A2 Section 2:
Bad Eilsen-Dortmund

Berlin

Services

Bad Eilsen — Schloss Arensburg
Services — Services
Bad Eilsen

Porta Westfalica

Vennebeck

A30 Rheine **ILLEGAL**

Exter

Herford-Ost

Herford — Services

Herford/ — Bad Salzuflen

Bielefeld

Niedergassel — Obergassel
Services — Services

Brackwede/ — Sennestadt

Gütersloh

Gütersloh — Services

Rheda/ — Wiedenbrück

Oelde

Vellern Services

Neubeckum/ — Beckum

Ahlen/Soest

Rhynern — Services

Hamm

A1 Köln **ILLEGAL** **Hamburg A1**

Venlo

A2 Section 3:
Dortmund-Venlo

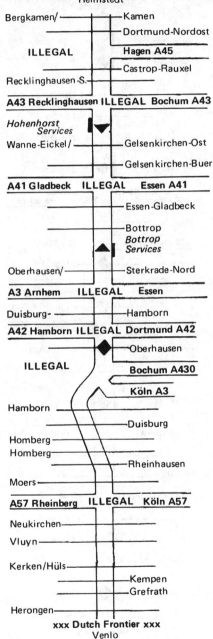

Helmstedt

Bergkamen/ — Kamen

Dortmund-Nordost

ILLEGAL — Hagen A45

Castrop-Rauxel

Recklinghausen-S.

A43 Recklinghausen ILLEGAL Bochum A43

Hohenhorst Services

Wanne-Eickel/ — Gelsenkirchen-Ost

Gelsenkirchen-Buer

A41 Gladbeck ILLEGAL Essen A41

Essen-Gladbeck

Bottrop

Bottrop Services

Oberhausen/ — Sterkrade-Nord

A3 Arnhem ILLEGAL Essen

Duisburg- — Hamborn

A42 Hamborn ILLEGAL Dortmund A42

Oberhausen

ILLEGAL

Bochum A430

Köln A3

Hamborn

Duisburg

Homberg

Homberg

Rheinhausen

Moers

A57 Rheinberg ILLEGAL Köln A57

Neukirchen

Vluyn

Kerken/Hüls

Kempen

Grefrath

Herongen

xxx Dutch Frontier xxx

Venlo

A3 Section 1:
Emmerich-Köln

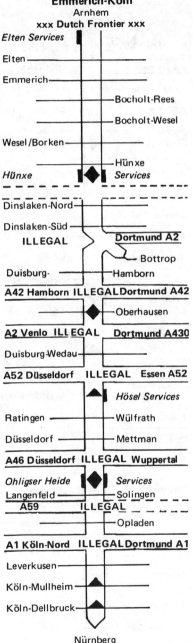

Arnhem

xxx Dutch Frontier xxx

Elten Services

Elten

Emmerich

Bocholt-Rees

Bocholt-Wesel

Wesel/Borken

Hünxe

Hünxe *Services*

Dinslaken-Nord

Dinslaken-Süd

ILLEGAL — Dortmund A2

Bottrop

Duisburg- — Hamborn

A42 Hamborn ILLEGAL Dortmund A42

Oberhausen

A2 Venlo ILLEGAL Dortmund A430

Duisburg-Wedau

A52 Düsseldorf ILLEGAL Essen A52

Hösel Services

Ratingen — Wülfrath

Düsseldorf — Mettman

A46 Düsseldorf ILLEGAL Wuppertal

Ohligser Heide *Services*

Langenfeld — Solingen

A59 ILLEGAL

Opladen

A1 Köln-Nord ILLEGAL Dortmund A1

Leverkusen

Köln-Mullheim

Köln-Dellbruck

Nürnberg

A3 Section 2: Köln-Limburg

Arnhem

Köln-Ost — ILLEGAL → Olpe A4

A4 Aachen — ILLEGAL

Köln - Flughafen / — Königsforst

Königsforst — *Services*

Siegburg / — Troisdorf
Siegburg — *Services*

Bonn / Siegburg

Logebachtal Services
Siebengebirge

Bad Honnef / — Linz

— Neustadt / Wied

Fernthal Services
— *Epgert Services*

Neuwied / — Altenkirchen

— *Urbacher Wald Services*
— Dierdorf

Sessenhausen Services
— *Landsberg an der Warthe*

Ransbach / — Siershahn

A48 Trier — ILLEGAL

Montabaur

Services — *Services*

— *Nentershausen Services*

Diez

Lahntal — *Services*

Limburg-Nord
Limburg-Süd

Regensburg

A3 Section 3: Limburg-Spessart

Arnhem

Werschau Services
Camberg — *Services*

— Camberg
— Idstein
— Niederhausen

Medenbach — *Services*

A66 Wiesbaden ILLEGAL **Frankfurt**

Raunheim

A67 Darmstadt — ILLEGAL

Frankfurt- — Flughafen

A5 Basel ILLEGAL **Giessen A5**

— Frankfurt-Süd

A49 Darmstadt ILLEGAL **Frankfurt A49**

Frankfurt-Ost / — Offenbach

— Hanau

Weiskirchen — *Services*

ILLEGAL — **Dortmund A45**

— Stockstadt

Aschaffenburg-W.

Aschaffenburg-O.

— Hösbach
— Weibersbrunn

Rohrbrunn

Spessart — *Services*

— Marktheidenfeld

Regensburg

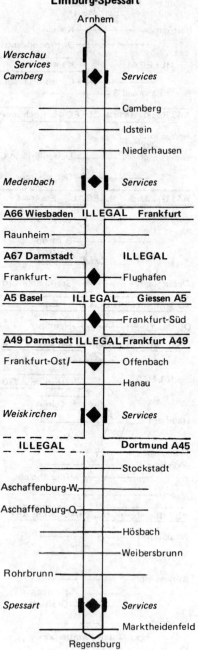

A3 Section 4:
Wertheim-Nürnberg

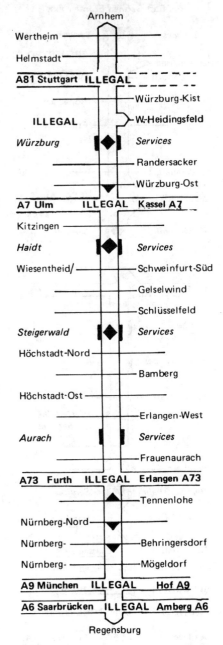

Arnhem

Wertheim

Helmstadt

A81 Stuttgart ILLEGAL

Würzburg-Kist

ILLEGAL

W.-Heidingsfeld

Würzburg   Services

Randersacker

Würzburg-Ost

A7 Ulm   ILLEGAL   Kassel A7

Kitzingen

Haidt   Services

Wiesentheid/   Schweinfurt-Süd

Gelselwind

Schlüsselfeld

Steigerwald   Services

Höchstadt-Nord

Bamberg

Höchstadt-Ost

Erlangen-West

Aurach   Services

Frauenaurach

A73 Furth   ILLEGAL   Erlangen A73

Tennenlohe

Nürnberg-Nord

Nürnberg-   Behringersdorf

Nürnberg-   Mögeldorf

A9 München   ILLEGAL   Hof A9

A6 Saarbrücken   ILLEGAL   Amberg A6

Regensburg

A4 (West):
Aachen-Köln

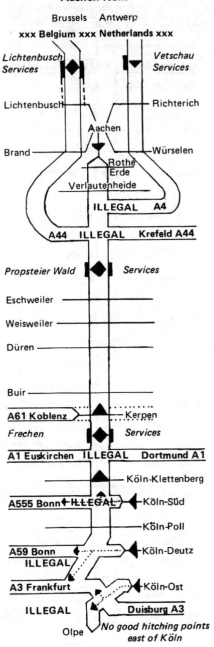

Brussels   Antwerp

xxx Belgium xxx Netherlands xxx

Lichtenbusch   Vetschau
Services   Services

Lichtenbusch   Richterich

Aachen

Brand   Würselen

Rothe
Erde

Verlautenheide

ILLEGAL   A4

A44 ILLEGAL   Krefeld A44

Propsteier Wald   Services

Eschweiler

Weisweiler

Düren

Buir

A61 Koblenz   Kerpen

Frechen   Services

A1 Euskirchen ILLEGAL   Dortmund A1

Köln-Klettenberg

A555 Bonn ILLEGAL   Köln-Süd

Köln-Poll

A59 Bonn   Köln-Deutz
ILLEGAL

A3 Frankfurt   Köln-Ost

ILLEGAL   Duisburg A3

Olpe   *No good hitching points
east of Köln*

91

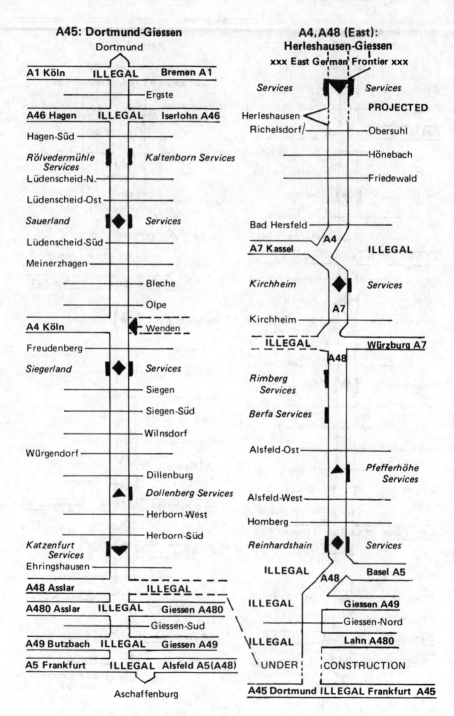

A45: Dortmund-Giessen

Dortmund

| A1 Köln | **ILLEGAL** | Bremen A1 |

Ergste

| A46 Hagen | **ILLEGAL** | Iserlohn A46 |

Hagen-Süd

Rölvedermühle Services ▮ ▮ *Kaltenborn Services*

Lüdenscheid-N.

Lüdenscheid-Ost

Sauerland ▮◆▮ *Services*

Lüdenscheid-Süd

Meinerzhagen

Bleche

Olpe

| A4 Köln | ◄ Wenden |

Freudenberg

Siegerland ▮◆▮ *Services*

Siegen

Siegen-Süd

Wilnsdorf

Würgendorf

Dillenburg

▲▮ *Dollenberg Services*

Herborn-West

Herborn-Süd

Katzenfurt Services ▮▼▮

Ehringshausen

| A48 Asslar | **ILLEGAL** |
| A480 Asslar | **ILLEGAL** | Giessen A480 |

Giessen-Sud

| A49 Butzbach | **ILLEGAL** | Giessen A49 |
| A5 Frankfurt | **ILLEGAL** | Alsfeld A5(A48) |

Aschaffenburg

A4, A48 (East): Herleshausen-Giessen

xxx East German Frontier xxx

Services ▼ *Services*

PROJECTED

Herleshausen ◄
Richelsdorf / Obersuhl

Hönebach

Friedewald

Bad Hersfeld **A4**

| A7 Kassel | **ILLEGAL** |

Kirchheim ◆▮ *Services*

Kirchheim **A7**

ILLEGAL Würzburg A7

A48

Rimberg Services ▮

Berfa Services ▮

Alsfeld-Ost

▲▮ *Pfefferhöhe Services*

Alsfeld-West

Homberg

Reinhardshain ▮◆▮ *Services*

ILLEGAL **A48** Basel A5

ILLEGAL Giessen A49

Giessen-Nord

ILLEGAL Lahn A480

UNDER **CONSTRUCTION**

| A45 Dortmund | **ILLEGAL** | Frankfurt A45 |

92

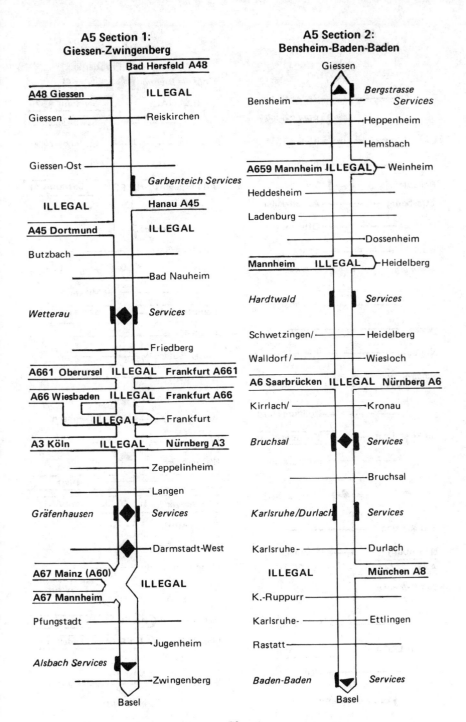

A5 Section 1:
Giessen-Zwingenberg

Bad Hersfeld A48

A48 Giessen — ILLEGAL

Giessen — Reiskirchen

Giessen-Ost

Garbenteich Services

ILLEGAL — Hanau A45

A45 Dortmund — ILLEGAL

Butzbach

Bad Nauheim

Wetterau — *Services*

Friedberg

A661 Oberursel ILLEGAL Frankfurt A661

A66 Wiesbaden ILLEGAL Frankfurt A66

ILLEGAL — Frankfurt

A3 Köln ILLEGAL Nürnberg A3

Zeppelinheim

Langen

Gräfenhausen — *Services*

Darmstadt-West

A67 Mainz (A60)

ILLEGAL

A67 Mannheim

Pfungstadt

Jugenheim

Alsbach Services

Zwingenberg

Basel

A5 Section 2:
Bensheim-Baden-Baden

Giessen

Bensheim — *Bergstrasse Services*

Heppenheim

Hemsbach

A659 Mannheim ILLEGAL — Weinheim

Heddesheim

Ladenburg

Dossenheim

Mannheim ILLEGAL — Heidelberg

Hardtwald — *Services*

Schwetzingen/ — Heidelberg

Walldorf / — Wiesloch

A6 Saarbrücken ILLEGAL Nürnberg A6

Kirrlach/ — Kronau

Bruchsal — *Services*

Bruchsal

Karlsruhe/Durlach — *Services*

Karlsruhe- — Durlach

ILLEGAL — München A8

K.-Ruppurr

Karlsruhe- — Ettlingen

Rastatt

Baden-Baden — *Services*

Basel

93

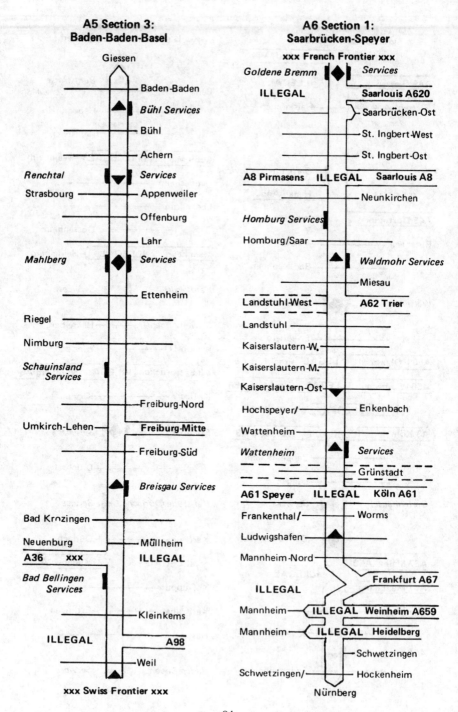

A5 Section 3:
Baden-Baden-Basel

Giessen

Baden-Baden
Bühl Services
Bühl
Achern
Renchtal — *Services*
Strasbourg — Appenweiler
Offenburg
Lahr
Mahlberg — *Services*
Ettenheim
Riegel
Nimburg
Schauinsland Services
Freiburg-Nord
Umkirch-Lehen — **Freiburg-Mitte**
Freiburg-Süd
Breisgau Services
Bad Krozingen
Neuenburg — Müllheim
A36 xxx — ILLEGAL
Bad Bellingen Services
Kleinkems
ILLEGAL — A98
Weil

xxx Swiss Frontier xxx

A6 Section 1:
Saarbrücken-Speyer

xxx French Frontier xxx
Goldene Bremm — *Services*
ILLEGAL — Saarlouis A620
Saarbrücken-Ost
St. Ingbert-West
St. Ingbert-Ost
A8 Pirmasens ILLEGAL Saarlouis A8
Neunkirchen
Homburg Services
Homburg/Saar
Waldmohr Services
Miesau
Landstuhl-West — A62 Trier
Landstuhl
Kaiserslautern-W.
Kaiserslautern-M.
Kaiserslautern-Ost
Hochspeyer/ — Enkenbach
Wattenheim
Wattenheim — *Services*
Grünstadt
A61 Speyer ILLEGAL Köln A61
Frankenthal/ — Worms
Ludwigshafen
Mannheim-Nord
Frankfurt A67
ILLEGAL
Mannheim — ILLEGAL Weinheim A659
Mannheim — ILLEGAL Heidelberg
Schwetzingen
Schwetzingen/ — Hockenheim

Nürnberg

94

A6 Section 2: Speyer-Nürnberg

Saarbrücken

A61 Speyer	ILLEGAL
Am Hockenheim Ring	Services
A5 Basel ILLEGAL	Frankfurt A5

Rauenberg/ — Wiesloch

— Sinsheim

Kraichgau — Services

— Steinsfurt

— Bonfeld

Heilbronn- — Obereisesheim

Heilbronn- — Neckarsulm

| A81 Stuttgart ILLEGAL | Würzburg A81 |

— Schwabbach

Öhringen —

Neuenstein —

— Kupferzell

Schwäbisch Hall —

Ilshofen —

Crailsheim —

— Rothenburg/Tauber

Services — Services
— Ansbach-West

— Ansbach-Mitte

— Ansbach-Ost

Neuendettelsau —

— Schwabach-West

— Schwabach-Ost

| A77 Roth ILLEGAL | Fürth A77 |

— Nürnberg-Süd

| A9 München ILLEGAL | Hof A9 |

| A3 Regensburg ILLEGAL | Würzburg A3 |

Amberg

A7 Section 1: Flensburg-Hamburg

xxx Danish Frontier xxx

Ellund Services —

— Flensburg

Wanderup —

— Schleswig-Schuby

— Schleswig-Jagel

— Eckernförde

Hüttener Berge — Services

Büdelsdorf —

Rendsburg — ILLEGAL

— Westensee

— Bordesholm

| ILLEGAL | Kiel A215 |
Neumünster- — Einfeld

Aalbek Services

— Neumünster

— Brokenlande Services

Neumünster- — Wittorf

Bad Bramstedt —

— Kaltenkirchen

Quickborn —

Holmmoor — Services

— Hamburg-Nord

Schnelsen —

| A23 Elmshorn | ILLEGAL |

— Hamburg-Stell.

Hamburg- — Wedel

Hamburg- — Altona

Hamburg- — Waltershof

Würzburg

95

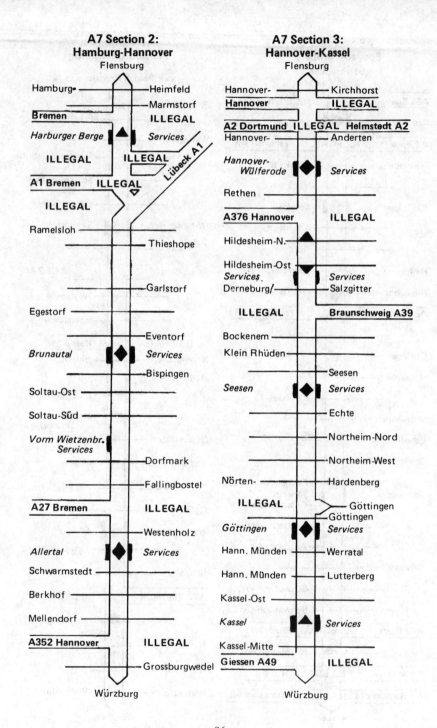

A7 Section 2: Hamburg-Hannover

Flensburg

Hamburg	Heimfeld
	Marmstorf
Bremen	ILLEGAL
Harburger Berge	Services
ILLEGAL	ILLEGAL
A1 Bremen	ILLEGAL
ILLEGAL	
Ramelsloh	
	Thieshope
	Garlstorf
Egestorf	
	Eventorf
Brunautal	Services
	Bispingen
Soltau-Ost	
Soltau-Süd	
Vorm Wietzenbr. *Services*	
	Dorfmark
	Fallingbostel
A27 Bremen	ILLEGAL
	Westenholz
Allertal	Services
Schwarmstedt	
Berkhof	
Mellendorf	
A352 Hannover	ILLEGAL
	Grossburgwedel

Lübeck A1

Würzburg

A7 Section 3: Hannover-Kassel

Flensburg

Hannover-	Kirchhorst
Hannover	ILLEGAL
A2 Dortmund ILLEGAL **Helmstedt A2**	
Hannover-	Anderten
Hannover-Wülferode	Services
Rethen	
A376 Hannover	ILLEGAL
Hildesheim-N.	
Hildesheim-Ost *Services*	Services
Derneburg/	Salzgitter
ILLEGAL	**Braunschweig A39**
Bockenem	
Klein Rhüden	
	Seesen
Seesen	Services
	Echte
	Northeim-Nord
	Northeim-West
Nörten-	Hardenberg
ILLEGAL	Göttingen
	Göttingen
Göttingen	Services
Hann. Münden	Werratal
Hann. Münden	Lutterberg
Kassel-Ost	
Kassel	Services
Kassel-Mitte	
Giessen A49	ILLEGAL

Würzburg

96

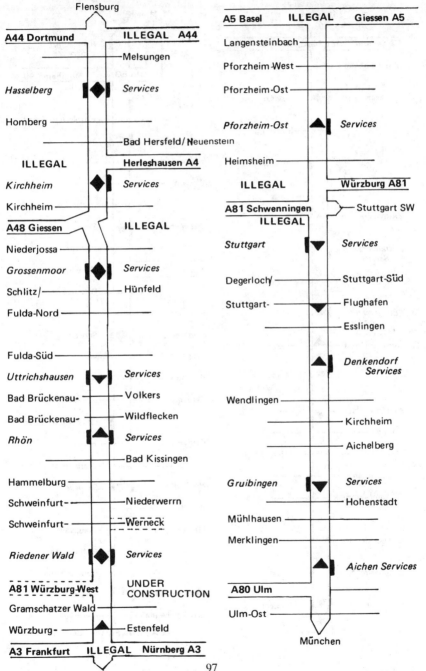

A7 Section 4:
Kassel-Würzburg

Flensburg

A44 Dortmund   ILLEGAL   A44

Melsungen

Hasselberg   Services

Homberg

Bad Hersfeld/ Neuenstein

ILLEGAL   Herleshausen A4

Kirchheim   Services

Kirchheim

A48 Giessen   ILLEGAL

Niederjossa

Grossenmoor   Services

Schlitz/   Hünfeld

Fulda-Nord

Fulda-Süd

Uttrichshausen   Services

Bad Brückenau-   Volkers

Bad Brückenau-   Wildflecken

Rhön   Services

Bad Kissingen

Hammelburg

Schweinfurt-   Niederwerrn

Schweinfurt-   Werneck

Riedener Wald   Services

A81 Würzburg-West   UNDER CONSTRUCTION

Gramschatzer Wald

Würzburg-   Estenfeld

A3 Frankfurt   ILLEGAL   Nürnberg A3

A8 Section 1:
Karlsruhe-Ulm

A5 Basel   ILLEGAL   Giessen A5

Langensteinbach

Pforzheim-West

Pforzheim-Ost

Pforzheim-Ost   Services

Heimsheim

ILLEGAL   Würzburg A81

A81 Schwenningen   Stuttgart SW
ILLEGAL

Stuttgart   Services

Degerloch   Stuttgart-Süd

Stuttgart-   Flughafen

Esslingen

Denkendorf
Services

Wendlingen

Kirchheim

Aichelberg

Gruibingen   Services

Hohenstadt

Mühlhausen

Merklingen

Aichen Services

A80 Ulm

Ulm-Ost

München

97

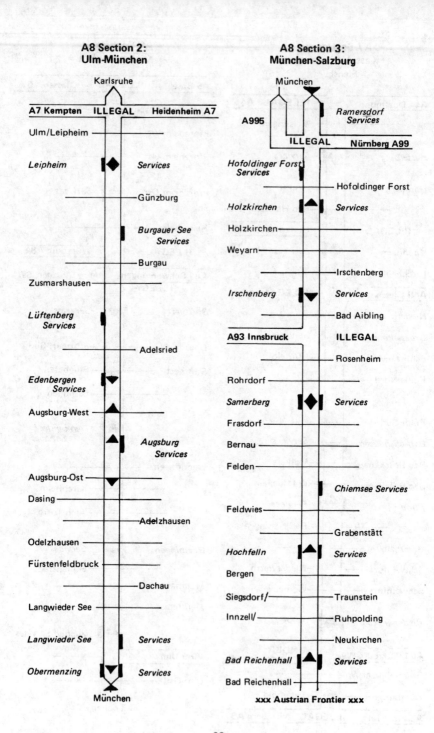

A8 Section 2:
Ulm-München

Karlsruhe

A7 Kempten   **ILLEGAL**   **Heidenheim A7**

Ulm/Leipheim

Leipheim   *Services*

Günzburg

Burgauer See Services

Burgau

Zusmarshausen

Lüftenberg Services

Adelsried

Edenbergen Services

Augsburg-West

Augsburg Services

Augsburg-Ost

Dasing

Adelzhausen

Odelzhausen

Fürstenfeldbruck

Dachau

Langwieder See

Langwieder See   *Services*

Obermenzing   *Services*

München

A8 Section 3:
München-Salzburg

München

A995   *Ramersdorf Services*

ILLEGAL   **Nürnberg A99**

Hofoldinger Forst Services

Hofoldinger Forst

Holzkirchen   *Services*

Holzkirchen

Weyarn

Irschenberg

Irschenberg   *Services*

Bad Aibling

A93 Innsbruck   **ILLEGAL**

Rosenheim

Rohrdorf

Samerberg   *Services*

Frasdorf

Bernau

Felden

Chiemsee Services

Feldwies

Grabenstätt

Hochfelln   *Services*

Bergen

Siegsdorf/   Traunstein

Innzell/   Ruhpolding

Neukirchen

Bad Reichenhall   *Services*

Bad Reichenhall

xxx Austrian Frontier xxx

98

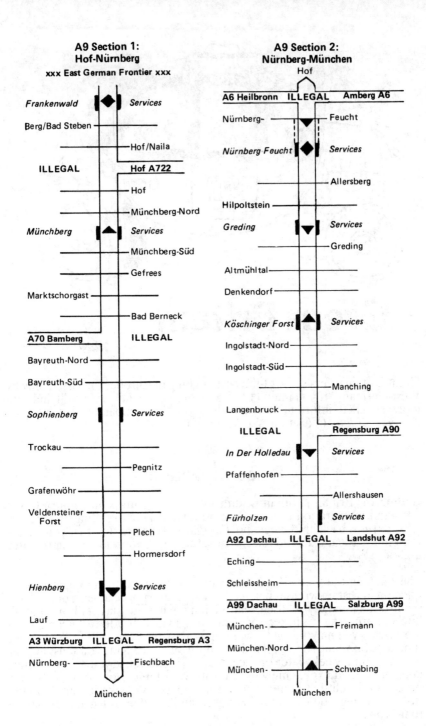

A9 Section 1:
Hof-Nürnberg
xxx East German Frontier xxx

Frankenwald — Services

Berg/Bad Steben

Hof/Naila

ILLEGAL — **Hof A722**

Hof

Münchberg-Nord

Münchberg — Services

Münchberg-Süd

Gefrees

Marktschorgast

Bad Berneck

A70 Bamberg — **ILLEGAL**

Bayreuth-Nord

Bayreuth-Süd

Sophienberg — Services

Trockau

Pegnitz

Grafenwöhr

Veldensteiner Forst

Plech

Hormersdorf

Hienberg — Services

Lauf

A3 Würzburg — **ILLEGAL** — **Regensburg A3**

Nürnberg- — Fischbach

München

A9 Section 2:
Nürnberg-München
Hof

A6 Heilbronn — **ILLEGAL** — **Amberg A6**

Nürnberg- — Feucht

Nürnberg-Feucht — Services

Allersberg

Hilpoltstein

Greding — Services

Greding

Altmühltal

Denkendorf

Köschinger Forst — Services

Ingolstadt-Nord

Ingolstadt-Süd

Manching

Langenbruck

ILLEGAL — **Regensburg A90**

In Der Holledau — Services

Pfaffenhofen

Allershausen

Fürholzen — Services

A92 Dachau — **ILLEGAL** — **Landshut A92**

Eching

Schleissheim

A99 Dachau — **ILLEGAL** — **Salzburg A99**

München- — Freimann

München-Nord

München- — Schwabing

München

99

Great Britain

Great Britain offers some of the best hitching in Europe, surpassed only by West Germany. If you intend to do a lot of hitching here, you will find a lot more detailed information and advice in the companion *Hitch-hikers' Manual Britain* (Vacation Work, £3.95).

Rules of Thumb

Getting In. Britain is the most difficult western European country to get into, and immigration officers have no qualms about sending anyone but EEC citizens back on the next boat or plane. Try to ensure that you have a fair bit of cash and a good reason for returning to your home country after a short stay.

The Law. In the early 1970s you could hardly hope to complete a day's hitching in Britain without being pulled up by the police at least once. They seem to have finally realised that hitching is here to stay and that not all hitchers are drug-traffickers or escaped convicts. If you're hitching on a motorway, you may just get a warning or possibly even a lift to the nearest junction. Spot fines are unheard of, so if you are caught, you must appear in court some weeks later or plead guilty (if you think you are) by letter, apologising and explaining why it wasn't your fault. Not surprisingly, this procedure is a little too unwieldy for the police to invoke if you are found just the wrong side of a motorway sign and are due to leave the country tomorrow.

Road Strategy. There are no tolls on the motorways, which makes them the best bet for long distances. For best results jump from services to services. Otherwise choose your junctions with care: those serving large towns are busy enough. On main roads you should also travel fast, and waiting times will rarely be over half an hour. Britain's road planners must have had hitch-hikers in mind when they decided on the distribution of roundabouts, which are far more common—both at motorway junctions and at other main road intersections—than in any other European country.

Route Planning. Main roads are prefixed A, secondary roads B, and minor roads are unnumbered. Unfortunately, the road system is a bit more complicated than that. A-roads can be either "Primary Routes" or "Class I connecting roads", and the former appear as thicker lines on the better class of maps. Motorways may be called M__or A__(M); the first kind have numbered junctions, the second do not. Finally, to complicate matters even further, the whole system is continually reviewed, so road numbers on signs may differ from those on maps. The E-numbers are not used at all.

The A1–A6 radiate from London to various points on the coast, and the A7-A9 originate in Edinburgh. Other roads get their first digit from the sector in which they start: the A27 starts between the A2 and A3, the B557 between the A5 and A6, etc. Motorways follow the same kind of pattern, except for the M5 (Exeter–Birmingham) and the M25 (London Orbital Motorway).

Maps. You get reasonable free maps of the whole country from either Little Chef restaurants or Trust House Forte hotels. If you can't find one of these, you can buy good detailed regional maps from petrol stations; there's not much to choose between the various brands. Town plans usually have to be paid for—even at tourist offices—but you might be lucky if you enquire at an estate agency.

Place Names. One point of difficulty—among English as well as aliens—are the strange Welsh and Scottish names. Welsh in particular presents problems, and the Welsh language is used alongside English on road signs. Although most Welsh town names look foreign, several of them are in fact only anglicised versions of an even more complicated Welsh original. Thus Blaenau Ffestiniog, Glyndyfrdwy and Llanrhaedr-y-Mochnant are pure Welsh forms. But Swansea is Abertawe, and you will find Cardigan referred to as Ceredigion, Cardiff as Caerdydd, etc., among Welsh speakers and alongside the English version on signposts.

Number Plates. There is a very complex system by which registration letters are allotted according to area—it usually involves the last two of the group of three letters, but these letters rarely resemble the names of the towns they represent. In addition if a vehicle moves permanently to another area it retains its original number. But it is a fairly safe bet that if the middle letter of the group of three is S, then the car was originally registered in Scotland, and if I or Z occurs then it is Irish.

Planned and Paid Lifts. There is no agency for putting drivers in touch with potential passengers. For journeys within Britain, the notice boards in

Students' Unions are the best bet; for trips abroad, try the *Travellers* section in the personal columns of *Time Out* or *City Limits*.

Hitchers who can satisfy a few conditions have the opportunity to get from London to Dover in style. Hertz Car Rentals have a heavy demand for cars at their Dover office, due to the constant stream of motorists returning without vehicles due to accidents or breakdowns abroad. The supplies are replenished from stocks in London, using casual delivery drivers. If you are over 21 with a reasonably clean driving licence and a credit card, Hertz will rent you a car from their branches in Russell Square (central London) or Heathrow Airport for £1, so long as you deliver it to Dover within a maximum of 12 hours and 150 miles. You have to pay for the petrol you use. Even so, for under a fiver you can get yourself, your companion, your luggage and any hitchers you pick up to Dover with speed and in comfort. To book a car call 01-262 1638 a day or two in advance. Your chances are best midweek; Fridays are impossible. Try to avoid emulating the hitcher just beginning a trip to Poland who got a £10 parking ticket before leaving London, thus rendering the operation highly uneconomic. If you do fall foul of a traffic warden, pay the fine yourself or it will be charged to your credit card.

Northern Ireland. Until an acceptable social and political solution is reached in the six counties of Ulster that are part of the United Kingdom, it is not advisable for any citizen of the British Isles to hitch-hike in the north of Ireland. Although you may set out to avoid religion and politics as topics of conversation, an enquiry as to your name and origin will enable any driver to form an opinion of your religious affiliation—even if you're a lifelong atheist. This may have consequences more unpleasant than summary eviction from the car. And those responsible for law enforcement are not used to seeing hordes of hitchers lining the motorways out of Belfast. The time spent convincing them of your innocence will be better spent on a train or bus.

Locals routinely hitch within closely-defined areas. Most foreigners (i.e. all but the Irish and British) are relatively immune to the conflict; but people whose appearance could conceivably be construed as that of a plain-clothed member of the security forces (and this seems to include almost anyone) are advised to stay well clear. If you're still not deterred, then the amount of time wasted at road blocks or the alarming incidence of traffic accidents should be enough to convince you to head for the more predictable roads of Britain or Eire.

Town Guide

(for key and explanation, see the introduction)

BIRMINGHAM

A47: Leicester
🚌 93, 94, 661 to A47/Newport Rd jn just before Castle Bromwich. Stand on A47.**

M6: London (M1), Leicester (M69)
🚌 as above but walk ½ mile N along Newport Rd to M6 jn. Stand on M6 approach road.***
🚌 962 (rush hour only), 962N (night) to M6 jn above.

NB: There is no entry to the M6 westbound from this jn.

A456: Kidderminster, Bristol (M5)
🚶 1 mile: SW from Paradise Circus along Broad St to Five Ways jn with A456/A4540. Stand on A456 slip road.*
🚌 9, 9N, 130, 131, 136, 137, 140 to Hagley Rd West (A455)/Quinton Expressway jn (A456). Stand on A456**, or 🚶 1 mile S to M5 jn. Stand on A456*** or M5 slip road.***

M6: The North
🚌 16N, 51 to A34/M6 jn at Great Barr. Stand on M6 slip road.***

BRIGHTON

A23: London (M23), Horsham (A281)
🚌 106, 107, 117, 137, 175 to Mill Rd/Vale Avenue/A23 jn at Robin Hood Garage. Stand by bus stop on A23.****

A27 (east): Lewes, Dover (A259, A20)
🚶 1½ miles: N from Palace Pier along Old Steine and Grand Parade, bear R along Lewes Rd (A27) to jn with Hollingdean Rd/Bear Rd. Stand on A27 at start of dual carriageway.**
🚌 10, 11, 25, 38, 49, 58, 59 to above jn.

A27 (west): Portsmouth, Southampton
🚌 2, 21, 22, 29, 62 to Upper Shoreham Rd/A27 rdbt 1 mile before Shoreham. Stand on A27.****

BRISTOL

M32: London, South Wales (M4), Midlands (M5)
🚶 ¾ mile: E along Newfoundland St to start of M32. Stand at start (by motorway sign) or on slip road. Sign pref.*
🚌 19, 21, 22, 62 to above jn.
🚌 10, 22, 23, 89-91 to M32 jn 2 at Eastville. Stand on slip road. Sign pref.**

A4018: Midlands (M5), The South West (M5), London (M4), South Wales (M4)
🚌 1, 28, 29, 87, 88 to Whitetree rdbt (Westbury Rd A4018). Sign pref.***
(🚶 from Stoke Bishop Halls of Residence: ½ mile).

A4: Bath, Salisbury (A36)
🚶 ½ mile: S from Temple Meads station over Bath Bridge and along Bath Rd (A4) to jn with Wells Rd (A37). Stand at lights on A4.**
🚌 1, 13, 30-34, 60 to above jn.

A37: Wells
🚶 🚌 as above but stand at lights on A37.**

CAMBRIDGE

A1134 (south): London (M11)
🚶 ½ mile: S along Trumpington St to double mini rdbt at jn with Lensfield Rd/Fen Causeway. Stand at start of Trumpington Rd (A1134).**

A1303 (west): St Neots (A45)
🚶 ½ mile: NW along Bridge St and Magdalene St, L along Northampton St to rdbt at jn with Queen's Rd/Madingley Rd (A1303). Stand on A1303.**

A1307 (north west): Huntingdon (A604)
🚶 1 mile: NW along Bridge St, Magdalene St, Castle St and Huntingdon Rd (A1307) to between New Hall and Fitzwilliam colleges on left. Stand on A1307.**
🚌 151, 155-158, 189-191 to colleges above.

A1134 (north): King's Lynn (A10)
🚶 1½ miles: NW along Bridge St and Magdalene St, R along Chesterton Lane and Chesterton Rd, L then R along one-way system, along Milton Rd (A1134) to rdbt at jn with Elizabeth Way. Stand on A1134.*
🚶 as above but continue along A1134 (Milton Rd) to Kings Hedges Rd/Green End rdbt, ¾ mile further. Stand on A1134. Sign pref.***
🚌 180, 181, 195 to second rdbt above.

A1303 (east): Ipswich (A45)
🚶 2½ miles: E along Jesus Lane, Maids Causeway and Newmarket Rd (A1303) to jn with Ditton Lane by Cemetery. Stand on A1303.**
🚌 111, 122, 150, 166 to above jn.

A1307 (south east): Colchester (A604)
🚶 2 miles: SE along St Andrews St, Regent St and Hills Rd (A1307) to rdbt at jn with Fendon Rd opposite New Hospital. Stand on A1307.***
🚌 113, 136, 143, 185, 186, 188, 193 to above rdbt.

CARDIFF (Caerdydd)

A48: Newport, London (M4)
🚶 1½ miles: N from Castle Green along Kingsway and North Rd (A470) to Gabalfa Interchange (A48/A469). Stand on A48 (Eastern Avenue) slip road. Sign pref.**
🚌 1, 2, 7, 8, 21-24, 28, 29, 36, 41, 43, 63 to above jn.
🚌 12, 56-59, 107 to Llanedeyrn Interchange (A4161). Stand on A48 slip road. Sign pref.***

A469: Caerphilly, Tredegar
🚶🚌 as above to Gabalfa Interchange but stand beyond jn at start of Caerphilly Rd (A469).**

A470: Swansea (M4)
🚶🚌 as above to Gabalfa Interchange but stand beyond jn at start of Northern Avenue. Sign pref.**

DOVER

A2: Canterbury, London (M2)
🚶 to Marine Parade/Jubilee Way (A2) rdbt outside Eastern Docks. Stand on A2.**
🚶 2 miles: NW from Town Hall along High St and London Rd, R along Green Lane, L along Melbourne Avenue and Honeywood Rd to A2/A256 rdbt. Stand on A2.****
🚌 561, 563, 564, 573, 574, 584-588 to above rdbt at Whitfield.

A256: Sandwich, Margate
🚶🚌 as above but stand on A256.**

A258: Deal
🚶 1 mile: NE along Castle Hill Rd and Deal Rd (A258) to jn with Jubilee Way (A2). Stand on A258.***
🚌 580, 594 to above jn.

A20: Folkestone, London (M20)
🚶 to York St/Priory St/Priory Rd/ St Martin's Hill (A20) rdbt near Priory station. Stand on A20.**

EDINBURGH

A1: Newcastle, London
🚶 2 miles: E along Princes St, Waterloo Place, Regent Rd, Montrose Terrace and London Rd (A1) to Portobello Rd fork. Stand on A1.*
🚌 15, 26, 44, 49, 86 to Milton Rd (A1)/Musselburgh Rd jn before Musselburgh. Stand on A1.***

A702: Carlisle, The South (M6)
🚶 3 miles: S along Lothian Rd, Earl Grey St, R at Tollcross along Home St, Leven St, Bruntsfield Place, Morningside Rd and Comiston Rd to Biggar Rd (A702)/A720 jn. Stand on A702.***
🚌 4, 7, 11, 15, 32, 79 to above jn at Fairmilehead.

A90: Perth (M90), The North (M90, A9) (via Forth Bridge)
🚶 2 miles: NW along Queensferry St, Queensferry Rd and Hillhouse Rd (A90) to jn with Telford Rd (A902). Stand on A90.**
🚌 18, 20, 22, 24, 29, 32 to above jn.

A8: Glasgow (M8), Stirling (M9)
🚶 to Haymarket Station. Stand on Glasgow Rd (A8) outside Bin Ends wine bar. Sign pref.*
🚌 31 to A8/Turnhouse Rd/Maybury Rd jn. Stand on A8.***

FOLKESTONE

M20: London
🚶 1½ miles: W from Central Station

along Cheriton Rd, R along Cherry Garden Avenue to rdbt at start of M20.***
Sometimes crowded on arrival of ferries—try just outside the dock gates.

GLASGOW

There are four major bus operators in Glasgow, and many of them use the same numbers. Operators are given below. Services 800+ are night buses.

M74: Carlisle, The South (M6)
🚌 44, 53-56, 151 (Central Scottish) to start of M74 by Calderpark Zoo. Stand at start of M74.**

A77: Kilmarnock, Ayr, Stranraer
🚌 38, 38A (SPTE) to Ayr Rd (A77)/Rouken Glen Rd/Eastwood Mains Rd rdbt at Eastwood Toll, 6 miles SW of City centre. Stand on A77.***

M8 (west): Greenock (A8)
🚶 ½ mile: W from Central Station along Waterloo St to M8 approach road. Sign pref.*
🚌 22-24, 28, 634, 635 (Western Scottish) to Renfrew Rd/Hillington Rd jn just before Renfrew, 5 miles W of city centre. Walk 200 yards S to M8 jn, stand on M8 slip road.***

A82: Dumbarton, Fort William
🚌 20, 801 (SPTE), 134, 146 (Central Scottish) to A82/Drumry Rd East rdbt near Drumry. Stand on A82.***

A80: Cumbernauld, Stirling (M80, M9)
🚶 3 miles: N from Glasgow Cross along High St and Castle St, R along Alexandra Parade for 1½ miles, L along Cumbernauld Rd (A80) to M8 jn 12. Stand just past jn with Provanmill Rd by cemetery on A80.**
🚌 1, 26, 33-37, 39, 40 (Midland Scottish) 6, 38, 65 (SPTE) to above jn.

M8 (east): Edinburgh
🚌 15, 216 (Eastern Scottish) to

M8/A8/M73 jn at Bargeddie, 8 miles east of city centre. Stand on A8 slip road.***

HARWICH (Parkeston Quay)

A120: Colchester, London (A12)
🚶 ½ mile: S out of harbour along Parkeston Rd to rdbt at jn with A120.***

LEEDS

M1: London, Hull (M62)
🚶 ¾ mile: S over River Aire along Nevill St or Bridge End to start of M1/M621. Sign pref.**
If you are heading for Hull, the A63/M62 route via Selby is slower but better for hitching.

M621: Halifax, Manchester (M62)
🚶 as above but stand on M621 approach road. Sign pref.**

A660: Otley, Skipton (A65)
🚶 1, 780, 782-784 to A660/A6120 rdbt at Lawnswood. Stand 100 yards along A660 beyond Otley Old Rd.***

A61: Harrogate
🚌 2, 3, 20, 21, 29, 31, 32, 34-36, 52, 53, 767-769, 781 to A61/A6120 rdbt at Moortown.****

A58: Wetherby, The North (A1)
🚌 741, 796-799 to A58/A6120 rdbt between Monkswood and Wellington Hill.****

A64: York, Scarborough
🚌 5, 11, 795 to northernmost A64/A6120 rdbt just before Whinmoor.****

A63: Selby, Hull (M62)
🚌 83, 84, 162-165, 401 to A63/A6120 rdbt near Whitkirk.****

LIVERPOOL

M62: Manchester, The South (M6)
🚌 6C, 6D, 40, 45, 62-65, 76 to

M62/A5080 jn at Broad Green.*
⊜ from Lime St to Broad Green.
*Your chances are much better at the
M57/M62 jn, described below:
hitching from the roundabout is legal.*
🚌 ⊜ to Broad Green then bus H5,
H12, H13, H15 to M57/M62 jn.****

M58: Wigan, The North (M6)
⊜ Merseyrail Northern Line to Old
Roan then L out of station and ¼
mile along Ormskirk Rd (A59) to
A59/M57/M58 jn.****

LONDON

A2: Canterbury, Dover
⊜ from Charing Cross, Waterloo
East or London Bridge to Eltham
Well Hall. L out of station and along
Well Hall Rd for ½ mile to
Westhorne Avenue (A205)/
Rochester Way (A2) rdbt.***

A20: Maidstone, Folkestone
🚌 21 from London Bridge to Eltham
Rd/Sidcup (A20) jn between Lea
Green and Eltham Green, then walk
¼ mile along A20 to Clifford's rdbt
at jn with Westhorne Avenue
(A205). Stand on A20.***
⊜ to Catford or Catford Bridge then
bus 160, 160A to rdbt above.

A23: Brighton, Eastbourne (A22)
⊜ from Victoria, Charing Cross,
Waterloo East or London Bridge to
Purley. L out of station to A22** or
L then R to A23.**

A3: Guildford, Portsmouth
🚌 72 from Hammersmith or 85 from
Putney Bridge to Robin Hood Gate
at south east of Richmond Park.
Stand at start of Kingston by-pass
(A3).***

**A316: Winchester (M3), The South
   West (M3)**
🚌 290 from Hammersmith to
Hogarth rdbt (A4/A316) by Fuller's
brewery.**
⊜ from Waterloo to Sunbury. Stand
on M3 slip road. Sign pref.***

**A4: Heathrow Airport, Bristol, The
   West (M4)**

⊜ to Hammersmith, under flyover to
A4 slip road. Sign pref.*
⊜ or ⊜ (North London Line) to
Gunnersbury. L out of station along
Chiswick High Road, under flyover
to M4 slip road. Stand by garage
beyond pedestrian crossing. Sign
pref.**

A40: Oxford, Cheltenham (M40)
⊜ to Hanger Lane. Stand on
Western Avenue (A40) slip road or
at lay-by on A40***

M1: Leeds, The North
⊜ to Brent Cross. Follow signs from
station to North Circular Rd (A406),
L for ½ mile along A406 to rdbt at
start of M1. Stand on M1. Invariably
crowded: sign pref.****
🚌 N94 (hourly every night) to above
rdbt at Staple's Corner.
🚌 113 from Oxford Circus, Baker
Street or Hendon Central to Apex
Corner. Under subway beneath rdbt
and downhill along Ellesmere
Avenue for 200 yards to "Service
Vehicles Only" track leading under
M1 to Scratchwood Services.****

A1: Peterborough, The North
🚌 113 to Apex Corner. Stand at
start of Barnet Way (A1).***

M11: Cambridge, Norwich (A11)
⊜ to Redbridge. Stand at start of
M11. Sometimes crowded: sign
pref.***
*If your destination is Norwich, do not
accept a lift continuing along the M11
beyond jn 9.*

A12: Colchester, Southend (A127)
⊜ to Gants Hill. Stand outside at
rdbt on Eastern Avenue (A12)***

MANCHESTER

**A5103: Chester (M56), The South
   (A556, M6)**
🚶 ½ mile: S from St Peter's Square
along Lower Mosley St and Medlock
St, under Mancunian Way (A57M)
to start of Princess Rd (A5103).
Stand at rdbt on A5103. Sign pref.**

If you are heading south on the M6, do not accept a lift that will drop you anywhere on the M56 except at the A556 jn.

M602: Liverpool (M62)
⚐ 1 mile: W from Regent Bridge along Regent Rd to rdbt at start of M602. Stand at rdbt.****
🚌 62, 64, 66-67 to above rdbt.

A627(M): Rochdale, Leeds (M62)
🚌 23, 24, 181 (night), 182 to start of A627(M) at Chadderton, NW of Oldham. Stand on slip road: Rochdale ***, Leeds.**
If you are heading for Leeds but are offered a lift to Rochdale, take it to the opposite end of the A627(M) for a better hitching spot.

M62: Leeds, Liverpool
🚌 52, 74 (night), 95-97 to Prestwich Hospital, then walk 200 yards N to A56/M62 jn. Stand on M62 slip road.**
🚎 to Besses O' Th' Barn near above jn.

A57: Sheffield (M67, A628, A616)
⚐ ¾ mile: SE from Piccadilly station along London Rd, across Mancunian Way jn and along Downing St and Ardwick Green South to rdbt at jn with Hyde Rd (A57)/Stockport Rd (A6). Sign pref.*

A6 (south east): Stockport, Derby
⚐ as above but stand on A6. Sign pref.*

NEWCASTLE UPON TYNE

A1(M): Durham, London
⊖ to Heworth then 🚌 130, 190, 192-4, 520, 525, 528, 530 to Leam Lane (A194)/A1(M) rdbt. Stand at start of A1(M).***

A696: Galashiels, Edinburgh (A68)
⊖ to terminus at Bank Foot. Stand outside station on A696.***

A6125: Berwick (A1), Edinburgh (A1)
⊖ to Regent Centre. Stand outside

station on A6125 ** or ⚐ ½ mile N to jn with Broadway.***

NEWHAVEN Harbour

A26: Lewes, London (A22)
⚐ ¼ mile: N out of harbour, under A259 flyover on New Rd (A26) to just beyond jn with Avis Way.**

A259 (east): Eastbourne, Hastings
⚐ ½ mile: N out of harbour, R along The Drove to Denton Corner. Stand beyond bend on Seaford Rd (A259).***

A259 (west): Brighton
⚐ 1 mile: N out of harbour, L along The Drove, over bridge and around one-way system, L along Brighton Rd to sharp bend by golf course. Stand opposite club house on A259.***

PORTSMOUTH

M275: Southampton (M27), London (A27, A3), Brighton (A27)
⚐ 1 mile: N from Portsmouth and Southsea Station along Commercial Road (initially pedestrian precinct) and Mile End Rd to Rudmore rdbt by Continental Ferry Port. Stand at start of M275. Sign pref. Southampton ***, London **, Brighton.*
🚌 1, 2, 7, 8, 24-26, 55 to Rudmore rdbt above.

A27: Brighton, London (A3M)
🚌 1-4, 7, 8, 22-24, 347, 350, 403, 450, 452, 702, 740-749 to M275/A27 jn at Hilsea. Stand on A27 slip road. Sign pref.**
🚎 to Warblington, then ⚐ ¼ mile: S from station, L along Emsworth Rd to A27 rdbt.***

SHEFFIELD

M1 (south): London, Doncaster (M18)
🚌 24, 69, 96, 208, 287, 924 to A6178/A631/M1 jn at Tinsley. Stand on M1 slip road. Sign pref. London ***, Doncaster.**

A57: Worksop, London (A630, M1), Doncaster (A630, M1, M18)

🚶 to Commercial St/Sheaf St/Duke St (A616)/Sheffield Parkway (A57) rdbt at Park Square by city centre, ½ mile north of station. Stand on A57. Sometimes crowded, sign pref.**

A61 (south): Chesterfield, Derby

🚶 to Suffolk Rd/Shrewsbury Rd/ Granville Rd/Queens Rd (A61) rdbt by city centre, ¼ mile south of Station. Stand on A61.**
🚌 201-203 to Sheffield Rd (A61) rdbt between Low Edges and Batemoor just inside county boundary; or 42, 53 to Low Edges Rd/A61 jn then ¼ mile S to above rdbt. Stand on A61.****

M1 (north): Wakefield, Leeds

🚌 277, 288 to Meadowhall Rd (A6109) jn with M1. Stand on M1 slip road.**

SOUTHAMPTON

M27 (east): Portsmouth, London (A33, M3)
M27 (west): The South West (A31)

🚌 63, 63A to bridge over M27 at Rownhams. Turn R along service road before bridge for M27 west, or after bridge for M27 east. Sign pref.***

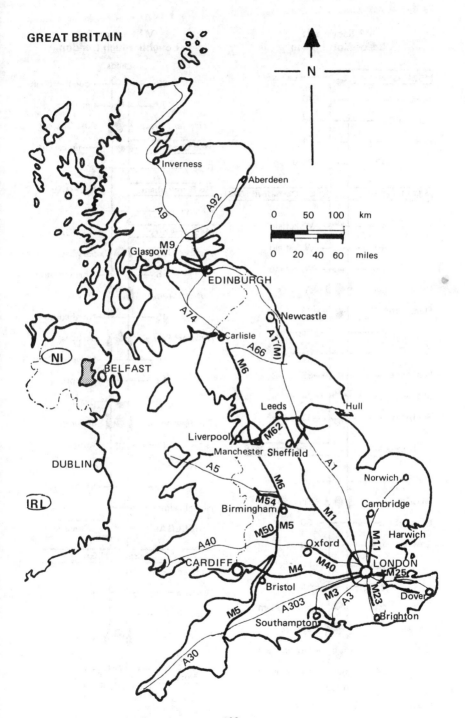

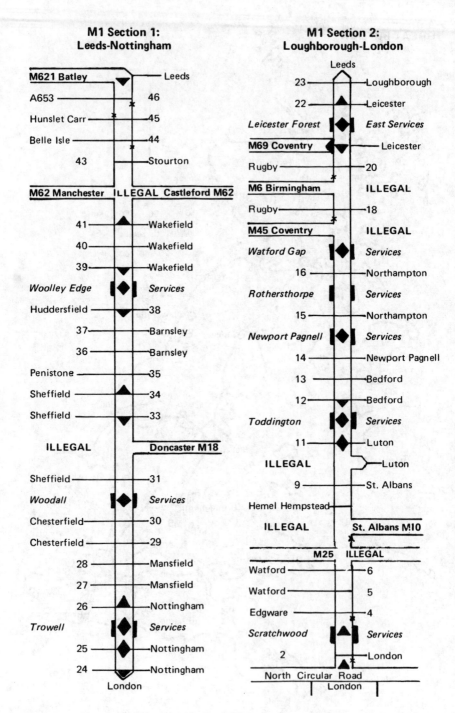

M1 Section 1:
Leeds-Nottingham

Leeds

M621 Batley
A653 — 46
Hunslet Carr — 45
Belle Isle — 44
43 — Stourton

M62 Manchester ILLEGAL Castleford M62

41 — Wakefield
40 — Wakefield
39 — Wakefield
Woolley Edge **Services**
Huddersfield — 38
37 — Barnsley
36 — Barnsley
Penistone — 35
Sheffield — 34
Sheffield — 33

ILLEGAL Doncaster M18

Sheffield — 31
Woodall **Services**
Chesterfield — 30
Chesterfield — 29
28 — Mansfield
27 — Mansfield
26 — Nottingham
Trowell **Services**
25 — Nottingham
24 — Nottingham

London

M1 Section 2:
Loughborough-London

Leeds

23 — Loughborough
22 — Leicester
Leicester Forest *East Services*
M69 Coventry — Leicester
Rugby — 20

M6 Birmingham ILLEGAL

Rugby — 18

M45 Coventry ILLEGAL

Watford Gap *Services*
16 — Northampton
Rothersthorpe *Services*
15 — Northampton
Newport Pagnell *Services*
14 — Newport Pagnell
13 — Bedford
12 — Bedford
Toddington *Services*
11 — Luton

ILLEGAL — Luton
9 — St. Albans
Hemel Hempstead

ILLEGAL St. Albans M10

M25 ILLEGAL

Watford — 6
Watford — 5
Edgware — 4
Scratchwood *Services*
2 — London
North Circular Road
London

110

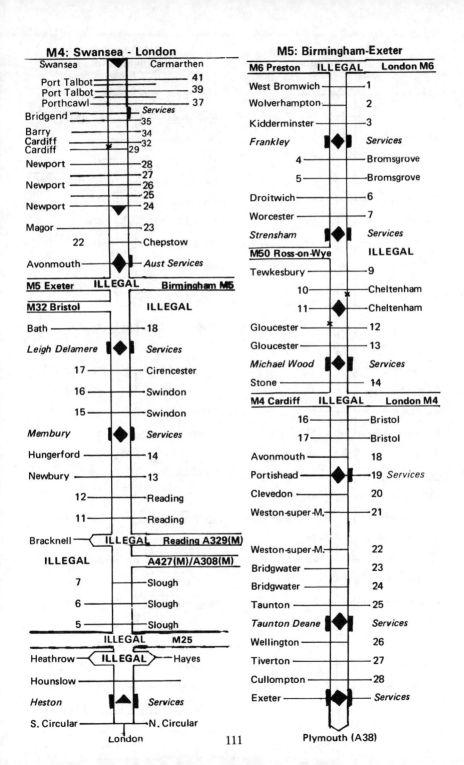

M4: Swansea - London

Swansea		Carmarthen
Port Talbot		41
Port Talbot		39
Porthcawl		37
		Services
Bridgend		35
Barry		34
Cardiff		32
Cardiff		29
Newport		28
		27
Newport		26
		25
Newport		24
Magor		23
22		Chepstow
Avonmouth		*Aust Services*

M5 Exeter   ILLEGAL   Birmingham M5

M32 Bristol   ILLEGAL

Bath		18
Leigh Delamere		*Services*
17		Cirencester
16		Swindon
15		Swindon
Membury		*Services*
Hungerford		14
Newbury		13
12		Reading
11		Reading
Bracknell		**ILLEGAL Reading A329(M)**
ILLEGAL		**A427(M)/A308(M)**
7		Slough
6		Slough
5		Slough

ILLEGAL   M25

Heathrow	**ILLEGAL**	Hayes
Hounslow		
Heston		*Services*
S. Circular		N. Circular

London

M5: Birmingham-Exeter

M6 Preston   ILLEGAL   London M6

West Bromwich		1
Wolverhampton		2
Kidderminster		3
Frankley		*Services*
4		Bromsgrove
5		Bromsgrove
Droitwich		6
Worcester		7
Strensham		*Services*

M50 Ross-on-Wye   ILLEGAL

Tewkesbury		9
10		Cheltenham
11		Cheltenham
Gloucester		12
Gloucester		13
Michael Wood		*Services*
Stone		14

M4 Cardiff   ILLEGAL   London M4

16		Bristol
17		Bristol
Avonmouth		18
Portishead		19 *Services*
Clevedon		20
Weston-super-M.		21
Weston-super-M.		22
Bridgwater		23
Bridgwater		24
Taunton		25
Taunton Deane		*Services*
Wellington		26
Tiverton		27
Cullompton		28
Exeter		*Services*

Plymouth (A38)

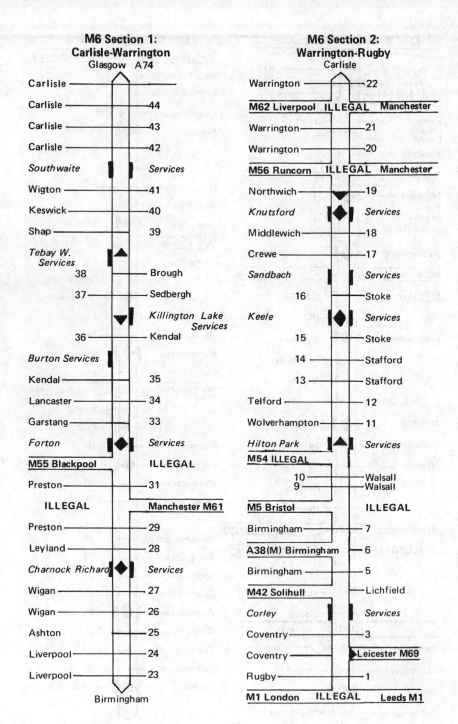

M6 Section 1:
Carlisle-Warrington
Glasgow A74

Carlisle	
Carlisle	44
Carlisle	43
Carlisle	42
Southwaite	*Services*
Wigton	41
Keswick	40
Shap	39
Tebay W. Services	
38	Brough
37	Sedbergh
	Killington Lake Services
36	Kendal
Burton Services	
Kendal	35
Lancaster	34
Garstang	33
Forton	*Services*
M55 Blackpool	**ILLEGAL**
Preston	31
ILLEGAL	**Manchester M61**
Preston	29
Leyland	28
Charnock Richard	*Services*
Wigan	27
Wigan	26
Ashton	25
Liverpool	24
Liverpool	23

Birmingham

M6 Section 2:
Warrington-Rugby
Carlisle

Warrington	22
M62 Liverpool ILLEGAL Manchester	
Warrington	21
Warrington	20
M56 Runcorn ILLEGAL Manchester	
Northwich	19
Knutsford	*Services*
Middlewich	18
Crewe	17
Sandbach	*Services*
16	Stoke
Keele	*Services*
15	Stoke
14	Stafford
13	Stafford
Telford	12
Wolverhampton	11
Hilton Park	*Services*
M54 ILLEGAL	
10	Walsall
9	Walsall
M5 Bristol	**ILLEGAL**
Birmingham	7
A38(M) Birmingham	6
Birmingham	5
M42 Solihull	Lichfield
Corley	*Services*
Coventry	3
Coventry	Leicester M69
Rugby	1
M1 London ILLEGAL Leeds M1	

Eire
Republic of Ireland

Ireland is not a place to hurry through. Although you could get across the island in a day, a more leisurely approach will be in keeping with the slow pace of native life. No Irish driver is in a hurry, and not many are going very far. So you are likely to move in short lifts, and even these will be punctuated by stops for drinks, meals or a chat with friends or relatives along the way. The blanket speed limit of 60 mph is largely superfluous as Irish drivers are in any case slow and safe.

Road Strategy. The motorway system is limited to a five-mile stretch of the N7 around the town of Naas, 20 miles south west of Dublin. There are only two junctions (one at each end) so motorway regulations are unlikely to be a problem. A few stretches of dual carriageway around Dublin. Cork and Limerick are the only other remotely fast roads. The general rule is simply to hitch from wherever you are and to take any lift, however short. A total of twenty rides for a 100 mile journey is not unusual. Competition can be intense in the most unlikely places; disappearing into the nearest bar for a few hours is a reasonable strategy.

Maps. The Irish Tourist Board, 150 New Bond St, London W1 charges £1 for its map of Ireland. Instead, invest an Irish punt in the more useful Esso map. Tourist offices in larger towns give away street plans.

Place Names. Most towns have an official Irish name and an accepted English version, and both should appear on signposts. Dublin is Baile Atha Cliath, Cork is Corcaigh. Pronunciation is sometimes difficult. For Naas, say "Nace"; for Portlaoise—"Portleash"; and Dun Laoghaire—"Dun Leary".

Town Guide

(for key and explanation, see the introduction)

DUBLIN (Baile Atha Claith)

N1: Dundalk, Belfast (A1)
🚶 2 miles: N along O'Connell St, Parnell Square and Frederick St, R along Dorset St and Drumcondra Rd (N1), over bridge to jn with Millbourne Ave. Stand on N1 beyond school.**
🚌 Airport service from Busaras to airport entrance (IR£2). Stand on N1.****

N11: Wexford, Rosslare (N25)
🚶 2 miles: S from Bank of Ireland along Grafton St, diagonally across St Stephen's Green, along Leeson St, Morehampton Rd and Donnybrook Rd to start of dual carriageway (Stillorgan Rd/N11).***

N7: Naas, Limerick, Cork (N8), Killarney (N8, N72), Waterford (N9)
🚶 1½ miles: W from Cornmarket

along Thomas St, James's St (call in at the Guinness Brewery) and Old Kilmainham to jn with South Circular Rd. Stand on Emmet Rd.** Or 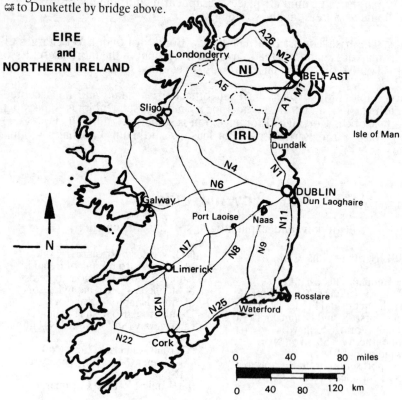 300m S to Davitt Rd.**

N4: Sligo, Galway (N6)

1½ miles: W along north bank of Liffey, continue along Parkgate St and Conyngham Rd (N4) to jn with South Circular Rd.***

CORK (Corcaigh)

N8: Portlaoise, Dublin (N7)
N25: Waterford, Wexford, Rosslare

1½ miles: E from Kent station along Lower Glanmire Rd (N25) to jn with Castle Ave.**

11 to terminus at above jn.

or as above but continue for 1¼ miles along N25 to rdbt at jn with N8. Stand on N8 *** or beyond bridge on N25.***

to Dunkettle by bridge above.

N71: Bandon, Bantry

2 miles: SW along Barrack St and Bandon Rd, bear L along Glasheen Rd and Wilton Rd, bear L along Bishopstown Rd to start of Bandon Rd (N71).**

8 to turn-off on Bishopstown Rd, 200 yards from above jn.

N22: Macroom, Killarney

2 miles: SW along Barrack St and Bandon Rd, bear R along Magazine Rd and Model Farm Rd (N22) to jn with Rossa Ave.***

5 to terminus at above jn.

N20: Limerick, Galway (N18)

1 mile: N along Upper St, John St, Watercourse Rd, Thomas Davis St and Dublin St to start of Redforge Rd (N20).**

5 to terminus on Redforge Rd.

EIRE
and
NORTHERN IRELAND

Londonderry

N1

BELFAST

A26

M2

A5

A1 M1

Sligo

IRL

Isle of Man

Dundalk

N4

N6

N1

DUBLIN
Dun Laoghaire

Galway

Port Laoise

Naas

N11

N7

N8

N9

Limerick

N20

N25

Waterford

Rosslare

N22

Cork

— N

| 0 | 40 | 80 miles |

| 0 | 40 | 80 | 120 km |

Greece

Greece is still one of the most beautiful places on earth to get stranded for a few hours, and the perfect place for a slow hiking and hitching trip on remote country roads. Although tourists have already overrun most of the country, there are still a few isolated corners where traffic can be counted on one finger and even the weekly bus will give you a free ride. The rush to get through life's daily chores is even less pronounced than in Spain or Ireland, so just relax and enjoy it.

On your travels you will often find yourself being treated as a status symbol, or at least a conversation piece. A driver will pick you up, then stop at every wayside café and even take long and bumpy detours to visit friends, simply in order to show you off. You will see him talking superciliously while his listeners occasionally glance over at you and nod their heads wisely, congratulating him on his kindness or bravery in picking you up. This treatment may slow your progress, but is worth tolerating, if only for the boost it so obviously gives to the driver's ego.

Of course, since Greece became a Mecca for tourists, most Greeks are used to low-budget travellers and may not give you the full star treatment. And working drivers in the middle of a hard day's labour are kind and helpful but not necessarily prepared to take you out of their way. To sample the traditional Greek ambience, get away from the thoroughly-beaten tourist track on to quieter country roads.

A note of caution, however: while motorists on main routes are now quite used to interpreting a raised thumb as a request for a lift, those in isolated areas may regard it as an offensive gesture. To play safe, always use a raised open palm.

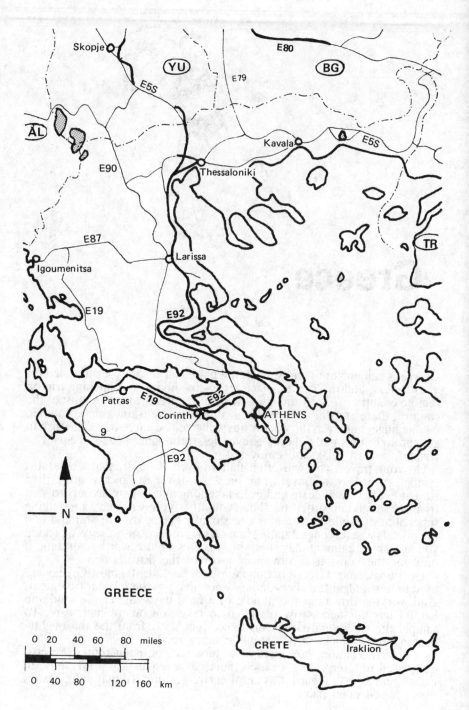

GREECE

0 20 40 60 80 miles

0 40 80 120 160 km

116

Rules of Thumb

Getting In. If you arrive in Greece on a cheap charter flight, immigration officials will demand to see evidence of accommodation bookings. Normally your travel agent will provide a reasonably genuine-looking voucher. If not, you may be turned away or charged the full economy air fare. But border guards on the land frontiers seem remarkably broad-minded about who they let in. They like to appear bureaucratic, studying your passport intently before stamping it, but they're quite harmless. If you arrive by sea from Italy or Israel, you'll probably be herded in without attention. Technically, you must declare all the currency you bring into Greece, but no-one seems to worry as long as you don't have an unreasonably large amount of cash. Travellers cheques will circumvent any such problems.

The Turkish frontier is undoubtedly the worst. Although no-one in their right mind would try to carry drugs in or out of Turkey, the Greek officials here suspect anyone who looks like an extra from *Midnight Express*.

The Law. Although it's technically illegal to do so, the standard procedure is to choose a nice piece of hard shoulder and wait for your lift to arrive. In practice few hitchers meet with any resistance, but in theory this is an arrestable offence. Being arrested in Greece is a highly expensive and unpleasant affair, so take great care; if possible, hitch only from one end of a motorway to the other.

Route Planning. Most of the time you won't have any choice of routes when hitching from one place to another. There aren't too many roads in Greece (particularly on the islands), so take the only road you can and just hope for enough traffic. Most roads tend to be unnumbered, but the E-numbers are shown on maps and signs.

Maps. Maps don't have to be too detailed to show all the hitchable roads, so you might as well make do with the free book of maps issued by the Greek National Tourist Office, 195 Regent St, London W1. This has the advantage of being in English. If you're in luck, you might also get city maps from the tourist offices in Athens, Thessaloniki or Patras. The city maps issued in London are hardly worth the trouble.

Place Names. Road signs give place names in both Greek and Roman script. But the Roman version may not be immediately recognisable since they are direct transliterations of the Greek rather than in anglicised form. The most important equivalents are given below, together with accents as an aid to pronounciation:

English	Greek	English	Greek
Athens	Athínai	Heraklion	Iráklion
Corfu	Kérkyra	Patras	Patrái
Corinth	Kórinthos	Rhodes	Ródos
Crete	Kríti	Salonica	Thessalóniki

Number Plates. The registration system was changed a decade ago. There are still some old plates around; the registration town or district is represented by the first letter or pair of letters on the blue strip at the top of the rear plate. The most important codes are A-Athens, B-Volos, π-Patras and Θ-Thessaloniki.

The new system thankfully uses Roman script (in fact the only letters used are those common to both Greek and Roman alphabet). But the system of coding is much more complex: the letters assigned to a particular town or district bear no resemblance to the place name. A full list is therefore not given, but since code letters are allocated in geographical/alphabetical blocks, a few simple clues can be given, based on the *first letter* of the two-letter code:

A   Cyclades, Dodecanese and Aegean Islands; Attica and Voiotia.
B   Athens   H   Crete
I   Epiros (NW mainland, Corfu and Levkas)
K   Thrace and E Macedonia (i.e. everything E of Thessaloniki)
M   Thessaloniki   N   Western Macedonia (Kozani/Florina)
P   Peloponnese, SW mainland and S Ionian Islands
T   E Central mainland (Grevena/Larissa/Lamia/Trikkala)

Town Guide

(for key and explanation, see the introduction)

ATHENS and PIRAEUS

8/E92 (west): Corinth, Patras (E19)
🚶 2km: W from Omonia Sq along Ag Konstantinou, Archilleos and Leof Athinon (8) to jn with Poseidippou by park.**
🚌 818 to Mandra/Thebes jn W of Dafni.***

1/E92 (north): Lamia, Thessaloniki
🚶 1km: N from Omonia Sq along Patission 28 Oktovriou (1) to jn with Leoforos Alexandras at Place Aigyptou.*
Θ (from Athens or Piraeus) to northern terminus. Stand on 1.**

Karen Mitchell recommends asking for a lift among the truck drivers around the docks at Piraeus; try the Plum Pudding bar at Zea Marine, or the customs house: if the drivers aren't in their cabs, they are probably eating in Dennis' cafe opposite.

HERAKLION

90 (west): Rethimnon, Chania
🚌 1 (westbound) to turn-off main road (97) for Matala then 🚶 200m to 90 flyover.**

97: Verenaton, Matala
🚌 as above but stand on 97**

90 (east): Agios Nikolaos
🚌 1 (eastbound) to jn signposted for Agios Nikolaos then walk 400m to jn with bypass.**

PATRAS

8/E19: Corinth, Athens
🚶 1km: S from Italy ferry terminal along Karolou Ai then L along Korinthou (8/E19) to jn with Agios Sofias. Stand on 8/E19.**

9: Pirgos, Olympia
🚶 3km: W from Italy ferry terminal

along Othonos-Amalias and follow
coast road (9) to edge of town. Stand
on 9.**

🚌 to Paralia.***

THESSALONIKI

1/E92: Athens
🚶 1km: NW from Arch of Galerius
along Egnatia, bear L at Platia
Vadari to jn with Politehnon.**

🚌 31 to terminus at Dendropotamus
on 1/E92.***

2/E20 (west): Edessa, Skopje (1/E5s)
🚶 3km: NW along Egnatia and
Monastirou (2/E20) to jn with 1/E92
just before rail bridge.**

🚌 18 along 2/E20 to Esso Pappas.
Stand on 2/E20.***

12/E20 (east): Serrai, Kavala (E5s)
🚶 2km: NW along Egnatia, then
bear R along Longada (12/E20) to jn
with Agios Dimitriou. Stand on 12/
E20.**

🚌 27 along 12/E20 to turn off for
Oreokastro. Stand on 12/E20.***

Italy

Italy has a comprehensive motorway network, and a correspondingly high volume of long distance traffic. Consequently, you will find that you can move very quickly, and your journey will probably include some enormously long lifts.

Lorry drivers—including the most unlikely looking characters—are prone to pick you up. Some lorries, especially kind with two trailers, are remarkably slow, so if you're on a hilly route, it may be advisable to jump out at the next services. But trucks' speed should not be prejudged according to size: some of the fastest movers on the road are 40-tonners with light loads. Many Italian lorries are right hand drive, so be careful when getting in and out. In the left-hand passenger seat, you may also be called on to negotiate such tricky things as toll payments.

Rules of Thumb

Getting In. Italy has the usual paranoia about impecunious hitchers, but the customs officers don't seem to be aware of the relative values of different notes. So if you take a lot of small denomination notes, rather than a few big ones, you're likely to be waved through. Don't cross the frontier in a lorry unless you want a long wait. The complexities of the paperwork are horrendous.

The Law. The Italian police tend to be fairly happy-go-lucky, which means they usually turn a blind eye but can be extremely unpleasant if they decide to turn officious. The only law to bother about is not hitching on motorways, and you'll be reminded of this by the *No Autostop* sign at every motorway entrance. Some signs also offer drivers a concise guide to the law on this subject and the penalties they may incur if they so much as contemplate picking you up. Toll-booth officials can on rare occasions be even more officious than the police, and you may find them turning you away from places where it is perfectly legitimate for you to stand. Annoyingly, this usually happens at the less busy slip roads, where they having nothing better to do. At the next slip road they may be asking the drivers to take you along.

Road Strategy. You will move fast on motorways, so long as you jump from service area to service area. Many services, however, provide only a skeleton petrol and snack service from about midnight to 6 a.m. Among motorway services, the best prospects are those that have restaurants. Some also have free showers to warm you up or clean you down; the best are operated by AGIP. The motorway network extends around all the major towns, so if you're travelling through you need never go into a town at all. Most of the towns' motorway ring roads (usually called *Tangenziale*) are toll-free, to encourage drivers to use them, rather than go through the town. But although they promote the flow of through traffic, they are not good hitching territory in their own right. Get out at a service area before the town, and wait for a lift going right through. All motorways south of Naples are toll-free, and thus carry a higher proportion of traffic.

On the motorways, you will find you are taken for granted—just part of the normal motorway scenery. Off the motorways, particularly in the south, you will be an object of great curiosity, and you may find it annoying to be waved at by the young kids riding past on their little mopeds. Such gestures are usually only friendly and should be tolerated. If you can stomach it, wave back and smile. It's not their fault that you're having a long wait.

Italians are proficient hitch-hikers and have an enviable knack of stopping traffic in the most unlikely (and illegal) places. All Italians are potential hitch-hikers, so don't be surprised to see priests, policemen or mothers with *bambini* standing with thumbs extended. However, most of the Italians that you find in direct competition with you will not be travelling far, and their usual method is to accept the first lift and cross other bridges when they get dropped at them.

Route Planning. Once off the *autostrade* (prefixed A) classified roads carry the prefix S.S. (*strada statale*), and these are divided into *Nazionale* (N) and *Provinziale* (P). Maps usually just write N or P, but road signs and milestones often use SS instead of or as well as N or P. Italy also has its share of E roads, although the original numbers have never been used on signs. The new numbering system, however, has already been adopted by the ACI (Italian Automobile Club).

Maps. The Italian State Tourist Board (ENIT), 1 Princes St, London W1 gives away copies of the ACI road map, which is sufficient for long-distance hitching. It also contains a number of useful town plans. The tourist office has some free city maps, but are likely to have run out of stocks of the more popular destinations. The best route planning maps are the AGIP booklets which are given out free at AGIP petrol stations. Reasonable planning maps can also be obtained from national and provincial tourist offices, as can more or less accurate and detailed road plans of the large towns. City and provincial tourist offices are never easy to find and tend to keep short hours. If you find one, and it's open, it's always worth asking if they have information and maps on other cities you plan to visit. If you're totally lost, the yellow pages of the telephone directory include a street plan, but these pages are often ripped out of directories in public phone booths. The Tabacco and LAC town plans offer greater detail and accuracy and can be bought from Roger Lascelles who also stocks the regional and national Tabacco and LAC road maps.

Place Names. Many Italian town names have special English versions, although some—like Leghorn and Placenza—are virtually obsolete.

Firenze	Florence	Padova	Padua
Genova	Genoa	Piacenza	Placenza
Livorno	Leghorn	Roma	Rome
Mantova	Mantua	Siracusa	Syracuse
Milano	Milan	Torino	Turin
Napoli	Naples	Venezia	Venice

French versions often take the same form as the English, but the following are worth noting:

Cuneo	Coni	Perugia	Péroux
Genova	Gênes	Piacenza	Plaisance
Livorno	Livourne	Venezia	Venise

German names like Mailand (Milan) and Venedig (Venice) sometimes cause problems, but other forms, like Rom, Florenz and Neapel, should be recognisable. The real trouble with German names comes in the Alto Adige, near the Austrian border, where German is a native language and nearly every town and village has two forms to its name. The most important ones are Bolzano (Bozen) and Merano (Meran). Finally, Trieste is called Trst by the Yugoslavs, who are a bit touchy about it.

Number Plates. Italian number plates can be identified by the first two letters on rear number plates. (These are more usually the last two letters on front plates). The exception to the rule is Rome, for which all four letters—ROMA—are used. The following list gives the abbreviations for all the Italian provinces, and a geographical indicator for each (e.g. SC = South central; Sic = Sicily, Sar = Sardinia).

AG	Agrigento (Sic)	AP	Ascoli Piceno (EC)	AV	Avellino (SW)
AL	Alessandria (NW)	AQ	L'Aquila (EC)	BA	Bari (SE)
AN	Ancona (EC)	AR	Arezzo (EC)	BG	Bergamo (NC)
AO	Aosta (NW)	AT	Asti (NW)	BL	Belluno (NE)

BN	Benevento (SW)	LI	Livorno (NW)	RE	Reggio E. (NC)
BO	Bologna (NC)	LT	Latina (WC)	RG	Ragusa (Sic)
BR	Brindisi (SE)	LU	Lucca (NW)	RI	Rieti (WC)
BS	Brescia (NC)	MC	Macerata (EC)	RO	Rovigo (NE)
BZ	Bolzano (NC)	ME	Messina (Sic)	ROMA	Rome (WC)
CA	Cagliari (Sar)	MI	Milan (NW)	SA	Salerno (SW)
CB	Campobasso (SE)	MN	Mantova (NC)	SI	Siena (WC)
CE	Caserta (SW)	MO	Modena (NC)	SO	Sondrio (NC)
CH	Chieti (EC)	MS	Massa (NW)	SP	La Spezia (NW)
CL	Caltanissetta (Sic)	MT	Matera (SE)	SR	Siracusa (Sic)
CN	Cuneo (NW)	NA	Naples (SW)	SS	Sassari (Sar)
CO	Como (NW)	NO	Novara (NW)	SV	Savona (NW)
CR	Cremona (NC)	NU	Nuori (Sar)	TA	Taranto (SE)
CS	Cosenza (SW)	OR	Oristano (Sar)	TE	Teramo (EC)
CT	Catania (Sic)	PA	Palermo (Sic)	TN	Trento (NC)
CZ	Catanzaro (SW)	PC	Piacenza (NC)	TO	Turin (NW)
EN	Enna (Sic)	PD	Padua (NE)	TP	Trapani (Sic)
FE	Ferrara (NE)	PE	Pescara (EC)	TR	Terni (WC)
FG	Foggia (SE)	PG	Perugia (C)	TS	Trieste (NE)
FI	Florence (NC)	PI	Pisa (NW)	UD	Udine (NE)
FO	Forli (NE)	PN	Pordenone (NE)	VA	Varese (NW)
FR	Frosinone (WC)	PR	Parma (NC)	VC	Vercelli (NW)
GE	Genoa (NW)	PS	Pesaro (EC)	VE	Venice (NE)
GO	Gorizia (NE)	PT	Pistoia (NC)	VI	Vicenza (NC)
GR	Grosseto (WC)	PV	Pavia (NW)	VR	Verona (NC)
IM	Imperia (NW)	PZ	Potenza (SW)	VT	Viterbo (WC)
IS	Isernia (SW)	RA	Ravenna (NE)		
LE	Lecce (SW)	RC	Reggio C. (SW)		

New codes have been introduced for certain cities, so the following will also be seen.

A1	Ancona	C3	Catanzaro	P4	Perugia
A2	L'Aquila	FL	Forli	P5	Potenza
B1,B2	Bologna	F2,F3	Florence	R2-R8	Rome
B3,B4	Bari	G1,G2	Genoa	T1-T5	Turin
B5	Bolzano	LC	Lecce	UN	Udine
CM	Como	MD	Modena	VN	Verona
CX	Cuneo	M1-M8	Milan	VS	Varese
CY	Catania	N1-N4	Naples	VZ	Vicenza
C1	Cagliari	PX	Padua	V2,V3	Venice
C2	Campobasso	P2,P3	Palermo		

Winter Hitching. A trip through northern Italy during January should dispel any ideas you may have about Italy being all sunshine and smiles. The mountains are especially hard hit, and the following Alpine passes will almost certainly be closed from November to March, maybe longer. They are listed approximately east to west:

Predil	Gardena	Stelvio	Moncenisio
Croce Carnico	Sella	Umbrail	Maddalena
Falzarego	Giovi	Spluga	
Pordio	Gavia	Piccolo San Bernardo	

Other passes either remain open for most of the winter, or are satisfactorily detoured by a tunnel or motorail service.

Town Guide

(for key and explanation, see the introduction)

BARI

A17 (north): Naples (A16), Rome (A16, A2), Ancona (A14)
A17 (south): Taranto
🚌 20 to motorway entrance at Modugno. Sign pref. North** South*

N16 (south): Brindisi, Otranto
🚌 12 to Sacrario Caduti d'Oltramare, then 🚶 on over bridge and stand either on slip road or on N16.*
🚌 12 to top of Via Martiri della Resistenza in Torre a Mare (ask people on the bus to tell you when to get off). 🚶 over bridge and down slip road. Stand on main road (N16).*

BOLOGNA

A1 (south): Florence, Rome
🚌 18, 19 to Rotonda Romagnoli on Viale Palmira Togliati. Stand on slip road to Asse Attrezzato Sud Ovest.**
🚌 19 to terminus at Casteldebole then 🚶 1.5km along Via Caduti di Casteldebole, R along Asse Attrezzato Sud Ovest and stand at motorway entrance.**
🚌 (infrequent rural service) to San Biagio, then 🚶 750m E along Via Pietro Micca to Cantagallo motorway services. Stand on southbound slip road.***

A1 (north): Milan, Verona (A22)
🚌 🚶 to either of the above jns.* Or to Cantagallo Services (*** on northbound slip road).
🚌 49 along Via Marco Emilio Lepido to Tangenziale. Stand on westbound slip road.**

A13: Padua, Venice (A4)
🚌 🚶 as for A1 (south) above to Cantagallo Services. Stand on northbound slip road.***
🚌 12 to motorway jn on Via Stalingrad. Stand on westbound slip road.*
🚌 22 to motorway jn on via Corticella. Stand on eastbound slip road.*

A14: Ancona, Bari
🚌 22 to motorway jn on Via Massarenti. Stand on southbound slip road.***

Signs are required when leaving Bologna in any of the above directions, with the possible exception of heading south from Cantagallo services.

BRINDISI

N16 (north): Bari, Naples (A17, A16), Rome (A17, A16, A2), Ancona (A17, A14)
🚌 7 to jn of Via Adriatica (N16) and Circonvallazione (where the bus comes off the ring road). Stand on Circonvallazione heading north.*

N7: Taranto
🚌 7 along Via Appia to jn with Cirrconvallazione. Stand on Via Appia (N7).*

N16 (south): Lecce, Otranto
🚌 as above and stand on Circonvallazione heading south.*
🚌 6 to Villagio San Paolo then 🚶 S along Via Provinziale Lecce to Circonvallazione jn. Stand on Circonvallazione.*

FLORENCE (Firenze)

A1 (south): Rome
🚌 23, 31, 32, 33 along Viale Europa to motorway jn at Piazza di Badia a Ripoli. Stand on southbound slip road. Sign pref.**

N2: Siena
🚶 1km: from Ponte Vecchio S along Via de Guicchiardini, Piazza dei Pitti, Via Romana to Porta Romana.

Stand on Via Senese (N2).*
🚌 B, 11A, 11B to above jn.
🚌 37 to Firenze Certosa motorway
jn. Stand at start of motorway.****

A11: Lucca, Genoa (A12)
A1 (north): Bologna, Milan, Venice
(A13, A4), Bolzano (A22)
🚌 29 (from station) to start of
autostrada on Viale L Gori, then 🚶
across rdbt and stand at autostrada
entrance. Sign pref. Lucca***,
Bologna.**

From this rdbt most traffic takes the
A11. For Bologna, take any lift and
ask to be dropped at the services on
*the motorway jn at Firenze-Nord.****

GENOA (Genova)

A12: La Spezia, Rome (A11, A1)
A10: Ventimiglia; A7: Milan
🚶 1.5km: from main station W along
Via S. Benedetto, Via Buozzi and
Via A. Cantore to motorway
entrance. Sign pref.***

Upon completion of new motorway
running N from Via A. Cantore 300m
E of this jn, stand at start of new
motorway for all points east.

MESSINA

A18: Catania; A20: Palermo (A19)
🚶 1km: from port up Via S.
Francesco d'Assisi to motorway
entrance. Sign pref.**

MILAN (Milano)

A1: Bologna, Florence, Rome
🚌 13, 20 or 🚌 84, 93 to Piazzale
Corvetto. Stand at entrance to
motorway.**

A7: Genoa, Ventimiglia (A10), Pisa
(A12)
🚌 95 (a circular route—you can get
it at Banda Neve ⊖ station) to Piazza
Maggi. Stand at motorway
entrance.**
🚌 91 to Piazza Belfanti, then 🚶
500m S along Via Spezia to above jn.

A4 (west): Turin, Aosta (A5)
A8: Varese, Como (A9)
🚌 14 (from Stazione Nord) along
Viale Certosa to second motorway
flyover. Stand on northbound slip
road. Sign pref.***
🚌 67 (from Conciliazione ⊖ station)
or 71 (from Buonarrotti) to Via Sant'
Elia/Via Benedetto Croce jn. 🚶
300m N to Piazza Kennedy. Stand at
entrance to motorway. Sign pref.***
🚌 1, 14, 19, 33 or 🚌 57, 61 to Piazza
Firenze, then 🚌 69 along Via
Gallarate to motorway flyover, then
🚶 300m N or S to either of above jns.

A4 (east): Brescia, Verona, Venice
🚌 🚌 🚶 as above for A4 west. Sign
pref.*
🚌 44 to Via Padova (terminus).
Stand on northbound slip road to
Tangenziale Est. Sign pref.***
⊖ 2 to above jn at Gobba.

NAPLES (Napoli)

A2: Rome, Bari (A16, A17)
A3: Salerno, Reggio di Calabria
🚶 800m: L out of Central Station
along Corso Amaldo Lucci, first L at
traffic lights along Via Galileo
Ferraris and stand at start of
motorway. Sign pref.***
🚌 14, 14r from Central Station to
Via Don Bosco, then 🚶 along Via
Don Bosco to motorway jn Sign
pref.***

PALERMO

N113 (west): Castelvetrano (A29),
Trapani (N187)
🚶 3km: N from Piazza R Settimo
along Via della Liberta, then L along
Viale Lazio to jn with Viale della
Regione Siciliana (by-pass). Stand
on by-pass. Sign pref.**
🚌 7, 8 (circular) to in above.

A19, N113 (west): Catania, Messina
(A20)
🚶 4km: S from Porta Maqueda along
Via Mequeda and Via Oreto to jn
with Viale della Regione Siciliana
(by-pass). Stand on by-pass. Sign
pref.**

🚌 1 to terminus on Via Oreto then 🚗 2km S to jn above.

🚗 2.5km: S from Porta Maqueda along Via Maqueda, L at Central Station along Via Lincoln to jn with Via Ponte di Mare (N113). Stand on N113 by Orto Botanico.**

REGGIO di CALABRIA

A3: Naples and all other points
🚗 1km: from port along Via S. Caterina to motorway entrance.**

ROME (Roma)

A1: Florence, Bologna, Milan
🚌 38, 58 to Via Conca d'Oro, or 🚌 137 to Viale Tirreno; then 🚌 335 to Via Salaria at Castel Giubileo, just before Grande Raccordo Annulare jn. Stand on eastbound slip road or on Grande Raccordo Annulare itself. Often crowded, especially in summer.**

🚌 56, 57, 319 to Piazza Vescovio, then 🚌 135 to above jn.

🚌 as above, but continue on 135 to end of line at Settebagni. 🚗 on 1km and stand on motorway slip road (less likely to be crowded). Sign pref.*

A24: L'Aquila, Pescara (A25)
🚗 1.5km: SE from Termini Station along Via Giovanni Giolitti to Piazza di Porta Maggiore. L along Viale di Scalo San Lorenzo and stand at start of motorway spur.**

🚌 19, 30 to above jn.

🚌 15 to Portonaccio and stand at motorway entrance.**

A2: Naples
🚌 152, 153, 155, 156, 157 to Grande Raccordo Annulare at Torre Nuova and stand on southbound slip road or on Grande Raccordo Annulare itself. Sign pref.*

🚌 Termini station-Grotte Celoni to above jn.

🚌 512 to terminus at Viale P. Togliatti, then 🚌 502, 503 along Via Tuscolana to Grande Raccordo

Annulare. Stand on northbound slip road or on Grande Raccordo Annulare itself. Sign pref.**

🚌 Termini station-Cinecitta, then 🚌 515, 551, 612 to above jn.

N8: Lido di Ostia
🚐 only costs 500l. all the way.

🚌 97 (from Trastavere) or 23 (from Castel San Angelo) to Via Guglielmo Marconi/Via Salvatore Pincherle jn. Then 🚗 S 200m along Via G. Marconi and stand on slip road to Via del Mare (N8).***

🚇 to San Paulo then 🚗 500m S along Via Ostiense to above jn.

N201: Fiumicino, Civitavecchia (A12)
🚌 128 (from Trastavere) to Via della Magliana. Stand at motorway entrance.**

🚌 8, 46 to Circ Cornelia, then 🚌 246 to Malagrotta. Stand on Via Aurelia.**

TRIESTE

N14, A4: Venice, Udine (A23)
🚗 2km: NW from station along Viale Miramare to edge of town. Sign pref.***

N58, 6: Ljubljana
🚗 1km: NE from station along Via C Ghega, and Via F Severo to jn with Via Marconi.**

🚌 to Fernetti, then 🚗 across border.**

Max Glaski recommends that for all points east you should turn L 400m before the border to catch the trucks leaving the customs compound. The minimum wait is 90 minutes, but lifts are long.

N14 (east), 2a: Rijeka (Fiume)
🚗 2km (mostly uphill): SE from Piazza Goldoni along Corso Garibaldi and Via Oriani, bear R along Via Molino a Vento then L along Via dell' Istra to N202 jn. Stand on N202 just before tunnel.**

🚌 to Pese then 🚗 across border.***

TURIN (Torino)

A21: Piacenza, Rome (A1), Savona (A6), Genoa (A6, A10)
🚌 35 to Piazza Benghasi, then 🛉
100m E along Via Corradino to jn
with Corso Trieste. Sign pref.
Piacenza***, Savona.*
🚌 Poirino, Santena or Trofarillo
(infrequent rural services) to above
motorway entrance.

A5: Aosta
A4: Milan, Verona, Venice
🚌 51 from Porta Susa Station up
Corso Vercelli to jn with Corso
Giulio Cesare, close to Stura station.
Stand at motorway entrance. Sign
pref.***
🚃 to Stura by above jn.

VENICE (Venezia)

N13: Mestre, Marghera, Padua (A4 west), Trieste (A4 east)
⚓ 1, 2, 4 to Piazzale Roma or 3, 17
to Tronchetto. Stand on Ponte della
Liberta at end of Piazzale Roma.
Sign pref.*

A4 (west): Padua, Milan, Bologna (A13), Rome (A13/A1)
6 from Piazzale Roma to Via Trieste
in Marghera, 🛉 200m along Via
Trieste, L along access road (parallel

and adjacent to motorway) to service
station. Stand at service station
(legal).* Or on westbound slip road
(illegal).*** Sign pref.

N309: Chioggia, Ravenna
🚌 🛉 as above, but continue walking
round rdbt (illegal) to N309 exit.
Stand on N309 (legal).***

A4 (east): Trieste, Udine (A23)
🚌 🛉 as above, but continue walking
round rdbt (illegal) to eastbound
services. Stand at service station exit
(legal).* Or on eastbound slip road
(illegal).**

VERONA

A4 (east): Padua, Venice
A4 (west): Milan, Bolzano (A22 north), Bologna (A22 south)
🛉 1km: S along Corso Porta to
Piazzale di Porta Nuova. Stand on
Viale del Piave. Sign pref.*
🛉 4km: as above, but continue S
along Viale del Piave, Via del
Lavoro and Viale delle Nazioni to
motorway entrance at Piazzale
Europa. Stand at approach to toll
booths (illegal), or if hassled, at
traffic lights on Viale delle Nazioni
(slightly less illegal). Sign pref.**
🚌 1, 8, 13 to above jn.

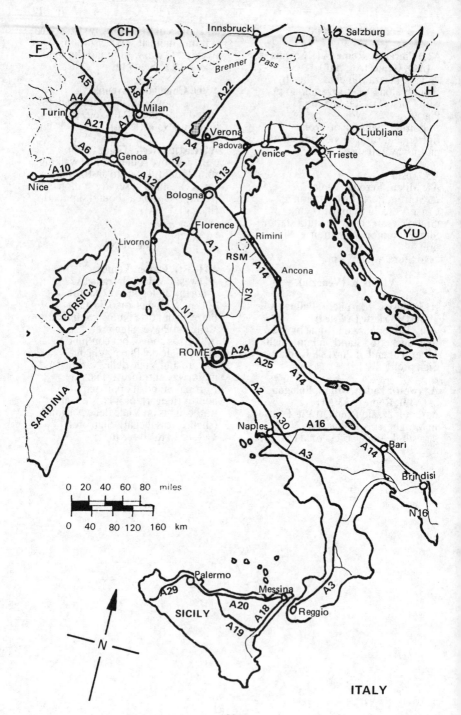

ITALY

A5, A4 Section 1: Aosta-Milano

Aosta
Nus
San Vincent — Chatillon
San Vincent — **Services**
Verres
Pont S. Martin
Quincinetto
Ivrea
A5
A5 Torino — ILLEGAL
Albiano
A4 Torino — ILLEGAL
A26 Genova — **A4**
Santhia
Santhia Services
Carisio
Balocco
Villarboit — **Services**
Greggio
Biandrate
Agognate
Novara
Services — **Services**
Galliate
Boffalora
Arluno
Rho
Roma (A1) ILLEGAL
Genova (A10)
Pero
A9 Milano — ILLEGAL Como A9
Trieste

A4 Section 2: Milano-Desenzano

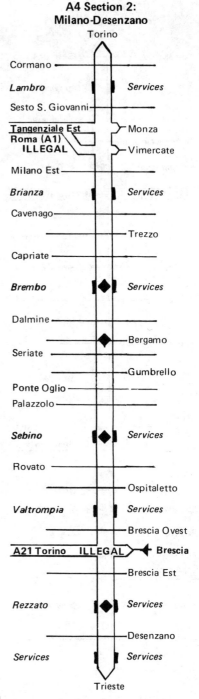

Torino
Cormano
Lambro — **Services**
Sesto S. Giovanni
Tangenziale Est — Monza
Roma (A1) ILLEGAL
Vimercate
Milano Est
Brianza — **Services**
Cavenago
Trezzo
Capriate
Brembo — **Services**
Dalmine
Bergamo
Seriate
Gumbrello
Ponte Oglio
Palazzolo
Sebino — **Services**
Rovato
Ospitaletto
Valtrompia — **Services**
Brescia Ovest
A21 Torino ILLEGAL — **Brescia**
Brescia Est
Rezzato — **Services**
Desenzano
Services — **Services**
Trieste

129

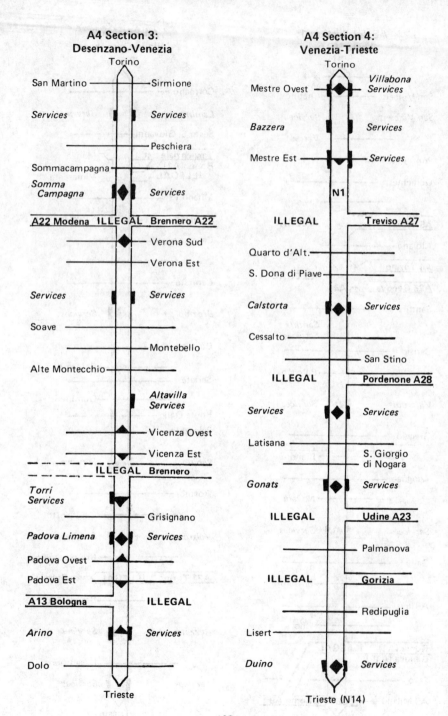

A4 Section 3: Desenzano-Venezia

Torino

San Martino —— Sirmione

Services — *Services*

—— Peschiera

Sommacampagna —

Somma Campagna — *Services*

A22 Modena ILLEGAL Brennero A22

—— Verona Sud

—— Verona Est

Services — *Services*

Soave ——

—— Montebello

Alte Montecchio —

Altavilla Services

—— Vicenza Ovest

—— Vicenza Est

ILLEGAL Brennero

Torri Services

—— Grisignano

Padova Limena — *Services*

Padova Ovest ——

Padova Est ——

A13 Bologna — **ILLEGAL**

Arino — *Services*

Dolo ——

Trieste

A4 Section 4: Venezia-Trieste

Torino

Mestre Ovest — *Villabona Services*

Bazzera — *Services*

Mestre Est —— *Services*

N1

ILLEGAL — **Treviso A27**

Quarto d'Alt. ——

S. Dona di Piave ——

Calstorta — *Services*

Cessalto ——

—— San Stino

ILLEGAL — **Pordenone A28**

Services — *Services*

Latisana ——

—— S. Giorgio di Nogara

Gonats — *Services*

ILLEGAL — **Udine A23**

—— Palmanova

ILLEGAL — **Gorizia**

—— Redipuglia

Lisert ——

Duino — *Services*

Trieste (N14)

130

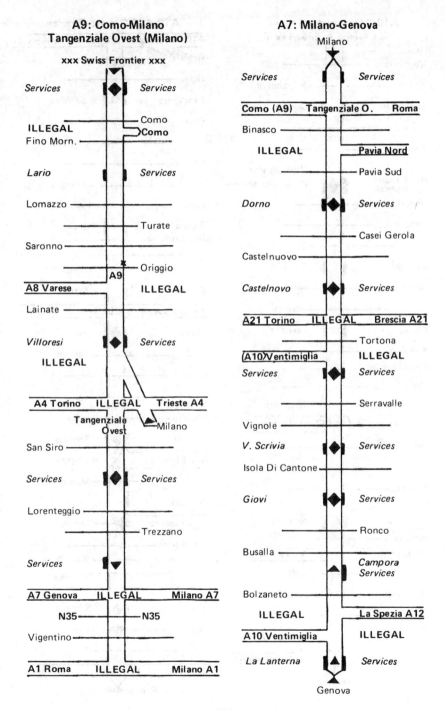

A9: Como-Milano
Tangenziale Ovest (Milano)

xxx Swiss Frontier xxx

Services 〔◆〕 Services

Como
Como
ILLEGAL
Fino Morn.

Lario 〔 〕 Services

Lomazzo

Turate

Saronno

Origgio
A9
A8 Varese   ILLEGAL

Lainate

Villoresi 〔◆〕 Services

ILLEGAL

A4 Torino   ILLEGAL   Trieste A4

Tangenziale
Ovest   Milano

San Siro

Services 〔◆〕 Services

Lorenteggio

Trezzano

Services 〔▼〕

A7 Genova   ILLEGAL   Milano A7

N35   N35

Vigentino

A1 Roma   ILLEGAL   Milano A1

A7: Milano-Genova
Milano

Services   Services

Como (A9)   Tangenziale O.   Roma

Binasco
ILLEGAL   Pavia Nord

Pavia Sud

Dorno 〔◆〕 Services

Casei Gerola

Castelnuovo

Castelnovo 〔◆〕 Services

A21 Torino   ILLEGAL   Brescia A21

Tortona
(A10)Ventimiglia   ILLEGAL
Services 〔◆〕 Services

Serravalle

Vignole
V. Scrivia 〔◆〕 Services

Isola Di Cantone

Giovi 〔◆〕 Services

Ronco

Busalla
〔▲〕 Campora
Services

Bolzaneto
ILLEGAL   La Spezia A12
A10 Ventimiglia   ILLEGAL

La Lanterna 〔▲〕 Services

Genova

131

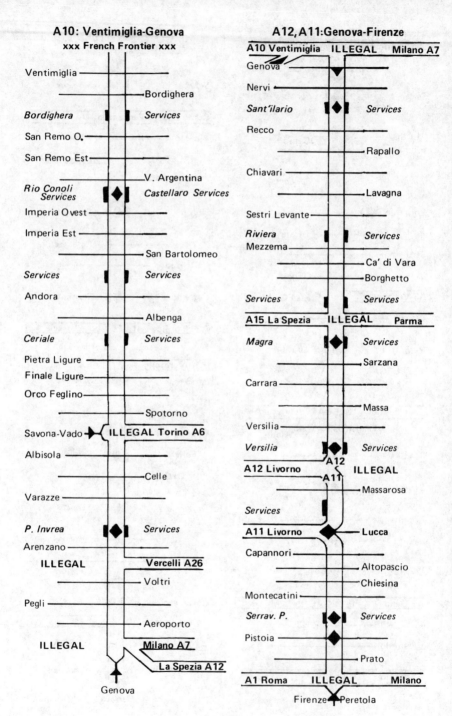

A10: Ventimiglia-Genova
xxx French Frontier xxx

Ventimiglia

Bordighera

Bordighera Services

San Remo O.

San Remo Est

V. Argentina

Rio Conoli Services Castellaro Services

Imperia Ovest

Imperia Est

San Bartolomeo

Services Services

Andora

Albenga

Ceriale Services

Pietra Ligure

Finale Ligure

Orco Feglino

Spotorno

Savona-Vado ILLEGAL Torino A6

Albisola

Celle

Varazze

P. Invrea Services

Arenzano

ILLEGAL Vercelli A26

Voltri

Pegli

Aeroporto

ILLEGAL Milano A7

La Spezia A12

Genova

A12, A11: Genova-Firenze

A10 Ventimiglia ILLEGAL Milano A7

Genova

Nervi

Sant'ilario Services

Recco

Rapallo

Chiavari

Lavagna

Sestri Levante

Riviera Mezzema Services

Ca' di Vara

Borghetto

Services Services

A15 La Spezia ILLEGAL Parma

Magra Services

Sarzana

Carrara

Massa

Versilia

Versilia Services

A12

A12 Livorno ILLEGAL

A11

Massarosa

Services

A11 Livorno Lucca

Capannori

Altopascio

Chiesina

Montecatini

Serrav. P. Services

Pistoia

Prato

A1 Roma ILLEGAL Milano

Firenze Peretola

132

A22: Brennero-Modena

xxx Austrian Frontier xxx

```
Vipiteno
                        Bressanone
Services    ◆   Services
                        Chiusa
Bolzano Nord
Bolzano Sud
Bolzano          Services
                        Egna-Ora
                        San Michele
Trento           Services
                        Trento
Rovereto Nord
Services    ◆   Services
Rovereto Sud
                        Ala-Avio
Services    ◆   Services
Rivoli-Cavaio
Garda       ◆   Services
                        Verona Nord
```

A4 Torino   ILLEGAL   Trieste A4

```
Services            Services
                        Nogarole Rocca
Mantova Nord
Mantova Sud
Services    ◆   Services
                        Pegognaga
Villanova-Rolo
                        Carpi
Services            Services
                        Campogalliano
```

A1 Milano   ILLEGAL   Roma A1

A1 Section 1: Milano-Reggio nell'Emilia

Milano

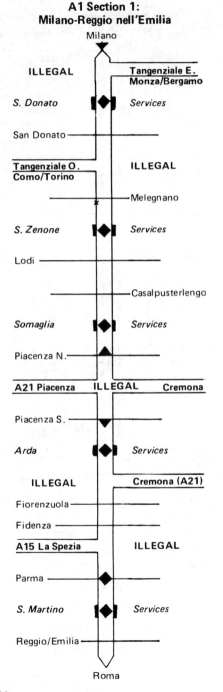

```
ILLEGAL         Tangenziale E.
                Monza/Bergamo
S. Donato   ◆   Services
San Donato

Tangenziale O.      ILLEGAL
Como/Torino
                        Melegnano
S. Zenone   ◆   Services
Lodi
                        Casalpusterlengo
Somaglia    ◆   Services
Piacenza N.     ▲
```

A21 Piacenza   ILLEGAL   Cremona

```
Piacenza S.     ▼
Arda        ◆   Services
ILLEGAL         Cremona (A21)
Fiorenzuola
Fidenza
```

A15 La Spezia   ILLEGAL

```
Parma       ◆
S. Martino  ◆   Services
Reggio/Emilia
```

Roma

133

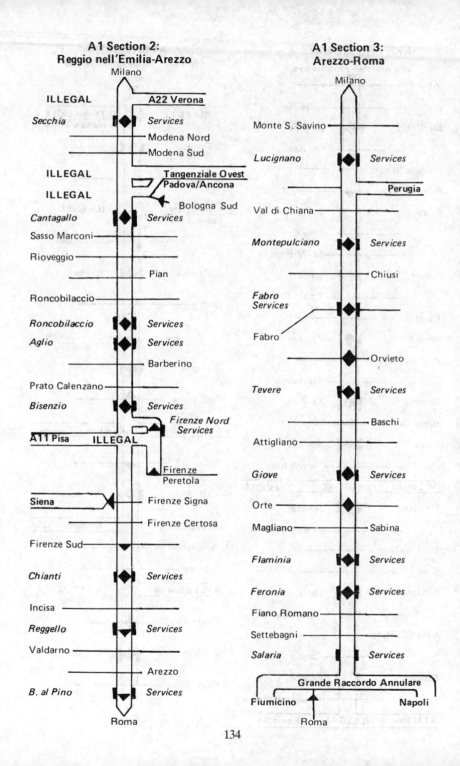

A1 Section 2:
Reggio nell'Emilia-Arezzo

Milano

ILLEGAL   A22 Verona

Secchia   *Services*

Modena Nord

Modena Sud

ILLEGAL   **Tangenziale Ovest**
Padova/Ancona

ILLEGAL

Bologna Sud

Cantagallo   *Services*

Sasso Marconi

Rioveggio

Pian

Roncobilaccio

Roncobilaccio   *Services*

Aglio   *Services*

Barberino

Prato Calenzano

Bisenzio   *Services*

Firenze Nord
Services

A11 Pisa   **ILLEGAL**

Firenze
Peretola

Siena   Firenze Signa

Firenze Certosa

Firenze Sud

Chianti   *Services*

Incisa

Reggello   *Services*

Valdarno

Arezzo

B. al Pino   *Services*

Roma

A1 Section 3:
Arezzo-Roma

Milano

Monte S. Savino

Lucignano   *Services*

Perugia

Val di Chiana

Montepulciano   *Services*

Chiusi

Fabro
Services

Fabro

Orvieto

Tevere   *Services*

Baschi

Attigliano

Giove   *Services*

Orte

Magliano   Sabina

Flaminia   *Services*

Feronia   *Services*

Fiano Romano

Settebagni

Salaria   *Services*

Grande Raccordo Annulare

Fiumicino   Napoli

Roma

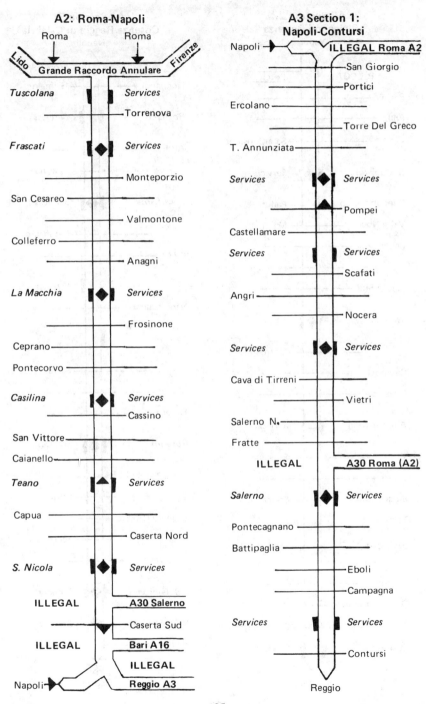

A2: Roma-Napoli

Roma   Roma

Lido   Grande Raccordo Annulare   Firenze

Tuscolana   *Services*

    Torrenova

Frascati   *Services*

    Monteporzio

San Cesareo

    Valmontone

Colleferro

    Anagni

La Macchia   *Services*

    Frosinone

Ceprano

Pontecorvo

Casilina   *Services*

    Cassino

San Vittore

Caianello

Teano   *Services*

Capua

    Caserta Nord

S. Nicola   *Services*

ILLEGAL   **A30 Salerno**

    Caserta Sud

ILLEGAL   **Bari A16**

    ILLEGAL

Napoli   **Reggio A3**

A3 Section 1: Napoli-Contursi

Napoli   **ILLEGAL Roma A2**

    San Giorgio

    Portici

Ercolano

    Torre Del Greco

T. Annunziata

Services   *Services*

    Pompei

Castellamare

Services   *Services*

    Scafati

Angri

    Nocera

Services   *Services*

Cava di Tirreni

    Vietri

Salerno N.

Fratte

ILLEGAL   **A30 Roma (A2)**

Salerno   *Services*

Pontecagnano

Battipaglia

    Eboli

    Campagna

Services   *Services*

    Contursi

Reggio

135

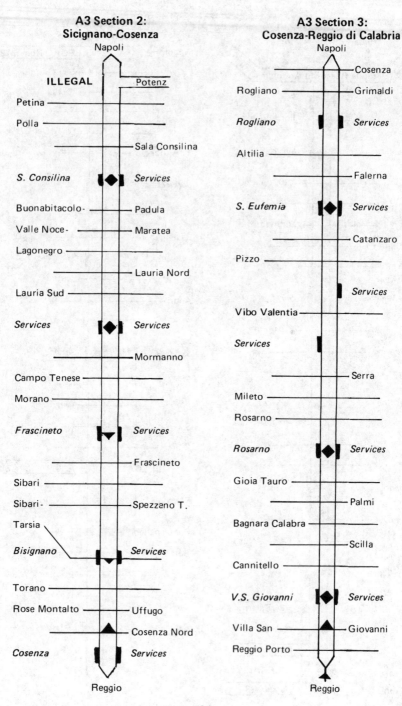

A3 Section 2: Sicignano-Cosenza

Napoli

ILLEGAL — Potenz

Petina ———

Polla ———

——— Sala Consilina

S. Consilina — *Services*

Buonabitacolo- ——— Padula

Valle Noce- ——— Maratea

Lagonegro ———

——— Lauria Nord

Lauria Sud ———

Services — *Services*

——— Mormanno

Campo Tenese ———

Morano ———

Frascineto — *Services*

——— Frascineto

Sibari ———

Sibari- ——— Spezzano T.

Tarsia ———

Bisignano — *Services*

Torano ———

Rose Montalto ——— Uffugo

——— Cosenza Nord

Cosenza — *Services*

Reggio

A3 Section 3: Cosenza-Reggio di Calabria

Napoli

——— Cosenza

Rogliano ——— Grimaldi

Rogliano — *Services*

Altilia ———

——— Falerna

S. Eufemia — *Services*

——— Catanzaro

Pizzo ———

Services

Vibo Valentia ———

Services

——— Serra

Mileto ———

Rosarno ———

Rosarno — *Services*

Gioia Tauro ———

——— Palmi

Bagnara Calabra ———

——— Scilla

Cannitello ———

V.S. Giovanni — *Services*

Villa San ——— Giovanni

Reggio Porto ———

Reggio

136

A14 Section 1: Bologna-Pesaro

A14 Section 2: Pesaro-Lanciano

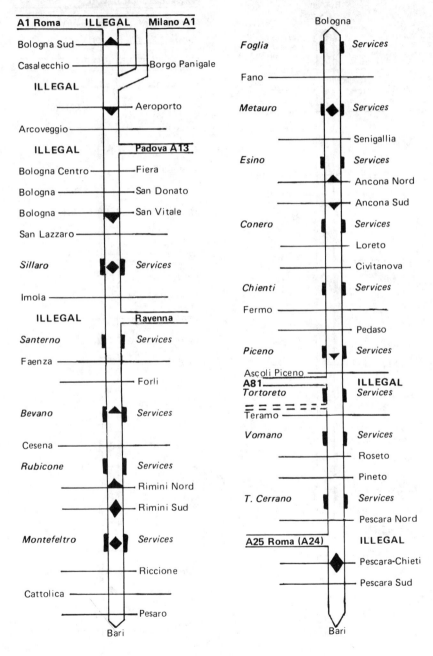

Section 1: Bologna-Pesaro

A1 Roma — ILLEGAL — Milano A1

Bologna Sud

Casalecchio — Borgo Panigale

ILLEGAL

Aeroporto

Arcoveggio

ILLEGAL — Padova A13

Bologna Centro — Fiera

Bologna — San Donato

Bologna — San Vitale

San Lazzaro

Sillaro — Services

Imola

ILLEGAL — Ravenna

Santerno — Services

Faenza

Forli

Bevano — Services

Cesena

Rubicone — Services

Rimini Nord

Rimini Sud

Montefeltro — Services

Riccione

Cattolica

Pesaro

Bari

Section 2: Pesaro-Lanciano

Bologna

Foglia — Services

Fano

Metauro — Services

Senigallia

Esino — Services

Ancona Nord

Ancona Sud

Conero — Services

Loreto

Civitanova

Chienti — Services

Fermo

Pedaso

Piceno — Services

Ascoli Piceno

A81 — ILLEGAL

Tortoreto — Services

Teramo

Vomano — Services

Roseto

Pineto

T. Cerrano — Services

Pescara Nord

A25 Roma (A24) — ILLEGAL

Pescara-Chieti

Pescara Sud

Bari

137

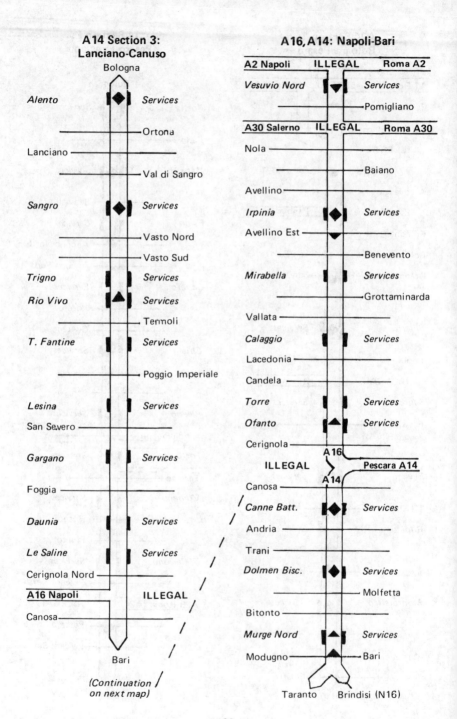

A14 Section 3:
Lanciano-Canuso

Bologna

Alento   ◆   *Services*

Ortona

Lanciano

Val di Sangro

Sangro   ◆   *Services*

Vasto Nord

Vasto Sud

Trigno   *Services*

Rio Vivo   ▲   *Services*

Termoli

T. Fantine   *Services*

Poggio Imperiale

Lesina   *Services*

San Severo

Gargano   *Services*

Foggia

Daunia   *Services*

Le Saline   *Services*

Cerignola Nord

A16 Napoli   ILLEGAL

Canosa

Bari

(Continuation on next map)

A16, A14: Napoli-Bari

A2 Napoli   ILLEGAL   **Roma A2**

Vesuvio Nord   ▼   *Services*

Pomigliano

A30 Salerno   ILLEGAL   **Roma A30**

Nola

Baiano

Avellino

Irpinia   ◆   *Services*

Avellino Est   ▼

Benevento

Mirabella   *Services*

Grottaminarda

Vallata

Calaggio   *Services*

Lacedonia

Candela

Torre   *Services*

Ofanto   ▲   *Services*

Cerignola   **A16**

ILLEGAL   **A14**   Pescara A14

Canosa

Canne Batt.   ◆   *Services*

Andria

Trani

Dolmen Bisc.   ◆   *Services*

Molfetta

Bitonto

Murge Nord   ▲   *Services*

Modugno   Bari

Taranto   Brindisi (N16)

San Marino

Hitching in the world's oldest republic—a 62 square kilometer chunk of the Appenines near the Adriatic coast at Rimini—is straightforward. The biggest difficulty is to filter out the local traffic from the overloaded Fiats and tourist buses carrying visitors between the coast and San Marino. Native drivers have the only vehicles with room to spare. They seem quite willing to transport young travellers to and from a country whose only attraction is being yet another nation to add to a total of those visited. Since San Marino isn't on the way to anywhere, you're almost certainly doing the same.

Malta

This group of islands can be very difficult to reach unless you find a cheap flight from Britain. Malta lies at the centre of the Mediterranean, and is served only by sporadic ferries (about £20, steerage class) from Syracuse or Catania on Sicily. If no sailing is anticipated in the near future, try asking around the cargo wharves at either Sicilian port. Better still, visit the yacht marinas of southern Italy in the hope of talking your way on to a Malta-bound private yacht as a temporary crew member.

Once you get to Malta, you'll find hitching around extremely easy. Just start walking to the edge of whichever village you happen to be in. Hitch on the left. If a native doesn't pick you up in the first minute, a tourist (in one of the very cheap hire cars) will probably stop for you in the next. Getting rides on the neighbouring island of Gozo is equally straightforward, although traffic is considerably lighter.

The only problems arise at the western edge of Valletta and in neighbouring Sliema, where the roads bear a passing similarity to fast dual-carriageways. If you encounter any difficulty, you can always invest 20p in a bus ride to anywhere on the island.

Language will not be a problem for those with a modicum of English. More worrying is the eccentric local driving style, combined with large numbers of tourists driving battered Ford Escorts over unfamiliar terrain. Be especially careful from whom you accept lifts: drunken tourists and speed-crazed natives should be avoided.

Spain and Portugal

Spain and Portugal are the slowest countries in western Europe for driving, let alone hitch-hiking, so you will only enjoy yourself if you forget about time and any deadlines you may have. Plan on a maximum of 300km a day, and don't be unduly upset if you don't get anywhere. If you get a lift without waiting more than an hour, count yourself lucky. Off the motorways you can't afford to turn down any lift, however humble. A horse and cart is an offer you can't refuse.

But hitching in both Spain and Portugal has markedly improved in recent years. The natives are richer and so there are more cars around, and political instability has given way to relatively stable democracies. This improvement can be expected to continue as both countries prepare to join the EEC. However, there may be sudden outbreaks of unrest (particularly in the Basque and Catalan areas of northern Spain) which can put paid to any chance of a lift in the immediate future.

Rules of Thumb

Getting In. Most border posts between Spain and Portugal close at night. Because of the one-hour time difference between the two countries (which can sometimes mean that one side of the border is open while the other is closed!), don't rely upon getting across outside the hours of 9am-7pm. The ferry over the southern frontier between Vila Real (Portugal) and Ayamonte (Spain) operates between these hours in winter, and for slightly longer in summer. Assuming you find both sides of a crossing point open, you should have no problem getting through. The border between France and Spain is also easy in terms of formalities, but expect to be searched for excess liquor if you pass through Andorra on the way.

Arriving from Morocco is a more daunting prospect. Don't be taken in by the fact the two North African towns of Ceuta and Melilla are classed as external Spanish territories. Although they have their own frontier posts with Morocco, the real search for drugs does not begin until you set foot on mainland Spain (in Algeciras if you sail from Ceuta, Malaga from Melilla). If you're caught with drugs, expect a haircut, no sympathy, and a long wait in jail while your trial is arranged (you'll be found guilty). Be careful of the company you keep on these crossings, as you can be jailed indefinitely on suspicion, and the suspicion will be considerable if a travelling companion turns out to be a smuggler. Also, do not carry any parcels or baggage through customs for anyone else unless you have inspected the contents.

The Law. Motorway hitching is illegal, as everywhere else. Since traffic police actually have something to charge you with if they catch you on a motorway, they will be delighted to relieve you of a few pesetas or escudos.

Should you be asked to pay an on-the-spot fine, give them the cash if you can afford it. Although you are theoretically allowed eight days in which to pay the fine, Spanish police in particular are horrified when someone refuses to hand over the cash immediately — they could impound your car if you had one, and may well incarcerate your rucksack or you instead!

Although you can expect harassment from the Spanish police even when you are standing somewhere legitimate, the Portuguese police are generally far more understanding, even sympathetic. Not so the Portuguese Minister for Tourism, who refers to hitch-hikers as the "tourist trash of Europe".

Road Strategy. Spanish drivers who are fortunate enough to own a fast car will tend to use toll (*peaje*) motorways where they exist rather than the parallel national road, leaving the latter for miscellaneous animals, tractors and lorries with terminal prognoses. You are advised to choose the former wherever possible. In Portugal, keep to the main routes radiating from Lisbon and the N125 coast road along the Algarve.

Around siesta time (1-5pm) don't expect too much native traffic. Perhaps because of the Circadian rhythms of the Iberians, hitching then seems to improve steadily towards nightfall.

Route Planning. Spain's network of motorways (*autopistas*) is still very ragged, although the A7 down the Mediterranean coast achieves quite a respectable length. The combination of the A2 and A68 also provides a through route from Barcelona to Bilbao. Most other motorways are still at the planning or construction stages, at least for part of their length. All the motorways (whose numbers carry the prefix A, except the Madrid ring motorway — M30) have a fair amount of traffic. This is also true of the six major national (N) roads that radiate from Madrid: NI to San Sebastian, NII to Barcelona, NIII to Valencia, NIV to Seville, NV to Badajoz and NVI to La Coruña. Few other N roads are practical propositions for hitch-hiking, and the same goes for the secondary or "complementary" roads, prefixed C.

The Portuguese road numbering system uses A for the embryonic motorway (*auto estrada*) system, and N for national roads. The E-numbers are found on signs in both Spain and Portugal.

Maps. The Spanish National Tourist Office (57 St George's St, London W1) provides a free *Mapa de Communicaciones* showing the road, rail and air networks of the whole country. It contains plans of the four largest cities, which are infinitely better than the illegible and misleading street maps contained in the glossy brochures produced by every city. Pester the local tourist offices for something better, which they often have hidden beneath the counter.

Portugal also produces some dire examples of cartography. The Tourist Office (1-5 New Bond St, London W1) has a dismal selection of booklets with feeble road maps and town plans. If you are hitching around a particular area of the Iberian Peninsula, invest in a Firestone Hispania regional map. These are available locally, or in advance from Roger Lascelles and specialist map shops.

For a free guide to all Spanish motorways (including details of service stations and limited access junctions), request the booklet *Guía de Autopistas de Peaje* from ASETA, Estabáñez Calderón 3, Madrid 20.

Place Names. The main variations between English and native versions are barely noticeable: we say Seville for Sevilla, Majorca for Mallorca, Lisbon for Lisboa and Oporto for Porto. However, Basque and Catalan names are gradually taking over in northeast Spain. They can be disconcerting until you get used to them. In Basque, San Sebastián becomes Donastia; Bilbao is Bilbo. In Catalan, Barcelona stays the same, but Gerona becomes Girona.

Number Plates. Portuguese number plates are not coded in any useful way, but the radiators of commercial vehicles bear a blue plate showing their city of registration. The first letter or two of Spanish plates are coded abbreviations of the province (or provincial capital) where the car was registered; the 53 codes are given below. The four external territories — in North Africa and the Atlantic — are asterisked: they are rarely seen on the mainland.

A	Alicante	CS	Castellon	LU	Lugo	SO	Soria
AB	Albacete	CU	Cuenca	MA	Malaga	SS	S Sebastian
AL	Almeria	GC*	Gran Canaria	ML*	Melilla	T	Tarragona
AV	Avila	GE	Gerona	MU	Murcia	TE	Teruel
B	Barcelona	GR	Granada	NA	Navarra	TF*	Tenerife
BA	Badajoz	GU	Guadalajara	O	Oviedo	TO	Toledo
BI	Bilbao	H	Huelva	OR	Orense	V	Valencia
BU	Burgos	HU	Huesca	P	Palencia	VA	Valladolid
C	La Coruña	J	Jaen	PM	Palma	VI	Vitoria
CA	Cadiz	L	Lerida	PO	Pontevedra	Z	Zaragoza
CC	Caceres	LE	Leon	S	Santander	ZA	Zamora
CE*	Ceuta	LO	Logrono	SA	Salamanca		
CO	Cordoba	LU	Lugo	SE	Sevilla		
CR	Ciudad Real	M	Madrid	SG	Segovia		

Planned and Paid Lifts. The only car-sharing agency is in Barcelona: call 333.35.46. Otherwise try the notice boards in universities.

Winter Hitching. The following roads are usually closed between November and May.

Pyrenees: La Bonaigua, Le Pourtalet, Portillon
Guadarrama: Navacerrada
Sierra Nevada: The road from Granada to Veleta, which (at 2 miles high) claims to be the highest road in Europe.

An alarming winter practice among some motorists in southern Spain is to drive up to the snow line in the mountains, build an enormous snowman on the bonnet of the car, then drive extremely fast down to the coast again. Steering is effected by leaning out of an open window. Accepting a lift from any car with a snowman on the bonnet is highly inadvisable.

Town Guide

(for key and explanation, see the introduction)

Spain

BARCELONA

A17, A7/E4 (north): Gerona, Andorra (N152)
⊞ or ⊞ or ⊖ 1 to Plaza de las Glorias, in north of city. Stand on Ave Meridiana. Sign pref.*
⊞ 2, 40 to Plaza de la Trinidad. Stand on Ave Meridiana. Sign pref.**

A19: Mataro, Lloret de Mar (NII) Gerona (NII)
⊞ or ⊞ or ⊖ 1 to Plaza de las Glorias. Stand on Ave de J A Primo de Rivera.*

C246: Sitges, Tarragona
⊞ 8, 9, 109 to Ave de J A Primo de Rivera (C246)/Paseo Zona Franca jn.**

A7 (south)/E26: Valencia, Madrid (NII/E4 west)
⊞ 7 from Plaza de Las Glorias to terminus on Avenida Diagonal (leading to A7). Sign pref.***

BILBAO (Bilbo)

N634, A8/E50 (east): San Sebastian, Madrid (N625, NI)
N634/E50 (west): Santander
⊞ to Plaza de Zabálburu in city

centre, 1km W of Estacion de Abando (Plaza de Espana) Stand at start of Ortiz de Zarate. Sign pref.**
⊞ 1km: NE from Plaza de F. Moyua along Alameda de Recalde to start of new bridge. Sign pref.*
⊞ 500m: E from Plaza de España over Puente G Mola to Plaza de G P de Rivera. Stand at start of Ave de Zumalacarregui (N634). Sign pref.*

GRANADA

N323/E103 (north): Jaen, Madrid (NIV/E25)
⊞ 2km: N along Gran Via de Colon and Ave de Calvo Sotelo, then R along Carretera de Madrid (N323) to jn with Avenue del Dr Oloriz.**
⊞ 3, 5 to exit at Carretera de Madrid. Stand on N323.**
⊞ from Monasterio San Juan de Dios to Pantano Cubillas (10km N).***

N342/E26 (east): Guadix, Murcia
⊞ 7 to Haza Grande. Stand on N342.**

N323/E103 (south): Motril
⊞ 1km: S from Puerta Real along Embovedado and Acera de Darro, over Puente Genil to start of Carretera de Motril (N323).**
⊞ 2km: as above but continue to jn with Camino de Ronda.***

N342/E26 (west): Antequera, Malaga (N331), Seville (N334)

🚉 2km: N along Gran Via de Colon and Ave de Calvo Sotelo to N432/N342 jn. Stand on N342.*
🚌 from main bus station to Santafé (10km W).**

N432: Cordoba

🚉 as above but stand on N432.*
🚌 from main bus station to Pinos Puente (15km NW).**

MADRID

NI/E25 (north): Burgos, San Sebastian (E3), Bilbao (N625)

⊖ 1 or 🚌 5, 27, 42, 49, 70, M3, M6, N10 to Plaza de Castilla. Stand on NI Sign pref.** Or 🚌 129 from Plaza de Castilla to Carretera de Burgos.**

NII/E4 (east): Zaragoza, Barcelona

🚉 2km: E from Plaza de Colon along Calle del Goya and L along Calle de General Paradilas to start of Ave de America (NII). Sign pref.**
⊖ 4, 7 or 🚌 11 to America by above jn.
⊖ 5 to Canillejas. Stand on N11 approach road.***

NIII/E101: Valencia

⊖ 6 to Conde de Casal. Stand on Ave del Mediterraneo (NIII) Sign pref.**
🚌 10, 14, 32, 56, 63, M9 to above jn.

NIV/E25 (south): Cordoba, Seville, Granada (N323/E103)

2.45km: SE from Plaza Cascorro along Calle Embajadores, R over Puente de Andalucia to start of Autovia Ciudad de Los Angeles (NIV).**
⊖ 3, 6 to Legazpi, then 🚉 300m over Puente de Andalucia to above jn.
🚌 6, 18, 22, 23, 47, 59, 76, 79, 85, 86, N5 to above jn.

N401: Toledo

🚉 3km: S from Plaza Mayor along Calle de Toledo, over Puente de Toledo and along Calle de Antonio Leiva to start of N401.***
⊖ 6 to Plaza Eliptica by above jn.
🚌 47, 55, 60, 78, 81, N6 to above jn.

NV/E4 (west): Badajoz, Lisbon (N4, N10)

🚉 1km: SW from Plaza de España along Cuesta de San Vicente to NV approach road at Puente del Rey.**
⊖ Ramal (shuttle) to Norte by above jn.
🚌 B, C, 25, 33, 39, 41, 46, 75, N8 to above jn.

NVI: La Coruña (E50)

🚉 1.5km: NW from Plaza de España along Calle de la Princesa and Ave del Arco de la Victoria to Plaza del Cardinal Cisneros. Stand at start of Ave Puerto de Herro (NVI).**
⊖ 3 to terminus at Moncloa then 🚉 500m NW along Ave del Arco de la Victoria to above jn.
🚌 83 from Moncloa to Carretera del Prado turn-off. Stand on NVI slip road.***

MALAGA

N340/E26 (west): Algeciras

🚉 3km: W along Alameda Principal, over bridge then L along embankment and R along Calle Cuarteles and Heroes de Sostoa (N340), past station to jn with Ronda Intermedia.**
🚌 3, 15, G to above jn.

N321/E26 (north): Granada (N342), Antequara (N331)

🚉 2km: E along Calle de la Victoria, bear L along Calle Cristo de la Epidemia (N321) to jn with Fuente Olletas.*
🚌 1, F to above jn.
🚌 2 to terminus at Cuidad Jardin. Stand on N321.***

N340/E103: Motril, Almeria

🚉 2km: E along Paseo del Parque, bear L then R at bullring along Paseo de Sancha and Ave Pintor Sorolla to jn with Paseo Maritimo. Stand on N340.*
🚌 17 to terminus on Carretera de Almeria then 🚉 E to lay by.**

PALMA de MALLORCA

PM1, C717: El Arenal, Santanyi

🚉 1.5km: E along Ronda Litoral

(coast road) to start of motorway.
Sign pref.**
🚌 17B to above jn.
🚌 17A, 17B to airport. Stand on
C717.**

C711: Soller
🚶 2km: N along Calle Capitan Salom
to jn with Camino Roig. Stand on
C711.**
🚌 19 to Faculdad de Ciencias. Stand
on Carretera de Valldemosa (C711).
**

C713: Inca, Alcudia
🚶 2km: NE along Calle de Aragon to
jn with dual carriageway. Stand on
C713.**
🚌 2, 3, 13 to above jn.

C715: Manacor, Arta
🚶 2km: E along Calle Heroes de
Manacor to jn with new dual
carriageway. Stand on C715.**
🚌 17A to above jn.

SAN SEBASTIAN (Donastia)

A8/E3 (west): Irun, Bordeaux
🚶 500m: E across Puente Santa
Catalina, along Calle Miracruz and
Ave Gral Mola to jn with Ave de
Navarra.**
🚶 1km: S along west bank of river,
follow Paseo Juan Olazabal to
motorway slip road.**
🚌 10 to near above jn.

A8/E50 (east): Bilbao, Santander (N634)
NI/E3 (south): Burgos, Madrid (E25)
🚶 1km: as above to motorway. Sign
pref. Bilbao*, Madrid**
🚶 2km: W along sea front, L along
Ave de Zumalacarregui, L along
Ave Tolosa. For Bilbao, stand on
motorway slip road.** For Madrid,
continue under motorway to jn with
exit roads.**
🚌 9 to near above jn.

SANTANDER

N634 (west): Santiago, Burgos (N623)
🚶 to Plaza Cuatro Caminos just
north of bull ring. Stand on N634.
Sign pref.*

N634 (east): Bilbao, Irun
🚶 as above. Sign pref.*
🚃 (narrow gauge from FEVE
station) to Solares, 10km S of
Santander. L out of station along
N632 for 500m to start of crawler
lane.**

SEVILLE (Sevilla)

NIV/E25 (east): Cordoba, Madrid
🚶 1km: NE along Calle del Sol and
Carretera de Carmona (NIV) to jn
with Antioquia/Santa Clara de
Cuba. Stand on NIV.*
🚌 14, 25, 32, 33 to above jn.

N334: Granada (N342/E26), Malaga (N331, N321/E26)
🚶 2km: E along Aguilas, Ave Luis
Montoto and Carretera de Malaga
(N334) to jn with Gral Alarcon.*
🚌 29 to above jn at Nazaret.

NIV, A4/E25 (south): Cadiz
🚶 1.5km: S from Catedral/Giralda
along Ave de la Constitution and
Ave de Roma, L along Paseo de las
Delicias (NIV) to jn with Ave Maria
Luisa. Stand on NIV.*
🚌 6, 19, 33 to above jn.

N431: Huelva, Faro (N125)
🚶 2km: W from Estacion de
Cordoba (Plaza de la Legion) along
Ave de Cristo, R along Calle Castilla
and over bridge to N630/N431 jn on
west bank. Stand on N431.**

N630/E102: Salamanca, Lisbon (N433/E52), Madrid (NV/E4)
🚶 as above but stand on N630.**

VALENCIA

A7/E26 (north): Barcelona
🚶 1.5km: NE over Puente del Real,
bear L along General Elio then R
along Ave de Blasco Ibáñez to start
of motorway.**

A7/E26 (south): Alicante, Granada (N340, N342)
🚶 1km: S from station along Calle
Alicante, Calle Gibraltar and Calle
Filipinas to rdbt at jn with Ave de

Peris y Valero/Ave de Ausias March
(N322).**

NIII/E101: Madrid
🛉 500m: W from Plaza Santa Lucia
along Angel Guimera and Calle
Linares to jn with Ave del Cid
(NIII).*

Portugal

LISBON (Lisboa)

A1, N1/E3: Coimbra, Porto (E50)
🚍 1, 8, 10, 19, 22 to Rotunda de
Aeroporto, a large rdbt northeast of
the city centre. Stand on A1
approach road.***

N6: Estoril, Cascais
⊖ to Rotunda. Cross Praça Marques
de Pombal and stand by park on Rua
J A de Aguiar. Sign pref.*

A2, N4/E4: Madrid, Faro (N5, N2)
⊖ as above. Sign pref.*
🚍 12, 18, 20 to Largo de Alcantara,
a rdbt on the western edge of the city
centre. Stand on A2 approach
road.**
⚓ from Estaçao Fluvial then 🚌 to
Setubal (about 75p in total), then 🛉
3km E along N10 to jn with A2.***

OPORTO (Porto)

**A1, N1/E50 (south): Coimbra,
      Lisbon**
🛉 1.5km: W from Hospital de Santo
Antonio along Rua de Don Manuel
II, R along Rua de Julio Dinis then L
along Rua do Campo Alegre to rdbt
at start of N1/E50 approach rd.**

N13/E50 (north): Viana, Vigo
🛉 2km: NW from Estaçao de
Boavista along Rua de 5 Outubro
(N13) to rdbt at jn with motorway
approach rd. Stand on N13.**

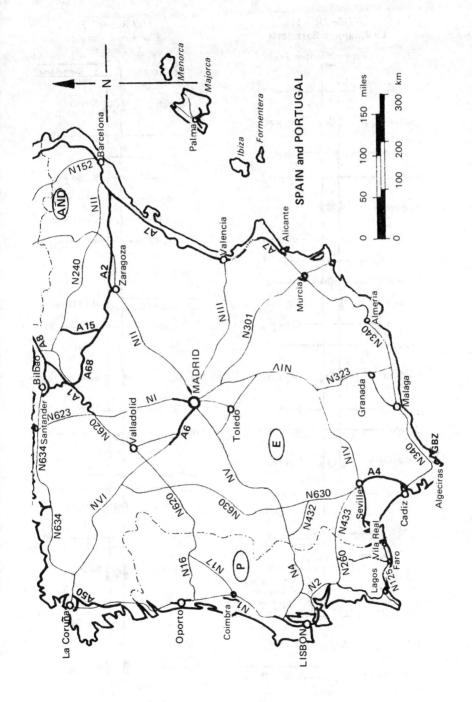

SPAIN and PORTUGAL

A7 Section 1:
La Junquera-Barcelona

xxx French Frontier xxx

La Junquera	14
La Junquera	*Services*
13	Rosas
Figueras	12
Emporda	*Services*
11	Ampurias
Gerona N.	10
Gerona S.	9
Girones	*Services*
8	Cassa
Lloret	7
La Selva	*Services*
6	Blanes
S. Celoni	5
Montseny	*Services*
Cardedeu	4
3	Granollers
2	Vich

ILLEGAL

1	Mollet
	Montcada Services

A18 Tarrasa   ILLEGAL   Barcelona A17

Valles	*Services*

ILLEGAL   Barcelona A2

Alicante

A7 Section 2:
Barcelona-Vinaroz

La Junquera

ILLEGAL   **Barcelona**

Llobregat	*Services*
Martorell	5
6	Gelida
7	S. Sadurni
8	Vilafranca
9	Villanueva
Sta. Margarita	10
Pe. nedes	*Services*

A2 Zaragoza   ILLEGAL

Vendrell	31
32	Altafulla
Medol	*Services*
33	Tarragona
Reus	34
35	Salou
Cambrils	37
Hospitalet	38
Hospitalet	*Services*
Ametlla	39
Baix Ebre	*Services*
Tortosa	40
41	San Carlos
Vinaroz	42
Benicarlo	*Services*

Alicante

148

A7 Section 3: Vinaroz-Alicante

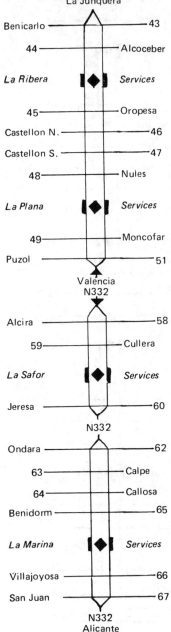

La Junquera

Benicarlo — 43
44 — Alcoceber
La Ribera ◆ Services
45 — Oropesa
Castellon N. — 46
Castellon S. — 47
48 — Nules
La Plana ◆ Services
49 — Moncofar
Puzol — 51

Valencia
N332

Alcira — 58
59 — Cullera
La Safor ◆ Services
Jeresa — 60

N332

Ondara — 62
63 — Calpe
64 — Callosa
Benidorm — 65
La Marina ◆ Services
Villajoyosa — 66
San Juan — 67

N332
Alicante

A2: Barcelona-Zaragoza

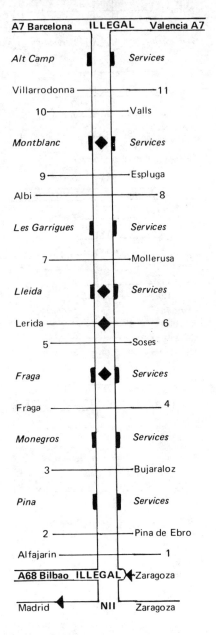

A7 Barcelona   ILLEGAL   Valencia A7

Alt Camp ■ ■ Services
Villarrodonna — 11
10 — Valls
Montblanc ◆ Services
9 — Espluga
Albi — 8
Les Garrigues ■ Services
7 — Mollerusa
Lleida ◆ Services
Lerida — 6
5 — Soses
Fraga ◆ Services
Fraga — 4
Monegros ■ ■ Services
3 — Bujaraloz
Pina ■ Services
2 — Pina de Ebro
Alfajarin — 1

A68 Bilbao   ILLEGAL ◀ Zaragoza
Madrid ◀ **NII** Zaragoza

149

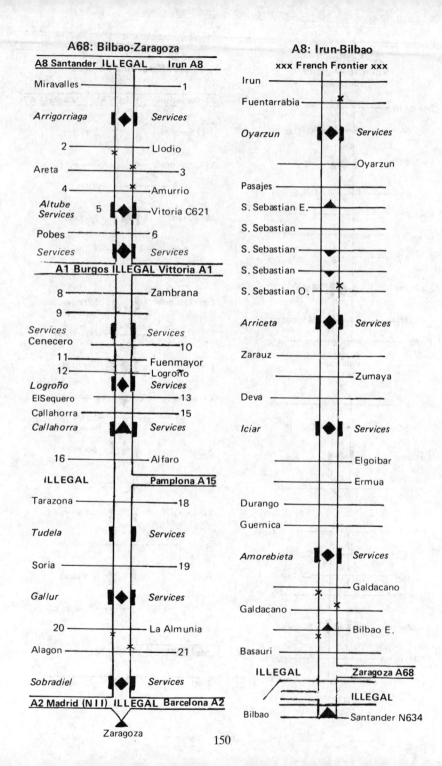

A68: Bilbao-Zaragoza

A8 Santander ILLEGAL   Irun A8

Miravalles ——————————— 1

Arrigorriaga   *Services*

2 —————×———— Llodio

Areta —————×———— 3

4 —————×———— Amurrio

Altube Services   5   Vitoria C621

Pobes ——————————— 6

Services   *Services*

A1 Burgos ILLEGAL Vittoria A1

8 ——————————— Zambrana

9 ———————

Services   *Services*
Cenecero ——————————— 10

11 ——————— Fuenmayor

12 ——————— Logroño

Logroño   *Services*

ElSequero ——————————— 13

Callahorra ——————————— 15

Callahorra   *Services*

16 ——————————— Alfaro

ILLEGAL   Pamplona A15

Tarazona ——————————— 18

Tudela   *Services*

Soria ——————————— 19

Gallur   *Services*

20 ——————————— La Almunia

Alagon ——————————— 21

Sobradiel   *Services*

A2 Madrid (N II) ILLEGAL Barcelona A2

Zaragoza

A8: Irun-Bilbao

xxx French Frontier xxx

Irun ———————

Fuentarrabia —————×——

Oyarzun   *Services*

————————— Oyarzun

Pasajes ———————

S. Sebastian E. ———————

S. Sebastian ———————

S. Sebastian ———————

S. Sebastian ———————

S. Sebastian O. —————×——

Arriceta   *Services*

Zarauz ———————

————————— Zumaya

Deva ———————

Iciar   *Services*

————————— Elgoibar

————————— Ermua

Durango ———————

Guernica ———————

Amorebieta   *Services*

—————×——— Galdacano

Galdacano —————×——

—————▲——— Bilbao E.

×

Basauri ———————

ILLEGAL   Zaragoza A68

ILLEGAL

Bilbao ——————— Santander N634

150

Gibraltar

Clearly a colony covering only 2½ square miles and whose only land frontier is closed to foreigners has rather limited hitching potential. However, the locals seem happy to give you a ride for a few hundred yards or the maximum possible distance between two points in the country: around a mile and a half. Hitch on the left.

For European hitch-hikers, the biggest problem is getting to or from Gibraltar. The accepted way from Spain is to take the ferry from Algeciras to Ceuta, hitch or bus the 60 miles to Tangier and travel back to Gibraltar on another ship. This, of course, is expensive and time-consuming. Until the border at La Linea re-opens to foreign visitors, the alternative is to insinuate your way on to a boat. You can choose between private yachts (preferably British-registered), or one of the clandestine freighters which keep the colony supplied with essentials from the Spanish mainland. See *Trains and Boats and Planes* in the introduction for suggested tactics.

It must be said that it is difficult to understand why any hitch-hiker would go to so much trouble in order to reach a fogbound ex-naval base whose main attraction is duty-free whisky. However, at the time of going to press, agreement was reached between Britain and Spain to re-open the frontier to foreigners. Assuming that this takes place, as planned, in February 1985, Gibraltar might be of interest to hitchers keen to increase their tally of countries visited.

Switzerland

[signature]

On paper, Switzerland looks a good bet for the hitch-hiker — an affluent society, plenty of traffic, an expanding motorway network, and a criss-cross of international routes. But in reality the lifts don't come easily, and the mountains are just another factor in slowing down your progress. Generally, the neater you look, the faster you will travel: appearance is important to the Swiss.

One thing you will notice about hitching in Switzerland is the absence of native hitch-hikers. Swiss young people are well trained to use public transport, and only the penniless or rebellious will be found by the roadside. Foreign hitch-hikers, mostly British and German, will occasionally be seen on the main through routes, but they are only likely to cause an obstruction at certain bottlenecks, like the border at Basel, or the roads out of Geneva or Zurich. In winter, you'll be the only one on the road.

Rules of Thumb

Getting In. A check on the amount of money you have may be all that is requested, but in most situations even that won't be asked. Another main concern is that you might try to find work in Switzerland, as they are very conscious of their immigration and unemployment problems.

The Law. An on the spot fine will be punishment for motorway hitching, although the police will inevitably be very polite and civilised and even a little apologetic about it. Don't litter your hitching spot with drinks cans, food wrappers or cigarette packets, as the Swiss are proud of their clean and tidy nation. Otherwise, you can expect little trouble or harassment.

Road Strategy. In Switzerland, the timing of your travels is crucial to your overall speed. Most Swiss are up at the crack of dawn and tucked up in bed as soon as it gets dark. An early start is therefore recommended, and you can expect a long wait in the evenings and at night. The strategy on motorways is to use busy slip roads (or get out on stretches of main road where motorways are still under construction), as service areas are thinly scattered and not heavily used.

Route Planning. The national road numbering system is three-fold. Major roads (including motorways) have N numbers. Other roads are either numbered (without a prefix) or un-numbered. The E numbers are also used on maps and signs.

Maps. Free route and town maps of an extremely high quality are given out by the Swiss Centre, Leicester Square, London W1 and most Swiss banks. The best maps come from the branches of the Union Bank of Switzerland (*Schweizerische Bankgesellschaft, Union de Banques Suisses* or *Unione di Banche Svizzere*). You don't even have to undertake any transaction, they are generally there to pick up for free. National and local tourist offices and also youth hostels give out free maps for the asking.

Place Names. As Switzerland has four native languages (if you include the 1% Romansch speakers), it is not surprising to find a lot of deviant town and canton names, including:

German	French		French	German
Basel	Bâle		Genève	Genf
Bern	Berne		Neuchâtel	Neuenburg
Biel	Bienne		Sierre	Siders
Graubünden	Grisons		Sion	Sitten
Luzern	Lucerne		Valais	Wallis

The Italian-speaking canton of Ticino is called Tessin in French. Italian also has its own names for several towns, e.g. Losanna for Lausanne.

Number Plates. Swiss number plates show the canton of origin, both in the abbreviated code (the first two letters) and the coat of arms. Since few of you will instantly recognise the cantonal coats of arms, the abbreviations are:

AG	Aargau	BS	Basel-Stadt	NE	Neuchatel	SZ	Schwyz
AI	Appenzell Inner-Rhoden	FR	Fribourg	NW	Nidwalden	TI	Ticino
		GE	Geneva	OW	Obwalden	UR	Uri
AR	Appenzell Ausser-Rhoden	GL	Glarus	SG	St Gallen	VD	Vaud
		GR	Grisons	SH	Schaffhausen	VS	Valais
BE	Bern	JU	Jura	SZ	Schwyz	ZG	Zug
BL	Basel-Land	LU	Luzern	SO	Solothurn	ZH	Zurich

Winter Hitching. Hitching in the Alps can be cold enough even in the summer, and in winter there is a real danger of exposure and hypothermia, so make sure you are prepared. Wrap up well and try to arrange your lifts so that you get dropped near civilisation, especially at night. Don't be surprised to find frost in your eyebrows and your face freezing over if you're standing in an exposed place.

Most mountain roads are impassable for much of the winter, and the following passes are closed at least between November and May:

Croix	Lukmanier	Splügen
Grimsel	Nufenen	Süsten
Klausen	Oberalp	Umbrail

The following passes are also closed in winter, but can be avoided by use of a tunnel (T) or rail transporter connection (R):

Albula (R)	Grand St Bernard (T) Simplon (T/R)
Furka (R)	St Gotthard (T/R)

These tunnels/rail connections are also widely used by native traffic in the summer, leaving mostly tourists to tackle the high passes.

Town Guide

(for key and explanation, see the introduction)

BASEL (Bâle)

N2/E4/E9 (south): Olten, Bern (N1/E4), Lucerne (N2/E9), Zurich (N3/E17)
⚐ 1km: E from SBB/SNCF station along Centralbahn Str, Nauenstr and Grosspeterstr to motorway approach road. Sign pref.***

N66/E9 (north): Mulhouse
🚌 15 to terminus on Elsasserstr then ⚐ 200m across French border. Stand on E9.***

A5/E4 (north): Frankfurt
🚌 2, 6 or 🚌 33, 36 or ⚐ to Badischbahnhof (German Railways Station, in NE of city). Then ⚐ 1km N along Schwarzwaldallee to motorway approach road.***

BERN (Berne)

N1/E4 (north): Zurich (E17), Basel (N2)
⚐ 2km: N over Kornhausbrücke, along Kornhausstr, R along Viktoria-Str to jn with Papiermühle-Str. Sign pref.**
🚌 9 to terminus at Young Boys stadium, then ⚐ 500m N along Papiermühle-Str to motorway jn Bern-Wankdorf. Sign pref.***
🚌 20 to terminus at Wyler, then ⚐ 500m E along Wilkeried-Str and L along Papiermühle-Str to above jn.

N6, 6: Interlaken, Lucerne (4)
🚌 5 to terminus at Bern-Ostring motorway jn.***

N12: Fribourg, Lausanne (N9/E2)
🚌 13, 14 to motorway jn Bern-Bümpliz. Stand on southbound slip road.**

1/E4 (south): Neuchâtel, Lausanne
🚌 14 to terminus at Gablebach. Stand on Murten-Str (1). Sign pref.***

GENEVA (Genève, Genf)

N1/E4 (north): Lausanne
🚶 2km: N along Rue de Montbrilliant to Place des Nations. Stand on Route de Ferney. Sign pref.**
🚌 F, O, Z, 14 to Place des Nations. 🚌 F to motorway jn on Route de Ferney. Stand on motorway slip road.***

1: Lausanne (via coast road)
🚶 2km: N along Rue de Lausanne (1) to jn with Avenue de France at Place Albert Thomas.***
🚌 S to terminus at above jn.

B41/E21b: Chamonix
🚌 C, 16 or 🚌 12 to Place L Favre, then 🚶 500m S along Rue J Pelletier and Route de Sous Moulin to start of motorway. Stand on slip road or approach road.***

1, A41/E4 (south): Chambéry, Lyon (A43/E13)
🚌 D to St-Julien on French border. Stand on E4.***

N206, N84/E46: Lyon, Macon (N79)
🚌 D as above but stand on N206.**
🚌 X to terminus at CERN on Route de Meyrin.***

N5/E45: Dijon, Paris (A6/E1)
🚌 F over French border to Ferney-Voltaire, then 🚶 500m to edge of town.**

LAUSANNE

N1/E4 (south): Geneva
🚶 2.5km: W along Ave du Mont d'Or and Ave Figuiers to rdbt at start of motorway. Sign pref.****
🚌 1, 4, 18 to rdbt above, just past Cimitière de Montoie.

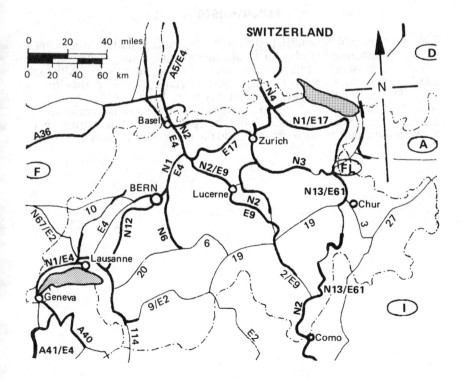

9/E2 (north): Vallorbe, Besançon (N67)

🚌🚶 as above to N1 rdbt. Sign pref.*
🚶 1km: NW along Ave d'Echallens to Montelan by Parc de Valency. Stand on 9.**
🚌 9 (westbound) to Montelan above.

1/E4 (north): Bern, Zurich (N1), Basel (N1, N2)

🚌 21-23, 51 to motorway jn on Route de Berne (1). Stand on 1.***

N9/E2 (south): Montreux

🚌 as above but stand on motorway slip road.**
🚌 9 (eastbound) to terminus on 9.***

ZURICH

N1/E17 (west): Bern (E4), Basel (N3)

🚶 2km: W from Hauptbahnhof along Museum Str, over Zoll-Brucke and along Sihl Quai and Hardturm Str to start of N1.***
🚌 4 to Sportplatz Hardturm by above jn.

N1/E17 (east): Winterthur, St Gallen

🚌 63, 94 to N1 approach road at Schulhaus.***

N3/E60: Lucerne (4), Chur (N13/E61)

🚶 1.5km: W from Hauptbahnhof along Bahnhof-Platz, over Post-Brücke and L along Kasernenstr and Stuffacher Quai, R along Manesse Str to start of N3. Sign pref.**
🚌 84 to Zürich Str/N3 jn south of Wollishofen. Stand on N3 slip road. Sihn pref.** Or, for Lucerne only, on Zürich Str.**

Liechtenstein

This tiny principality sandwiched between Switzerland and Austria bears a strong resemblance to Poland in its attitude to hitch-hiking. Both countries officially encourage hitching in their tourist literature. Although Liechtenstein does not operate an official hitching scheme, getting lifts is easy. The cars that stop are considerably more luxurious than in Poland since Liechtenstein is a very rich country — the most industrialised in Europe. There are no real frontier controls on the border with Switzerland, and the border with Austria is manned by Swiss officials.

Scandinavia

Scandinavia is not exactly a hitcher's paradise, with slow roads, a high cost of living and a general absence of long distance traffic that is willing to pick up hitch-hikers. Although the four countries of mainland Scandinavia — Denmark, Finland, Norway and Sweden — are fiercely independent, they have certain common traits of interest to hitchers. (One notable feature of each Nordic country is the apparent ability of every native to speak near-perfect English.)

In compiling this chapter it has therefore been necessary to present the information at two levels, first at a general level (points covering all countries) and then taking each country separately.

Rules of Thumb

The Law. The police are quite tolerant and you shouldn't have too much trouble. Even if you're caught hitching on motorways, remain polite and you're likely to get away with a warning rather than a spot fine which they are entitled to impose. Vagrancy laws aren't likely to be applied unless you busk in Oslo or beg for money. Even if you do, the police may well just warn you to move on.

Road Strategy. Neither the roads nor the traffic are really conducive to efficient hitch-hiking. The motorway network is patchy and inconclusive, even around the heavily-populated areas in the south. Most stretches of motorway are merely glorified bypasses. In the north, the traffic is so sparse as to be measured in terms of the number of cars per day or week, rather than the several hundred a minute you might find leaving the capital

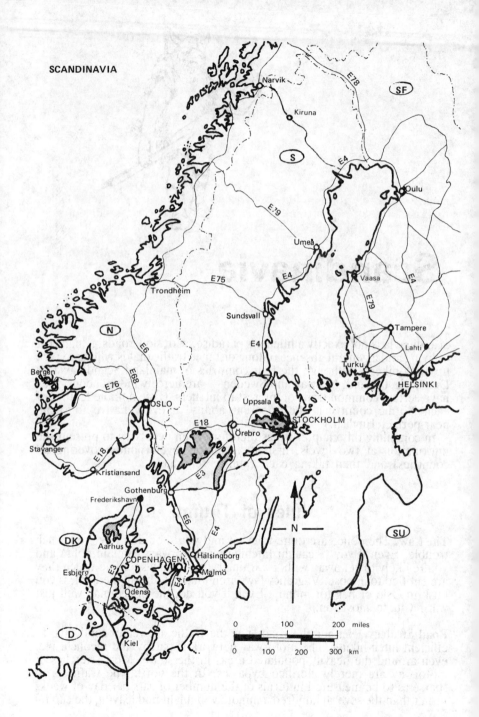

SCANDINAVIA

cities in the evening rush hour. Add to this the typical Scandinavian attitude that hitch-hikers are little more than shameless beggars, and you could be waiting a long time. Luckily, the young people in Scandinavia, especially Sweden, have a very outward-going approach, and they or their parents will eventually stop for you. In the north, where traffic really thins out, hitch-hikers still have a certain amount of novelty value, so that could attract a few lifts for you.

Route Planning. The thicker the line on the map, the more important the road is: if you stick to main roads you shouldn't have any great problems. Apart from E-roads, the national road numbering systems are virtually the same in all countries: major roads have numbers, minor roads don't. As a clue to sub-classification of numbered roads, the numbers with fewer digits are generally more important. While this is only a vague distinction in Norway or Finland, it is a definite rule in Denmark and Sweden, where roads with three-digit numbers are considered to be inferior in quality and traffic flow. A lot of significance is attached to the E-routes, and their numbers appear on signs and road maps often in place of national numbers.

Maps. Any maps that you pay for (either in advance or within Scandinavia) are going to be expensive. Fortunately, the tourist offices listed below provide a fair selection of route planning and city maps. You can fill in any gaps by collecting road maps free from local tourist offices.

Denmark: 169 Regent St, London W1 Finland: 66 Haymarket, London SW1
Norway: 21 Cockspur St, London SW1 Sweden: 3 Cork St, London W1

One publication which may help to pass the time is the Finnish *Holiday Triangle* brochure. This is effectively a board game of the Helsinki-Tampere-Turku triangle, which allows you to chart your progress. Examples: "The police catch you and fine you — miss three turns"; and "You can't go on until you get the right number to reach Helsinki in one go".

Denmark

Denmark is probably the fastest of the Scandinavian countries, if only because of the short distances and relatively high density of traffic.

Getting In. Drug and weapon searches are not infrequent on the Danish borders. Foot passengers who don't look as if they're going to go by train at Rødbyhavn are often victims, so try and get yourself fixed up with a lift on the ferry from Puttgarden. Searches for excess drink and tobacco seem to be confined to Scandinavians returning home, although some of the ferries between parts of Scandinavia now have a perforated ticket system which means that you can't buy more than your quota of duty free goods. It's worth stocking up with liquor and tobacco, either for your own use or as gifts for drivers.

Place Names. Copenhagen is København in Danish, and Köpenhamm in Swedish.

Planned and Paid Lifts. A notice on the notice board of *Use It* at Magstraede 14 in Copenhagen should put you in touch with someone willing to offer a ride in return for a share of petrol costs.

Town Guide

(for key and explanation, see the introduction)

AARHUS

10/E3 (north): Aalborg, Frederikshavn
🚌3 to terminus at Nydamsvej. Stand on Randersvej.***

10/E3 (south): Kolding, Esbjerg (1 west), Copenhagen (1 east)
🔲2km: SW from Town Hall along Frederiks Alle, across Harald Jensens Plads and along Skanderborgvej to jn with Marselis Blvd.**
🚌5 to terminus at Alderslyst. Stand on Skanderborgvej.***

COPENHAGEN (København)

19/E4 (north): Helsingor
🚌6, 24, 27, 84 to Hans Knudsens Plads. Stand on Lyngbyvej.**
🚆(S-Bahn) B, F to Ryparken then 🔲 200m S to above jn.

2/E4 (south): Rødbyhavn
🚌16, 22, 121, 132 or 🚆(S-Bahn) A to Ellebjerg. Stand on Folehavn at jn with Gammel Køge Landevej.***

1/E66: Roskilde, Odense
🚆(S-Bahn) B, Bb to terminus at Tastrup. Stand on Roskildevej.***

E6: Trelleborg
⛴ to Malmö then see *Malmö*.

ESBJERG

1/E66: Kolding, Copenhagen
🔲3km: E from ferry terminal along Østre Havnevej, L along Jernbanegade, R at end over railway bridge and along Storegade to Kirkevej.***
🚌1, 11, 12 to above jn.

12: Tondier (11)
🔲1km: E from ferry terminal along Østre Havnevej and Gammelby Ringvej to jn with Darumvej.**
🚌10 to above jn.

ODENSE

1/E66 (east): Nyborg, Copenhagen
🔲3km: SE from river along Frederiksgade, L along Nyborgvej (1) to jn with Munkerisvej.***
🚌4 to above jn by Motel Munkeris.

1/E66 (west): Kolding, Esbjerg
🔲2km: W along Vestergade, Vesterbro and Middelfartvej (1) to jn with Kløvermosevej.***
🚌4, 7 to above jn beyond Hanges Plads.
*A new motorway bypass is under construction to the south of Odense. This will reduce the star ratings above to **, but they will still be feasible for hitching.*

Finland

Hitching within Finland is good. Display a flag and even people who can't speak English will probably pick you up. There's not the competition with countless other hitchers that you might have in, say, Germany, nor are there the gargantuan lorries that can't stop. If you hitch outside the months of April–September, remember that the weather and the shortage of daylight may well be constraining factors.

Getting In. You will have little trouble when entering direct from Sweden or Norway, but expect a bit more attention, if only for the curiosity of it, if you arrive from Russia.

The border areas with the Soviet Union are a little sensitive, so if your vocation in life happens to be spotting the lesser spotted skitehawk — which coincidentally happens to have chosen to nest on the Finno-Soviet border — you'd better keep the police informed before you start, just to avoid any misunderstanding. Finland protects its neutrality jealously. All frontier posts between Finland and the USSR are closed from 8pm to 8am.

Number Plates. The black and white plates issued since 1972 are coded to show the district of registration. The first of the three letters indicates the district capital, according to the following code:

A Helsinki	L Rovaniemi	R Kotka	U Helsinki
H Hämeenlinna	M Mikkeli	S Joensuu	V Vaasa
K Kuopio	O Oulu	T Turku	X Jyväskylä

Place Names. The western coastal area of Finland contains a high proportion of native Swedish speakers. Many towns, particularly along the south and west coasts, have dual names, sometimes with only negligible differences (eg Vaasa=Vasa) Some less obvious variations are listed below.

Finnish	*Swedish*	*Finnish*	*Swedish*
Helsinki	Helsingfors	Maarianhamina	Mariehamn
Karjaa	Karis	Oulu	Uleåborg
Kaskinen	Kaskö	Pietarsaari	Jakobstad
Kokkola	Karleby	Porvoo	Borgå
Kristiinankaupunki	Kristinestad	Turku	Åbo
Lappeenranta	Villmanstrand	Uusikaarlepyy	Nykarleby

Town Guide
(for key and explanation, see the introduction)

HELSINKI

1/E3 (west): Turku
🚌 4, 4S to Munkkinieme aukio 6km NW of centre then 🚶 800m N along Hoplaksvagen to start of motorway.**

3/E79: Tampere, Vaasa
🚌 10, 10N, 10S to terminus on Mannerheimintie 6km NW of centre, then 🚶 500m N to start of motorway.***

4/E4: Lahti
🚌 6, 8, 9, 10N to Hameentie (4)/
Sturenkatu jn 4km N of centre.***

7/E3 (east): Porvoo, Kotka
🚌 1, 1A, 6, 10N along Hameentie to
bridge over motorway spur, then 🄷
250m E along Aleksis Kiven Katu to
start of spur.**

TAMPERE

3/E79 (north): Vaasa
11: Pori, Turku (41)
🚌 11, 29 to start of motorway on
Paasikiventie. Sign pref.***

9/E80 (north): Jyväskyla, Kuopio
🄷 500m: NE from station along
Itsenaisyydenkatu to jn with
Sammonkatu. Stand on
Teiskontie.**

12: Lahti
🄷 1km: SE along Rautatienkatu, L
along Vuolteenkatu, R along
Pinninkatu, then under railway and
stand at start of Iidersranta.**
🚌 5, 22, 23, 24, 30 to Iidesranta/

Kalevantie jn. Stand at start of
Messukylänkatu.**

**3/E79 (south): Helsinki, Turku (9/
E80 south)**
🄷 as above, but stand at start of
Lempääläntie.**
🚌 21, 26 (or 1 from Harmala
campsite) to start of motorway at
Taatala.**

TURKU

1/E3: Helsinki
🄷 2km: SE along Kaskenkatu,
Kaskigaten, Kaskentie and
Kaskivagen to jn with
Uudenmaantie at start of
Nylandsvägen (1).***
🚌 6, 11 to above jn.

8: Rauma, Pori, Vaasa
🚌 19 to jn of Suikkilantie and
Raumanvaltatie.***

9/E80: Tampere
🚌 21, 23 to Tolpontie/Ring Road jn.
🄷 E along Ring Road and stand on
northbound slip road to
Tampereenvaltatie.***

Norway

Be prepared for long waits, although the friendliness and excellent English
of most of the people who pick you up will almost make up for it.
Wherever and whenever you're hitching, take some warm clothing packed
near the top of your rucksack. It can get cold at high altitudes and in the
evenings. In summer the volume of traffic should be high enough to enable
you to move fairly quickly, but on minor roads and in winter, traffic is
sparse: this may invoke greater sympathy. Road surfaces get worse the
further north you go, although the standards are quite adequate in the
south.

Getting In. The officials are used to long hair and you'll be extremely
unlucky to be searched for drugs or weapons. If you arrive from the
Russian border with a rucksack over your shoulder, customs men will
probably like to have a chat, but only because they've probably never seen
anyone hitching out of the Soviet Union.

From Sweden or Finland you're unlikely to see a customs officer, let
alone be stopped by one.

Number Plates. Two systems exist side by side, each offering coded identification of the district of registration. In the old system, the district is represented by a single letter at the beginning of the number plate. In the new system, the code consists of the initial pair of letters: the pairs of letters are allocated in alphabetical blocks. The list below gives the new codes first, followed by one of the principal towns in the district, then (in brackets) the old single-letter code. As a clue to location, the alphabet progresses geographically from AA in the south-east to ZX in the far north.

AA-BB	Frederikstad (B)	ND-PB	Rjukan (H)	UE-VC	Alesund (T)
BC-CZ	Lillestrøm (C)	PC-PL	Arendal (I)	VD-XC	Trondheim (U)
DA-FR	Oslo (A)	PM-RD	Kristiansand (K)	XD-XU	Namsos (V)
FS-HR	Hamar (D)	RE-SL	Stavanger (L)	XV-YY	Narvik (W)
HS-JT	Lillehammer (E)	SM-TR	Bergen (O)	YZ-ZL	Tromsø (X)
JU-KY	Drammen (F)	TS-TU	Odda (R)	ZP-ZX	Alta (Y)
KZ-NC	Larvik (Z)	TV-UD	Førde (S)		

Winter Hitching. If you want a definition of the word "bleak", stand somewhere in the open country on the Bergen-Trondheim road in the middle of winter. Due to snow, the following mountain passes close from September or October to June or July.

Ardalsveien	Gaular	Sognefjell
Dagaliveien	Hardangervidda	Trollstig
Djupvass	Hemsedal	Valdresflyene
Dyrskar	Saltfjell	Videseter
Eagle's Road	Seljestad	Vikafjell

Town Guide

(for key and explanation, see the introduction)

BERGEN

7/E68: Oslo
⚐ to start of E68 200m SE of bus station.

KRISTIANSAND

E18 (east): Oslo
⚐ 500m: N along Vestre Strandgate to bypass (E18 east) slip road.***

E18 (west): Stavanger
⚐ to Vesterveien, by station.**

OSLO

E18 (west): Drammen, Stavanger,

Bergen (7, 5/E68)
🚌 1, 2 or 🚌 30, 31, 41, 72, 73 (direction Majorstua) to Olav Kyrres Plass and stand on Bygdøy Allé.**
⊖ to Skøyen and stand on Drammensveien.***

E6 (north): Lillehammer, Trondheim
🚌 1, 7 (direction Sinsen) or ⊖ to Carl Berners Plass. Stand on Trondheimsveien.**
🚇 T-Bane to Furuset then ⚐ 500m S to E6.**

E18 (east): Stockholm, Gothenburg (E6 south)
⚐ 1km: E from Radhusplassen along Radhusgata and stand at start of

Bispegata.** Or 🚶 up to the rdbt and
stand on eastbound slip road.**
🚶 as above but continue along
Bispegata, R along Oslogate and
stand just past start of
Mossveien.***
🚌 to Bekkelaget near E18 jn.***

STAVANGER

E18: Kristiansand, Oslo
🚶 1km: SW from station along
Kannikgata to start of E18 dual
carriageway on left.**
🚌 (hourly rural service) to Sandnes
on E18, 10kmS.***

TRONDHEIM

E6 (south): Oslo
🚌 44 to terminus and 🚶 100m to
main road.***
🚶 300m: from Sandmoen campsite to
above jn.

**E6 (north): Narvik, Tromsø (E78).
E75: Sundsvall, Stockholm (E4)**
🚶 1km: NE from Bakkebru along
Innherredsveien to jn by Ringve
Museum.***
🚌 1, 30 to above jn.

Sweden

Swedish drivers tend to be slow as well as fairly reluctant to pick people up,
so expect to move around slowly and don't be surprised if you have long
waits. Your chances will be improved if you display a flag.

Getting In. The Swedish authorities are particularly afraid of illegal
immigrants (or people entering legally but staying on to work), so be
prepared for some heavy questioning if you mention that you might want
to stay for more than a cursory visit. Otherwise, you should have little
trouble: searches are rare.
    If you enter direct from one of the other Nordic countries, you will only
encounter problems if you arrive on the ferry from Denmark. To avoid
long queues at customs, take a "local" ferry to Hälsingborg or Malmö,
rather than one that connects up with an international through train.

Place Names. Gothenburg is Göteborg in Swedish.

Planned and Paid Lifts. Stockholm has a part-time car-sharing agency
known as *Liftar-Service,* which charges a registration fee of 10kr. Dial
758.33.15 between 4 and 6pm for information. The staff speak English.

Town Guide

(for key and explanation, see the introduction)

GOTHENBURG (Göteborg)

E6 (north): Oslo
🚶 to Olskroks torget NE of centre
and stand on approach to

Tingstadstunnel (E6).**
🚌 2, 5 or 🚌 21, 24, 29 to Hjalmar
Brantings Platsen. Stand on
Norgevägen (leading to E6). Sign
pref.***

E3 (east): Örebro, Stockholm
🚌 6, 7 to Redbergsplatsen. Stand on Riddaregatan (E3).**

40: Boras, Jönköping, Stockholm (E4)
🚌 5 to St Sigfrids Plan. Stand on Kungsbackaleden.** Or 🚶 700m along Kungsbackaleden, across traffic lights and stand on slip road.***

E6 (south): Malmo
🚶 2km: SE along Sodra Vagen to jn with Skärs Led at start of Mölndalsvägen.***
🚌 4, 10 to above jn.

If your ultimate destination is mainland Denmark, it is simpler and cheaper to take the ⛴ direct to Frederikshavn, than to take the ⛴ from Hälsingborg or Malmö and then another to the mainland.

HALSINGBORG

E4: Stockholm, Gothenburg (E6 north)
🚌 12A, 12B to rdbt at end of Drottninghögsvägen. Stand on northbound slip road to Ängelholmsleden.**
🚌 19 to above rdbt at end of Bergavägen. Or continue to end of line, then 🚶 200m to end of Garnisonsgatan. Stand on northbound slip road.***
🚌 14 to Lagmansgatan and stand on eastbound slip road to Malmöleden. Sign pref.**
🚌 22 to end of Rusthällsgatan and stand on eastbound slip road to Malmöleden. Sign pref.**

E6 (south): Malmö
🚌 14, 22 to above slip roads to Malmöleden. Sign pref.**

MALMO

E6 (north): Gothenburg, Stockholm (E4)
🚶 1km: S from Central Station then L along Norra Vallgatan and Hornsgatan. Stand on approach road (legal),* or at start of

Stockholmsvägen (illegal).**
🚌 30, 33, 40, 52, 55 to Lundavägen/Hornsgatan jn then 🚶 back along Hornsgatan to above jn.
🚌 40 to terminus at Arlöv then 🚶 back to rdbt. Stand on northbound slip road.***

E6 (south): Trelleborg
🚌 32, 36 along per Albin Hanssonsweg to start of Inre Ringvägen. 🚶 E along ring road to rdbt. Stand on southbound slip road to Trelleborgsvägen.***

ÖREBRO

E3/E18 (east): Stockholm
🚌 1 along Øster Bangatan to Norrplan. Stand on eastbound slip road to Västerleden.***

51: Norrköping
🚌 12 to Almby Plan. Stand on Norrköpingsvägen.**

E3 (west): Gothenburg, Oslo (E18)
🚌 11, 17 to Kungsgaten/Anggatan jn. Stand at start of Kungsgatan.***
🚌 12 up Ekersvägen to motorway jn. Stand on southbound slip road.***

STOCKHOLM

E3 (south): Örebro, Gothenburg, Oslo (E18)
E4 (south): Jönköping, Malmö
⊖ to Hornstull. Stand at approach to Liljeholmsbron Bridge leading to Södertaljevägen. Sign pref.**
🚌 130 to start of motorway on Södertäljevagen.**
⊖ 14, 24, to Midsommarkransen then 🚶 100m S along Erikslundsgatan to jn above.

E18: Örebro, Oslo, Gothenburg (E3)
⊖ to Hallonbergen then 🚶 1km to Enköpingsvägen.
🚌 501, 509, 526, 591, 592, 607 to Enköpingsvägen/Uppsalavägen jn at Jarva. Stand on E18 slip road.**

E4 (north): Uppsala, Umeå
🚌 as above but stand on E4.**

E3 (north): Norrtälje, Kapellskär
Ⓔ 15 or 🚌 151, 601, 602, 607, 612,
614, 618, 670-72, 690, 691 to
University. Stand on E3.**

UPPSALA

E4 (south): Stockholm, Norrtälje (77)
🚌 22, 24, 132 to rdbt at S end of
Kungsgatan. Stand on
Stockholmsvägen.***

55: Enköping, Örebro (E18)
🚌 1, 2 to Bärbyleden/
Enköpingsvägen (55) jn at
Rickomberga.**

E4 (north): Sundsvall, Umea
🚌 20, 101 to N end of
Svartbäcksgatan. Stand on Tycho
Hedens Väg.***

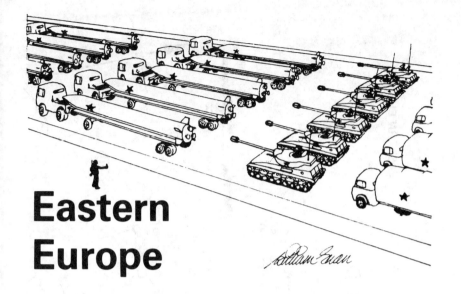

Eastern Europe

A hitching trip in Eastern Europe is not everyone's idea of a holiday: there are visa difficulties, exchange restrictions, and a scarcity of traffic even on the few main roads. The good news is that the difficulties are getting less and less as the various governments gradually become attuned to the benefits of promoting tourism. Visas are easier to obtain, currency restrictions are being waived or slackened, and the consequent increase in tourists from the West has led to a more enlightened attitude towards long-haired freaks and other species of hitch-hiker. Although traffic is still pretty thin on the ground, at least the drivers are beginning to understand what you're up to, and some of them will respond favourably. Eastern Europe is still not as free and tolerant as the West, and the culture difference will be noticed immediately. But the problems are not as great as many people imagine, and it is hoped that the following pages will at least put things into perspective.

Apart from Albania, where hardly anything is permitted, there are no actual laws against hitch-hiking. However, the visa conditions in the USSR make a hitching trip well-nigh impossible: before you can get a visa, you must pre-book your accommodation for every night of your stay. You will also be expected to book your train or air journey, or to arrive in your own car.

But in the other countries, hitch-hiking is tolerated, and in Poland it is actually encouraged. Wherever you go, however, you will find two basic factors that restrict your overall speed. First, the state of the roads: there are few motorways of the standard we expect in the West, and even the extensive East German network is in a terrible state of disrepair. Second, the volume of traffic: what little there is, is both slow and not going far. In most parts, however, people are willing to pick you up, so waits of over an

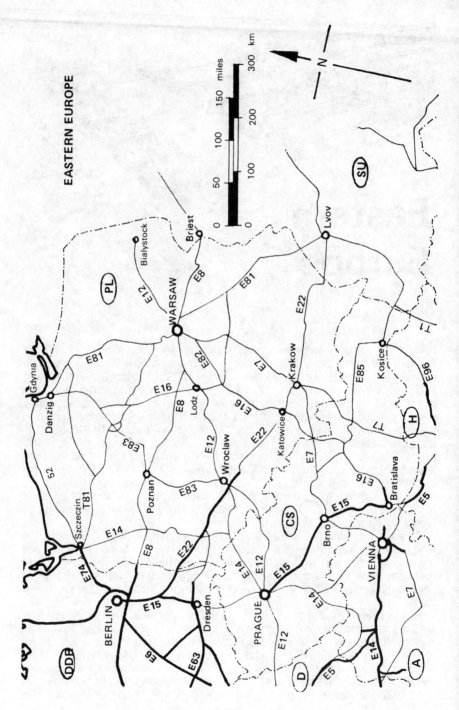

EASTERN EUROPE

168

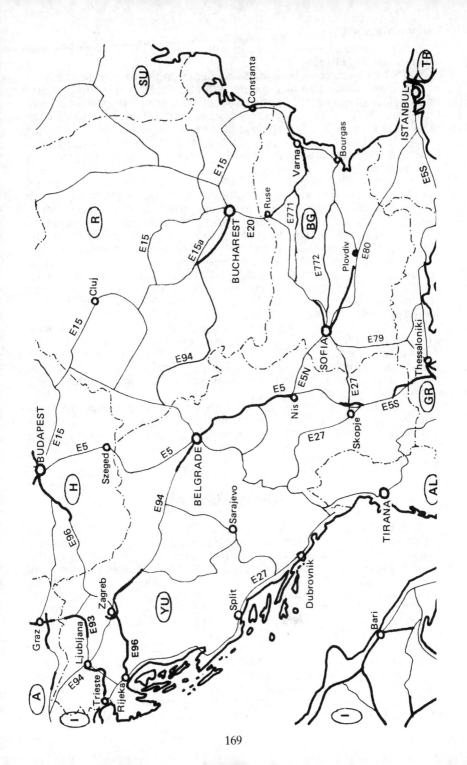

hour are still uncommon. Thus you will move around in short lifts with short waits in between.

You may be surprised by quite a few things on the road. Like the types of driver and vehicle that pick you up. Your typical lift will be either a lorry or a single man in a car. But at times a four-seater car with a family of eight plus granny will pull up to squeeze you in. Or you will ride in the back of an army lorry with the local troops. Tractors and horse-drawn carts frequently offer lifts and should be accepted. Strangest of all — and it has happened — was the hitch-hiker who was picked up by an ambulance, complete with a patient on his way to hospital.

You may well be equally surprised by the other hitch-hikers you see on the road. As well as the scores of students and other young people, you may see soldiers with their rifles slung over their shoulders, or a smartly-dressed secretary hitching to work, or an old peasant woman with a basket of squawking chickens. On market days, the roads out of the market town will be lined with a motley assortment of country folk and their miscellaneous livestock. Note also how the hitch-hikers react to approaching cars. In some parts, especially Hungary and rural Yugoslavia, a mild wave of the thumb will get you nowhere, but if you wave your arms around frantically and run shouting into the middle of the road, you will soon get a lift because this is what the native drivers are used to.

Most of the hitching competition is strictly local, consisting of natives who don't want to wait an hour for the bus. You'll probably get a lift along with some local hitchers. They will offer a few coins to the driver, but long-distance hitchers are usually exempt. However, some drivers in Poland during the hitching season may get a little upset if they don't receive their *Autostop* coupons.

The timings of your trip can be very important: Sundays are fairly inactive, especially in Poland. As for the best time of day to hitch, this is definitely the early morning (from 5.30 to 10), and it's well worth getting up early.

Rules of Thumb

Getting In. Frontier officials are particularly wary because of the black market that exists for western currencies, particularly in East Germany and Poland. The high black market rates are both cause and effect of the customs man's interest in your financial status: he will want to know how much you have, in what currency, and what you intend to do with it. At some frontiers you must fill in a currency declaration form: this you must then keep, along with the receipts you pick up for all exchange transactions, until you leave the country. It follows that anything you want to gamble on the black market should not be declared when you enter the country, or there will be a gap in your accounts. If you want to play the black market, be careful with whom you deal; you may be approached by police informers who will get commission on your conviction. For the best rates, offer only a small amount of money at first: if the dealer thinks you might part with more later, he will give you a good rate of exchange. Stick to the well known western currencies — US dollars, sterling, Swiss francs or West German marks — but be warned of the above average penalties for dealing in Deutschmarks in East Germany. Rather than actively indulging in illegal currency exchange, many westerners find it safer to spend undeclared dollar bills on goods and services at a very favourable rate of exchange.

Since most Eastern European countries either ban or restrict the import and export of their own currency notes, it follows that there is no big demand for them outside their home territory. Thus, for instance, East German marks can be picked up very cheaply at banks in West Berlin, and Polish zlotys circulate widely but stealthily in Prague and Vienna. The risk in smuggling them back into their home country is not as great as playing the black market, but you can expect to be searched if the customs men have nothing better to do (especially crossing from West to East Berlin).

Apart from paperwork and money, you might find the occasional customs officer worrying about what's in your rucksack. Most countries clamp down on western capitalist propaganda (like *Playboy* or the *Beano*) and on banned Russian authors, like Pasternak and Solzhenitsyn. Anything overtly anti-Communist will be either deported along with you or will be destroyed while you serve your jail sentence. *Europe — a Manual for Hitch-hikers* has been successfully transported across the frontiers of Eastern Europe.

You are not likely to be searched for anything else, although drugs and weapons are occasionally presented as excuses for harassment. The USSR has a horror of people smuggling western clothes, so don't turn up with a suitcase full of blue jeans. The same paranoia about blue jeans also exists in Yugoslavia, especially along the Italian frontier.

The above may all sound very daunting, but things really are better than they were. Nowadays, for instance, you are unlikely to be hassled just because you have long hair or no means of transport. Also, the above comments only really apply to the first border you cross between West and east: once you're inside the Communist bloc, frontiers are a lot easier.

Having handled the bureaucratic procedures likely to confront you at frontiers, it is worth adding another cautionary note about the volume of traffic crossing these frontiers. It is very small. Even where there is traffic, it is unlikely to want to take you across the border, for fear of getting fouled up in your customs and immigration problems. Drivers have enough hassles of their own without having to wait for you as well. These are not the only reasons to stick to main roads (or trains) for crossing frontiers. A minor road that looks a likely crossing point on the map may well only be open to local residents. Foreigners, especially westerners, are invariably channelled along the main international routes.

The Law. Although the police will frequently stop to look at your passport and admire your visa, they are unlikely to do more, especially if you are polite and offer your western cigarettes around. As elsewhere in Europe, it is illegal to hitch-hike on motorways, but the police will rarely even ask you to move.

A warning is also in order concerning photography. The pretty bridge you want to snap may be a strategic communications link, and the magnificent view from the top of the hill you've just climbed may include a secret rocket base. Think twice before clicking your shutter, as your motives, like those of bird-watchers and train or plane spotters, may be sadly misunderstood.

Route Planning. Traffic is extremely light throughout Eastern Europe, so if you want to get anywhere, you have to stick to the thick red lines on the map. The E-road numbers will be prominently marked on maps if not on road signs. Although the USSR has not given official blessing to the E roads, the designated routes continue, at least in spirit, to such fanciful destinations as Leningrad, Moscow and Kiev.

In addition to the E-roads, there is a network of T-roads: these are a complementary network of linking roads not covered by E-numbers. T-roads are international, but only within the Eastern bloc. As far as hitch-hiking is concerned, anything other than E- and T-roads are bad risks, unless you really want a walking holiday.

The national road numbering systems are generally quite straightforward: main roads are numbered, minor roads are not. Motorways tend to have A numbers (but D in Czechoslovakia and M in Hungary) if they have a prefix at all. In Romania main roads have numbers prefixed by DN. Bulgaria has gone over entirely to the new E-numbers for its major road network, but unfortunately these differ from the current internationally-agreed system.

Maps. The best maps of Eastern Europe belong to NATO, and hence are difficult to obtain. The tourist office of each country supplies a free route planning map. These show all the roads along which a sensible hitch-hiker might wish to travel, but very little else. If you want anything more detailed, then you'll have to buy a good German- or Swiss-made map of the country concerned before entering Eastern Europe. However, the city plans obtainable from tourist offices in London can be surprisingly clear and informative. Their addresses are:

Bulgaria: 18 Princes St, W1	Czechoslovakia: 18 Old Bond St, W1
East Germany: 20 Conduit St, W1	Hungary: 6 Conduit St, W1
Poland: 25 Mortimer St, W1	Romania: 77 Gloucester Place, W1
Yugoslavia: 143 Regent St, W1	

Place Names. Most of the Eastern European languages are inter-related and of Slavonic origin (Hungarian and Romanian are the main exceptions), but the Cyrillic script is only used in the USSR, Bulgaria and parts of Yugoslavia. Because of linguistic incompatibility, many town names have been given anglicised versions, including the following:

Belgrade	Beograd	Moscow	Moskva
Bucharest	Bucuresti	Prague	Praha
Danzig	Gdansk	Warsaw	Warszawa

Because a lot of Eastern Europe was once under German or Austro-Hungarian control, it is not surprising to find a lot of towns bearing German names, including:

Bratislava	Pressburg	Posen	Poznan
Brno	Brünn	Prague	Prag
Ljubljana	Laibach	Szczecin	Stettin
Maribor	Marburg	Warsaw	Warschau
Moscow	Moskau	Wroclaw	Breslau

Some Yugoslav towns close to the Italian frontier also have Italian names, e.g. Rijeka=Fiume and Koper=Capodistria.

Bulgaria

It is not unknown to get a lift straight through from Yugoslavia to Turkey, and thus to miss out on the dubious pleasures of hitching around this sparsely-populated country. To make life interesting for hitchers who try it, the E-road numbers differ from the rest of Europe and the roadsigns are mostly in Cyrillic script; there is a devastating lack of traffic off the main routes; and when you finally get a lift in an ancient truck (probably built before suspension was invented) along the pot-holed dirt tracks that pass for roads, you'll begin to suspect that there must be some better form of transport. To compensate, this is a country where few western hitchers are seen but all are welcomed, and which is blissfully lacking in tourists away from the Black Sea coast.

Getting In. If you are sufficiently confident of your ability to get through Bulgaria inside 48 hours, you can get a transit visa at the frontier for £5. Otherwise, you should obtain a visa in advance from a Bulgarian consulate for £10. There is no minimum currency exchange requirement, but (in common with all other Eastern bloc countries) you have to show upon entry how much money you have and explain how you've spent it upon departure. Travellers from Turkey can expect to be searched for drugs.

Road Strategy. Identifying the road you want is not easy. If you can't read Cyrillic script, you'll have to rely largely on road numbers. Unfortunately, the E-roads in Bulgaria are numbered according to the new system, which is not used elsewhere in Europe. The main east-west thoroughfare is the E80 (known as the E5N to the rest of Europe). The north-south route from Thessaloniki via Sofia to Ruse (E20) becomes the E79 in the south-east and the E83 in the north-west. The Black Sea coast road through Burgas and Varna is the E87. Even on these roads, you can expect to move in unpredictable fits and starts; away from the E-roads, you can expect to grind to a complete standstill.

Number Plates. The town of registration is indicated by the first letter or two on the number plate, in Cyrillic script. Sofia is **C**.

Town Guide

(for key and explanation, see the introduction)

SOFIA

E80 (west): Kalotina, Belgrade (E5N)
⊞ 2km: W along Kiril i Metodi, bear R along Valčo Ivanov to just beyond bridge over railway.**

E79 (north east): Ruse (E83), Varna (E83, E771, E70)
⊞ 2km: NE along Blvd Zaimov and Botevgradsko Šose to edge of city.**

E80 (east): Plovdiv, Burgas (E772)
⊞ to Orlov most, just beyond zoo at edge of city centre. Stand at start of Blvd Lenin.

E79 (south west): Thessaloniki (E20), Skopje (E870, E27)
⊞ 4km: SW along Totleben and Blvd Deveti Septemvri to jn with ring road.**

Czechoslovakia

Compared with other Eastern European nations, Czechoslovakia is fairly densely-populated and has a high standard of living. This is reflected in the relatively high volume of traffic. Prague has rush-hour jams to rival western capitals, and the roads through Plzen on Sunday evenings are choked with West German weekend visitors on their way home.

Getting In. To get into Czechoslovakia you will need a visa issued by the Czech Embassy (£5). Unless you've pre-booked and prepaid your accommodation or obtained currency exchange vouchers in advance, you will also have to change $10 or the hard currency equivalent for every day of your stay, before you are allowed to leave the customs area. It is important that you have small notes or low-denomination travellers cheques for this: unless you have the exact amount it will be taken up to the next round figure you have. In theory you can reconvert this excess but the procedure is so slow that you might as well spend it before you leave. Hitching is tolerated and customs officials, if not too busy, may even help you get a lift, but only after wasting at least an hour of your time with bureaucratic procedures and searches of your belongings.

Number Plates. The first two letters on number plates indicate the town of registration. The larger towns, listed below, are allocated more than one pair of letters:

Bratislava	BA/BH/BL/BT/BY	Kosice	KE/KS
Brno	BI/BM/BO/BS/BZ	Liberec	LB/LI
Ceske Budejovice	CB/CE	Olomouc	OC/OL/OM
Gottwaldov	GT/GV	Ostrava	OS/OT/OV
Hradec Kralove	HK/HR	Pardubice	PA/PU
Karlovy Vary	KR/KV	Plzen	PJ/PM/PN/PS
Karvina	KA/KI	Prague	AB-AZ/PH/PY/PZ
Kladno	KD/KL	Zilina	ZA/ZI

Smaller, less well known towns have only one pair of letters each, and in most cases both letters are derived from the town's name. The abbreviations are given below in four lists, each representing a geographical region of the country, starting in the west (NW Bohemia) and working through to Slovakia in the east.

North-west Bohemia
CH, CL, CV, DC, DO, JN, LN, MO, RO, SO, TC, TP, UL.
South-east Bohemia
BE, BN, CK, CR, HB, JC, JH, KH, KO, KT, MB, ME, NA, NB, PB, PE, PI, PT, RA, RK, SM, ST, SY, TA, TU, UO.
Moravia
BK, BR, BV, HO, JI, KM, NJ, PR, PV, SU, TR, UH, VS, VY, ZN, ZR.
Slovakia
BB, BC, BJ, CA, DK, DS, GA, HN, KN, LC, LM, LV, MI, MT, NR, NZ, PD, PO, PP, PX, RS, RV, SE, SK, SL, SN, TN, TO, TT, TV, VK, VV, ZH, ZV.

Town Guide

(for key and explanation, see the introduction)

BRATISLAVA

2/E15 (north): Brno, Prague
🚌 11, 12, 26, 33, 40, 41, to Brnenska Mlynska dolina jn at start of Lamačska cesta.**

61/E16: Zilina, Košice (18/E85)
🚌 15, 22, 24, 34, 37, 39 to Trnavska cesta/Bajkalska jn.**

2, 1/E15 (south): Györ, Budapest
🚌 C to turn-off for Čunovo, then [x] 1km SE along 2/E15 to Hungarian border.***

9: Vienna
🚌 26, C along Viedenska cesta to jn with Rusovska cesta, then [x] 1km SW along Viedenska cesta to Austrian border.***

BRNO

D1/E15 (north-west): Prague
D2/E15 (south-east): Bratislava
52,7/E7 (south): Vienna
[x] 2km: SW along Tatranska, Nove Sady, Renneska, Svancarova, and

Krematorni to jn with Jihlavski (2)**. Take any lift to 2/D1/D2 jn 3km south-west.
🚌 50, 62 to above jn.

PRAGUE (Praha)

11, 33/E12 (east): Wroclaw
🚌 5, 8, 25 to terminus at Hloubetin. Stand on slip road to 11.**

D1/E15 (south-east): Brno, Linz (3/E14)
⊖ to Mladeznica then 200m NE to start of D1.**

D5, 5/12 (west): Plzen
🚌 4, 9, 15 to terminus at Kozire then bus 164, 184, 219, 225, 230, 249 to jn at Bily Beranek. Stand on 5 (leading to D5).***

8/E15 (north): Teplice, Dresden
🚌 12, 14, 29 to terminus at Kobylisy. Stand on Rude Armady (8).** Or 🚌 162 for 1km N along 8 to where bus turns off at Dolni Chabry. Then walk 100m N to exit from camp site.***

East Germany

East Germany has a comprehensive network of motorways, although a few repairs to the surface of the transit routes to West Germany would greatly reduce travelling times. Compared with other eastern countries, there is also a good deal of long-distance traffic. If you can be bothered to meet the complex visa regulations, you'll find hitch-hiking widely practised and very easy. Unfortunately, the visa requirements are such that most hitchers will only see the country from hermetically-sealed cars on the pot-holed *autobahnen* linking West Germany with West Berlin.

Getting In. If you want to stay in the GDR for more than a single day, you will need a tourist visa, available for hard currency to the value of M15 (approx £3.80) at the frontier. At the same time you will have to book and pay for your hotel or camping site accommodation. Accommodation can be booked at the border, but you will, of course, be told that only the dearer hotels are available. If you book in advance you should be able to get a better deal.

If you are hitching from West Germany to West Berlin, or from West Berlin to Poland or Czechoslovakia, you can get through on a transit visa (M5 or about £1.25, payable in hard currency), but your lift must go all the way through. On a transit visa you are not allowed to get out and change cars in East Germany. A through lift is easy enough on routes between West Germany and West Berlin, but well nigh impossible if you're going to Poland or Czechoslovakia. You'll have no trouble with searches if you travel on a transit visa, especially if you're in a West German car.

The above applies only to transit journeys to or from West Berlin. On other transit journeys — from West Germany to Poland or Czechoslovakia — you are at liberty to hitch within East Germany. If you are unable to complete your journey through East Germany in a single day, you must book accommodation at specific hotels or campsites; details are available at *Reisebüro der DDR* frontier offices. You have a maximum of two nights/three days to leave East Germany for a country other than the one you arrived from; in other words, you can't surreptitiously use a transit visa in place of a regular visa.

Number Plates. East German number plates start with two letters, the first of which denotes the town of origin, according to this code:

A	Rostock	I	Berlin	S	Leipzig
B	Schwerin	K	Halle	T	Karl-Marx-Stadt
C	Neubrandenburg	L	Erfurt	U	Leipzig
D	Potsdam	M	Magdeburg	V	Halle
E	Frankfurt/Oder	N	Gera	X	Karl-Marx-Stadt
F	Erfurt	O	Suhl	Y	Dresden
G	Cottbus	P	Potsdam	Z	Cottbus
H	Magdeburg	R	Dresden		

Town Guide

(for key and explanation, see the introduction)

EAST BERLIN

96/E6 (north): Sassnitz, Rostock (E64)
🚃 (S-Bahn) to Pankow-Heinersdorf. Stand at start of motorway.**

A6/E74: Schwedt, Szczecin
🚌 24, 28 to Weissensee, then 🚌 41 to Lindenburg. When bus turns off Bernauerstr, alight and 🚶 1km to motorway slip road. Sign pref.**

A5/E8 (east): Frankfurt/Oder, Warsaw
A4/E15/E22: Cottbus, Dresden, Prague (170, 8)
A3/E6 (south): Leipzig
A2/E8 (west): Magdeburg
🚃 (S-Bahn) to Alt Glienicke. Stand at start of motorway. Sign pref.**
For destinations in West Germany, it is easier to travel via West Berlin.

Hungary

Hungary has exactly the right combination of factors to make hitch-hiking almost impossible: very few cars, hardly any long-distance traffic (especially off the E5, E15 and E96 around Lake Balaton) and a reluctance for drivers to pick up hitch-hikers. Frantic gesticulations will get you lifts faster than a dignified wave of the thumb, but you can still only expect to move around in short lifts.

Getting In. Hungary has abandoned its complicated compulsory exchange regulations, in the hope that tourists will flock in. A visa is required from a Hungarian Consulate, price £5 for the 30-day version or £3 for a 48-hour transit visa; you can also get it at the border or at airports but it will cost £1 extra and may involve a little delay. You cannot obtain visas on trains, nor on the hydrofoil from Vienna.

Town Guide

(for key and explanation, see the introduction)

BUDAPEST

The city on the west bank of the Danube is Buda; the eastern part is Pest.

M1/E5/15: Györ, Vienna
M7/E96: Szekesfehervar
🚶 3km: SW from Szabadsag bridge along Bartok Bela ut, bear R along Hamzsabegi ut, then L along Budaorsi ut to start of motorway. Sign pref.**
🚌 40, 41, 53, 72, 87 to above jn.

2/T7: Vac, Krakow
🚶 2km: N from Marx ter in Pest along Vaci ut (2) to jn with Robert Karoly korut.**
🚌 55, 84 or 🚌 3, 3V, 33V to above jn.

M3, 3/E96 (north): Miskolc, Kosice
⊖ 1 to terminus at Mexikoi ut then 🚇
500m N (follow signs) to M3
approach road.**
🚌 1, 25 to start of M3.**

4/E15 (east): Oradea (42), Debrecen (T1)
🚇 3km: SE from Kalvin ter in Pest
along Ulloi ut (4) to jn with
Hungaria Korut. Stand on 4.**
⊖ line 3 to Hatar ut, then stand
beyond petrol station at start of
Voros Hadsereg ut.***

5/E5 (south): Szeged, Belgrade (22)
🚇 to Boraros ter in south of Pest.
Stand on Soroksari ut.**
🚌 66 to Ocsai ut (5)/Haraszti ut (51)
jn. Stand on 5.**

6: Paks, Pecs
🚇 1km: SW from Szabadsag bridge
along Bartok Bela ut, L along
Fehervari ut (6) to jn with Schonherz
ut. Stand on 6.**
🚌 3, 103 to terminus on Nagyteteny
ut (6). Stand on 6.***

Poland

Poland is a unique country as far as hitch-hiking is concerned. As a form of transport, hitching is not only tolerated but even encouraged and officially organised through a committee that comes close to being a "Ministry of Hitch-hiking". The scheme was started in 1958 and has been evolving ever since, with direct participation from members of various government bodies, youth organisations, the press, media and trade unions. About 35,000 hitch-hikers a year participate in the scheme, but only about 1,000 of these are foreigners, mostly from western Europe and Scandinavia. Detailed statistical analysis has revealed that recent participants included a 92-year old doctor and an 86-year old professor of economics.

Getting In. A visa is required which you can get from the Polish Consulate in most European capitals for £10. You have to exchange $10 per day if you are under 26 or a student; $15 if you are older. People who pre-book and pre-pay their accommodation are exempt from this daily exchange. Alternatively, travel agents can sell you currency vouchers which you exchange for Polish zlotys on entry into Poland. More favourable rules apply for those who want to spend a couple of months studying in Poland or who have Polish relatives.

Rules of Thumb

Hitch-hiking as an organised means of transport is in the hands of the *Spoleczny Komitet Autostop* ("Social Autostop Committee" is the official translation), ulica Narbutta 27a, 02-536 Warsaw. If you write to them — several weeks, or preferably about three months, in advance — they will send you a complete package, including maps and multi-lingual handbooks. Briefly, this is how the system operates:

First of all the restrictions: you must be 17 or over (or 16 if you have your parents' written permission); and the official season lasts only from May

1st-September 30th. Participation in the scheme during this period includes full insurance against accidents while hitch-hiking. To participate, you must buy a book of coupons, costing 200 zlotys (about £1). The book of coupons can be obtained by filling out the registration card at one of the offices affiliated to the scheme. These include any of 260 branches of the PTTK (Central Board of Polish Country Lovers' Society), plus various offices of youth organisations in main towns and at some border points. Individual coupons are valid for rides of 25km, 50km and 80km. The full book of coupons adds up to 2,000km. It is valid for only one hitching season.

You give the driver the correct amount of signed and dated coupons, according to how far he takes you. He in turn will collect the coupons throughout the season, then, in October, will send his collection to the Social Autostop Committee. The coupons are counted, sorted and (to quote the SAC handbook) "divided into groups according to type of car, number of kilometres travelled, and then drawn. The drawing system is based on the principle that the more coupons were sent by one person, the higher are his chances of winning an award. The "champions" receive awards without drawing."

So much for the theory. How does the scheme work in practice? Some drivers do only stop because they believe you have coupons, and may ask you for more than their entitlement over the coffee (an expensive luxury) they've just bought you. But many other motorists positively scorn your precious book of coupons. They consider helping a foreign visitor to be reward enough. They might also consider the prizes (which have an average value of only £6) to be derisory.

The truth is that hitching in Poland is extremely good, even if you're travelling out of season or without the aid of coupons. The official scheme helps to elevate hitching to a noble art (see *Social and Ideological Comments*, below) and to raise the consciousness of motorists. In practice you might as well distribute your coupons liberally among those who collect them, since the rides you get from drivers who shun coupons will help to eke out your 2,000km allowance. And if you should run out, there's always a nearby branch of the PTTK where you can replenish your stocks for a pound.

Social and Ideological Comments. The Social Autostop Committee's handbooks make fascinating reading, as the following quotes illustrate:

Polish autostop is a purely social organisation. It is self-supported and represents a democratic form of tourism in the widest meaning of the word. Autostop facilitates seeing relics of the past, beauty of nature and modern achievements. Moreover, autostop is an excellent school of life: it develops self-dependence, accustoms young people to hardships and surprises of the journey, develops the ability to cope with various conditions.

The statistical autostop participant is a sociable person; he usually wanders in groups consisting of 2-3 persons; about 15 per cent travel with their families. It may now be said that an average autostop participant is more handsome. Although quite often his almost manly face is adorned with a beard and sideburns and his head is protected with bushy hair, he is more neat, has a better tourist equipment and his behaviour is more correct than it used to be with his predecessors in the first years of autostop.

A comforting fact should be noted: in spite of their high mobility, the autostop participants almost never fall victims of traffic accidents (an average for one season is not more than one death), and slight bodily injuries (not more than 5-6) happen usually during bathing in rivers and lakes, practising sport, etc. This should be explained by several reasons: autostop participants travel usually by day in good weather, along main routes, on which cars are driven by experienced drivers. Moreover, according to the opinion of the press, the autostop participants **faultlessly evaluate from a distance the driving skill of a less competent driver.** Such a low number of accidents is also influenced by the fact of multiple warnings inserted in the autostop book.

Targets which the Social Autostop Committee set for itself in this organised action have been reached. This was made possible by the help and friendliness of drivers, goodwill of authorities and work of many social activists. Moreover, it must be noted that until now not a single attack on the driver by the autostop participants took place.

Route Planning. Unlike the rest of Eastern Europe, your choice of road will not affect your chances enormously. Motorways are as potholed and uncomfortable as other roads, and do not carry significantly more traffic. On smaller roads in isolated areas the first vehicle will almost certainly stop. The main routes out of towns present unusual but not insurmountable problems. The best hitching spots out of any large city are each laden with a score or more of other hitchers. Every time a vehicle with even the slightest possibility of taking a passenger passes, this mass of humanity surges out on to the road, forcing the driver to swerve. Despite such intimidation, plenty of motorists give lifts. A western hitcher (as you so obviously will be) automatically receives preferential treatment from both drivers and native hitchers (who in any case are probably heading only 10km along the road).

The Law. There are few motorways, but enforcement of regulations is lax. It is doubtful whether a passing police car would bother you; if the police do take the trouble to pull you up, they'll probably apologetically request you to walk back up the slip road.

During periods of internal political unrest your freedom of movement should remain unhindered so long as you avoid obvious trouble spots. Motorists will be keen to hear your political views. What you tell them depends on whether you think they're a government agent or a supporter of Solidarity.

Maps. You will get a free road map of Poland in the package from the Social Autostop Committee. This is far more useful than the usual tourist office hand-out, being uniquely designed for hitch-hikers. On the reverse are basic street plans of the 49 provincial capitals (listed below), giving the numbers of buses and trams to take to get out of town to a suitable hitching spot on all the main routes.

Number Plates. The first two letters of the number plate represents one of the 49 provinces. Each province is allocated two pairs of code letters, as in the following table:

BA/BP	Biala Podl.	BG/BY	Bydgoszcz	CE/CZ	Czestochowa
BB/BL	Bielsko Biala	BK/BT	Bialystok	CH/CM	Chelm

CI/CN	Ciechanow	LL/LU	Lublin	SD/SE	Siedlce
EG/EL	Elblag	LM/LO	Lomza	SK/SN	Skierniewice
GD/GK	Gdansk	NO/NS	Nowy Sacz	SL/SP	Slupsk
GO/GW	Gorzow	OE/OP	Opole	SU/SW	Suwalki
JE/JG	Jelenia Gora	OK/OS	Ostroleka	TA/TN	Tarnow
KA/KT	Katowice	OL/ON	Olsztyn	TB/TG	Tarnobrzeg
KE/KI	Kielce	PA/PI	Pila	TO/TU	Torun
KG/KO	Koszalin	PC/PL	Plock	WA/WS	Warsaw
KK/KR	Krakow	PK/PT	Piotrkow	WB/WY	Walbrzych
KL/KZ	Kalisz	PM/PR	Przemysl	WK/WL	Wloclawec
KM/KN	Konin	PN/PO	Poznan	WO/WR	Wroclaw
KS/KU	Krosno	RA/RD	Radom	ZA/ZM	Zamosc
LC/LG	Legnica	RE/RZ	Rzeszow	ZE/ZG	Zielona Gora
LD/LZ	Lodz	SA/SI	Sieradz		
LE/LS	Leszno	SC/SZ	Szczecin		

Town Guide

(for key and explanation, see the introduction)

DANZIG (Gdansk)/GDYNIA

E81: Warsaw
🚌 112, 120, 136, 164, 166, 181, 186
to anywhere suitable on
Elbanska.***

E16: Lodz, Poznan (E83)
🚋 to Pruszcz Gdansk then 🚶 500m S
to E16/bypass jn.**

52: Slupsk, Szczecin
🚋 to terminus at Wejherowo then 🚶
500m N to 51.***

KRAKOW

E7 (north): Warsaw
🚌 105, 150, 217, 247 to Lubianska/
Listopada jn. Stand on
Listopada.***

E22 (east): Tarnow, Przemysl
🚌 103, 133, 143, 173 or 🚋 3, 6, 9, 13,
24 to Kamienskiego/Wieliczka jn.
Stand on Wieliczka.***

**E7 (south): Brno (46), Budapest (T7),
   Zakopane (15)**
🚌 101, 133, 135, 141, 145, 201, 235
or 🚋 8, 19, 24 to Brozka/
Zakopianska jn. Stand on
Zakopianska. Sign pref.**

E22a: Katowice
🚌 118, 173, 208, 218 to
Korownikova/Fizykov/Pasternik jn.
Stand on Pasternik.***

F22 (west): Katowice, Wroclaw
🚌 to above jn. Stand on Fizykov.***

POZNAN

E8 (east): Warsaw
🚌 57, 66, 105 to Browarna/
Warszawska jn. Stand on
Warszawska.***

38: Lodz, Katowice (37)
🚌 54, 62, 65 to edge of town. Stand
on B Krzywoustego.**

**E83 (south): Wroclaw, Zielona Gora
   (44)**
🚌 56, 80, 103, 116 to edge of town.
Stand on Glogowska.**

**E8 (west): Frankfurt an der Oder,
   Berlin, Szczecin (E14)**
🚌 61, 102, 114 to Lutycka/ Jaroslawa
jn. Stand on Jaroslawa. Sign pref.**

**E83 (north): Bydgoszcz, Gdansk
   (E16)**
🚌 73, 112 to Baltycka/ Gnieznienska
jn. Stand on Gnieznienska.**

WARSAW (Warszawa)

E8 (west): Poznan, Berlin, Wroclaw (E12)
🚌 105, 106, 129, 149, 163, 194 to Dzwigowa/Polczynska (E8) jn.***

E81 (north): Danzig, Bydgoszcz (T81)
🚃 5, 6, 15, 17, 27 to start of Pulkowa at Mlociny.***

E12 (east): Bialystok
🚌 119, 120 to anywhere suitable on Generalska.**

E8 (east): Siedlce, Briest, Lublin (E81)
🚶 3km: E along Jerozolimskie and Waszyngtona to rdbt at Grochow. Stand on Grochowska (E8).**
🚌 115, F to Patriotow/ Bronislava Czecha (E8) jn.***

E7: Krakow, Katowice (E82, E16)
🚶 2km: S along Grojecka to Lopuszanska/Fr Hynka jn. Stand at start of al Krakowska (E7).**
🚃 2, 7, 9, 14 to terminus at Okecie. Stand on E7.***

Few people, including the police, are aware of the bye-law that forbids hitch-hiking within Warsaw's city boundaries.

WROCLAW

E12 (east): Lodz, Warsaw

🚌 104 to Kochanowskiego/B Krzywoustego jn. Stand on B Krzywoustego.***

34: Opole, Katowice (E22)
🚌 101, 122 or 🚃 3, 5, 19 to anywhere suitable on Krakowska.**

E22 (east): Katowice, Krakow
🚌 107, 113 or 🚃 17 to E22 jn on al Armii Radzieckiej (E12). Stand on E22.***

E12 (south): Klodzko
🚌 as above but stand on E12.**

E83 (west): Jelenia Gora, Prague (E14)
🚌 as above. Stand at E83 jn just beyond E22.***

E22 (west): Cottbus, Berlin
🚌 as above. Stand on westbound slip road to E22.***

42: Zielona Gora
🚌 129 or 🚃 3 to Kosmonautow. Stand just past railway bridge.**

E83 (north): Poznan
🚌 108 to anywhere suitable on Zmigrodzka.***

Bus and tram routes on the main routes of the other 44 provincial capitals are marked on the town maps issued free by the Biuro Autostop PTTK, 02-536 Warsaw, ul Narbutta 27a.

Romania

Hitch-hiking in Romania is about as bad as in neighbouring Hungary, so expect long waits and short lifts.

Getting In. Tourist visas ($10) and transit visas ($5) are obtainable at the frontier. You must exchange $10 for each day of your stay.

Getting Out. The Romanians like to keep their money to themselves, and you are forbidden to bring a single leu in or out of the country. They will very likely search you thoroughly on the way out to satisfy themselves that you are not trying to ruin their economy.

Number Plates. The letter or pair of letters in the middle of Romanian number plates indicate the province of origin. Provinces are sometimes, but not always, named after their principal towns; in the table below, the provincial capital is always given, even where the letters are an abbreviation for the name of the province.

AB	Alba Iulia	CV	Covasna	OT	Slatini
AG	Pitesti	DB	Tirgoviste	PH	Ploesti
AR	Arad	DJ	Craiova	SB	Sibiu
B	Bucharest	GJ	Tirgu Jiu	SJ	Zalau
BC	Bacau	GL	Galati	SM	Satu Mare
BH	Oradea	HD	Deva	SV	Suceava
BN	Bistrita Nasaud	HR	Odorheiul Sec	TL	Tulcea
BR	Braila	IF	Giurgiu	TM	Timisoara
BT	Botosani	IL	Calarasi	TR	T Magorelf
BV	Brasov	IS	Iasi	VL	Rim Vilcea
BZ	Buzau	MH	Turnu Severin	VN	Pocsani
CJ	Cluj	MM	Baia Mare	VS	Birlad
CS	Resita	MS	Tirgu Mures		
CT	Constanta	NT	Piatra Neamt		

Town Guide

(for key and explanation, see the introduction)

BUCHAREST (Bucuresti)

A1/E94/E15a: Pitesti
🚌 9, 11, 13, 25, 26, 35, 37 to Soseaua Grozavesti/Soseaua Cotrocen jn on edge of Gradina Botanica. Stand at start of Bulevardul Armata Poporului (leading to A1).***

DN1/E15 (north): Ploesti
🚌 3, 4 to terminus at Plata Scinteii, 3km N of centre. Stand on Soseaua Baneasa (DN1).***

DN2/E15/E20 (east): Constanta
🚌 1, 4, 21 to turn-off on Soseaua Colentina (DN2).**

DN5/E20 (south): Giurgiu, Sofia
🚌 7, 12, 17, 25, 32 to Soseaua Oltenitei/Soseaua Giurgiului (DN5) jn 3km S of centre. Stand by park on DN5.***

Yugoslavia

Yugoslav drivers won't pay you much attention. They are quite used to the queues of hitchers, and occasionally a driver may stop just out of curiosity. However, the supply of lifts is quite simply inadequate, and waits of a day or more are commonplace. A lift in anything under an hour is fairly close to a miracle. One exception: females either singly or in pairs will get around fast, but not necessarily pleasantly, and usually in very short lifts.

Getting In. Europeans don't need a visa, but other nationalities will have to gct one; they can be arranged at the border for a small charge. Coming back from Turkey or Greece, you are unlikely to be refused entry, but the officials may be a bit more hesitant if you arrive from Italy or Austria and have no money to speak of.

Road Strategy. Summer in Yugoslavia makes you wonder whether there is anybody left in Germany. Every other car seems to be German registered, and it is well worth writing "Bitte" on your sign. There are also plenty of other tourists driving around in hire cars. Your national flag will be a great asset.

Route planning is not very difficult. If you want to see any traffic, choose either the *autoput* (loosely translated "motorway") right through the centre, or the coast road. The latter is more pleasant in every way, but you face a long detour inland through Titograd and Skopje if you're travelling on to Greece. If you want a leisurely walking holiday without a car in sight, choose virtually any other road. One peculiarity about the coast road is that all the lay-bys and other useful hitching spots are on the inland side of the road, so travelling north is likely to be faster than travelling south.

Number Plates. The two letters before the red star are an abbreviation of the town of registration. The best known towns are:

BG	Belgrade	MB	Maribor	SK	Skopje
BR	Bar	NI	Nis	ST	Split
BT	Bitola	NS	Novi Sad	SU	Subotica
DU	Dubrovnik	RI	Rijeka	TG	Titograd
LJ	Ljubljana	SA	Sarajevo	ZG	Zagreb

Most of the other towns are pretty obscure, so a complete list would not mean much to the average hitch-hiker. Instead, the code letters alone are given below. Using the *autoput* (E94/E5/E5S) as an axis, the country is divided into four parallel zones: the list for each zone reads from north-west to south-east. The letters listed above are included (in **bold**) for reference.

1. North-east of the autoput
CE, **MB**, MS, KN, VZ, CK, KZ, BJ, KC, VT, DA, SP, NA, OS, VK, SO, **SU**, **NS**, KK, ZR, PA, PO, ZA.
2. Autoput: Würzenpass to Gevgelija (E94/E5S)
KR, **LJ**, NM, **ZG**, SI, KT, NG, SB, SM, SA, **BG**, SD, KG, SV, KS, **NI**, LE, VR, KU, **SK**, TV, ST.
3. Inland between autoput *and coast*
GO, KA, OG, BI, PD, BL, JC, LI, DO, ZE, TZ, **SA**, GZ, PV, VA, TU, CA, KV, BP, IG, KM, PE, DJ, PJ, PR, GL, UR, PZ, TE, OH, **BT**.
4. The coastline and immediate hinterland
KP, PU, **RI**, GS, ZD, SI, **ST**, MA, MO, **DU**, NK, KO, CT, **TG**, **BR**.

Town Guide

(for key and explanation, see the introduction)

BELGRADE (Beograd)

1/E94 (west): Zagreb, Ljubljana
⚑ 2km: S along Kneza Milosa to Drugi Bulevar sliproad.*
🚌 32, 33, 39 to above jn.
⚑ 1.5km: S from station along Slobodana Penezica-Krcuna to Autoput slip road. Sign pref.**
🚌 3, 4, 29, 501, 502 to above jn.
🚌 36, 44 to Studentska/Autoput jn 5km W of city. Stand on Autoput.**
⚑ 1km: from Camp Beograd to above jn.

11/E5: Novi Sad, Budapest (5)
🚌 14, 15, 16, 36 to Bulevar Lenjina/Beogradskaput (11) jn. Stand on 11.**
🚌 14, 17, 45 to Marsala Tita/Matije Gupca/Cara Dusana (11) jn at Zemun, 6km NW of city. Stand on 11.***

13/E94 (east): Timisoara (59)
🚌 38 to jn on north side of Danube. Stand on 13.***

1/E5: Nišs, Skopje (E5S), Sofia (E5N)
🚌 9, 10, 12, 17, 29, 47 to Autoput jn. Locate and stand on appropriate slip road.**

LJUBLJANA

1/E94 (east): Zagreb, Belgrade
🚌 3 to terminus on Dolenjska cesta.**

6/E93 (south): Trieste, Rijeka (6c, E27)
🚌 1, 6 to terminus on Trzaska cesta.**

1/E94 (north): Klagenfurt, Villach (1a)
🚌 1 to terminus on Cetovska cesta at Vizmarje.**

6/E93 (north): Maribor, Graz
🚌 8 to terminus on Titova cesta.**

RIJEKA

2a/E27 (west): Trieste, Ljubljana (10)
⚑ 3km: NW along Ulica Borisa Kidrica past rail station to edge of city.*
🚌 from local bus station at Beogradski trg to Matulji, on 2a/E27 10km NW of city.**

13/E96: Zagreb, Belgrade (1/E94)
⚑ 2km: SE from Titov trg over river, along Ulica Proleterski Brigada and 2/E27 to start of E96 motorway.**
🚌 to Pecine near above jn.

2/E27 (south): Split, Dubrovnik
⚑ 🚌 as above but stand on 2/E27.*
🚌 to Kraljevica, on 2/E27 20km SE of city.**

SARAJEVO

10 (north): Tuzla, Belgrade (1/E94)
⚑ 2km: N along Dure Dakovica (10) to jn with Kosevsko B.**
⚑ 200m: from Camping "Student" to above jn.

5 (east): Gorazde
⚑ or 🚎 1, 2, 3 to Bentbasa (5)/Obala Vojvode Stepe/P Kocica jn in east of city. Stand by bridge on 5.**

5 (west): Banja Luka, Mostar (10 south)
🚎 3, 4, 6 to terminus at Ilidza, then ⚑ 500m along Sarajevska, over bridge and stand on Blazujski Drum.***

SKOPJE

2/E27 (north): Priština, Titograd
⚑ 2km: N along Maršala Tita (2) to edge of town.**

2/E27 (east): Sofia, Belgrade (1/E5S north), Thessaloniki (1/E5S south)
⚑ 2km: E along Kei D Vlahov to jn

with Bulevar Krste Misirkov by park and bridge on north bank of Vardar. Sign pref.*

SPLIT

2/E27 (north): Rijeka, Ljubljana (10/ E93)
🚌 37 to Trogir (15km NW of city, cost 50 dinars). Stand at lights on 2/E27.***

2/E27 (south): Dubrovnik, Titograd
🚌 55-61 to jn with by-pass (5km SE of city). Stand on 2/E27.***

ZAGREB

1/E94 (east): Belgrade
🚌 2, 3, 15 to terminus on Beogradska Avenija.**

7/E96: Karlovac, Rijeka
🚌 10, 14 to terminus at Gradsko Kupatiste then 🚶 500m S over bridge to start of Jadranska Avenija.**

1/E94 (west): Ljubljana, Maribor (1b)
🚌 9, 12 to terminus then 🚶 200m S along Fallerova Setatiste to Ljubljanska Avenija. Sign pref: Ljubljana**, Maribor.*

Index to Cities and Towns Listed

Some cities and towns have both native and English placenames. Where these differ significantly, both are listed below for easy reference.

Aachen 80
Aarhus 160
Amsterdam 49
Andorra La Vella 74
Antwerp 42
Arnhem 49
Athens 118

Barcelona 142
Bari 124
Basel 154
Belgrade 185
Bergen 163
Berlin (East) 177
Berlin (West) 80
Bern 154
Bilbao 143
Birmingham 102
Bologna 124
Bonn 80
Bordeaux 62
Boulogne 63
Bratislava 175
Bremen 81
Brindisi 124
Bristol 103
Brno 175
Bruges 43
Brussels 43
Bucharest 183
Budapest 177

Caerdydd 104
Calais 62
Cambridge 103
Cardiff 104
Cologne 81
Copenhagen 160
Cork 114

Danzig 181
Dieppe 63
Dover 104
Dublin 113
Dunkerque 63
Düsseldorf 82

East Berlin 177
Edinburgh 104
Esbjerg 160

Firenze 124
Florence 124

Folkestone 104
Frankfurt 82

Gdansk 181
Gdynia 181
Geneva 155
Gcnoa 125
Ghent 43
Gibraltar 151
Glasgow 105
Gothenburg 162
Granada 143
's Gravenhage 49
Graz 37
Groningen 49

Hague, The 49
Halsingborg 165
Hamburg 82
Hannover 83
Harwich 105
Helsinki 161
Heraklion 118
Hook of Holland 50

Innsbruck 37
Iraklion 118

København 160
Köln 81
Krakow 181
Kristiansand 163

Lausanne 155
Leeds 105
Le Havre 63
Liège 43
Lille 63
Linz 37
Lisbon 146
Liverpool 105
Ljubljana 185
London 106
Luxembourg 44
Lyon 64

Maastricht 50
Madrid 144
Malaga 144
Malmö 165
Manchester 106
Marseille 64
Messina 125

Milan 125
Monaco 74
Munich 83

Nantes 65
Naples 125
Newcastle 107
Newhaven 107
Nice 65
Nuremburg 84

Odense 160
Oporto 146
Örebro 165
Oslo 163

Palermo 125
Palma 144
Paris 65
Perpignan 65
Piraeus 118
Porto 146
Portsmouth 107
Prague 175

Reggio di Calabria 126
Rijeka 185
Rome 126
Rotterdam 50

Saarbrücken 84
Salonica 119
Salzburg 38
San Marino 139
San Sebastian 145
Santander 145
Sarajevo 185
Seville 145
Sheffield 107
Skopje 185
Sofia 174
Southampton 108
Split 186
Strasbourg 66
Stavanger 164
Stockholm 165
Stuttgart 84

Tampere 162
Thessaloniki 119
Torino 127
Toulouse 66
Trieste 126

Trondheim 164
Turin 127
Turku 162

Uppsala 166
Utrecht 50

Valencia 145
Valletta 139
Venice 127
Verona 127
Vienna 38

Warsaw 182

West Berlin 80
Wien 38
Wroclaw 182

Zagreb 186
Zeebrugge 44
Zurich 156

Thank you for your unbelievably useful book, which helped me hitch from Newcastle to Malta (with a little help from ferries) with the minimum of trouble—*Kathy Ricketts, Newcastle-upon-Tyne*

I could never have got out of London without it—*John Telford, Tennessee*

The greatest time-saver since front-fastening bras—*Alan Thatcher, New Zealand*

I wish to congratulate you on a masterful piece of literature which must, in time, go down in history as being influential on the directions of many people's lives. Anne and I have covered over 2,000 miles so far this summer, and have found the hitching very easy and enjoyable—*Rob Woon, Harwich*

I've been using *Europe: a Manual for Hitch-hikers* for about a year now, and have found it to be invaluable in my travels, especially when confronted with the complexities of the West German Autobahn system—*Steve Bristow, Scunthorpe*

I'd just like to add my congratulations to the many others you've probably already received on an excellent book. As far as I'm concerned, hitch-hiking is the only way to travel. It was one of the most exhilarating and incredible experiences I've ever had—
Alan Ng, Ontario

PA